Fundamental Concepts
and Problems
in
Business Ethics

Fundamental Concepts and Problems in Business Ethics

ROGENE A. BUCHHOLZ

The University of Texas at Dallas

PRENTICE HALL, Englewood Cliffs, New Jersey

LIBRARY OF CONGRESS
Library of Congress Cataloging-in-Publication Data

Buchholz, Rogene A.
  Fundamental concepts and problems in business ethics / Rogene A.
Buchholz.
    p.   cm.
  Includes bibliographies and index.
  ISBN 0-13-332504-0
  1. Business ethics. 2. Decision-making--Moral and ethical
aspects. 3. Business ethics--Case studies. I. Title.
HF5387.B83 1989
174'.4--dc19   88-14062
                                                          CIP

Editorial/production supervision: Kim Gueterman
Cover design: Bruce Kenselaar
Manufacturing buyer: Ed O'Dougherty

 © 1989 by Prentice-Hall, Inc.
A division of Simon & Schuster
Englewood Cliffs, NJ 07632

Printed in the United States of America

10 9 8 7 6 5 4 3 2

ISBN   0-13-332504-0   01

Prentice-Hall International (UK) Limited, *London*
Prentice-Hall of Australia Pty. Limited, *Sydney*
Prentice-Hall Canada Inc., *Toronto*
Prentice-Hall Hispanoamericana, S.A., *Mexico*
Prentice-Hall of India Private Limited, *New Delhi*
Prentice-Hall of Japan, Inc., *Tokyo*
Prentice-Hall of Southeast Asia Pte. Ltd., *Singapore*
Editora Prentice-Hall do Brasil, Ltda., *Rio de Janeiro*

Contents

6 SHOULD ETHICAL STATEMENTS BE TAKEN SERIOUSLY? 81

7 ISN'T IT ALL A MATTER OF SELF-INTEREST? 93

8 IS THE CORPORATION A MORAL AGENT? 105

9 CAN A CORPORATION BE MADE MORAL? 115

10 DOES BUSINESS ETHICS HAVE A FUTURE? 140

CASES

INDEX   233

Preface

The study of business ethics is not a new concern. There have been many articles and books written on the subject ever since management emerged as a professional activity in corporations and as business organizations grew in size and power so as to affect many aspects of modern society. Several attempts have been made over the years to develop a moral philosophy for management and delineate a set of ethical principles to guide management decision making. These efforts reflect a continuing concern about ethical issues in business, a concern that has accelerated in the past several years in both schools of business and management and the corporate world.

While many of the issues are the same, what is new about today's concern is the development of business ethics as a field of study in its own right, not as a peripheral subject to be added onto existing courses as time and interest permit. Over the past few years, a large and growing body of literature has developed, journals in business ethics have been established to promote writing and research in the area, many business schools have added business ethics courses to their curriculum, and several centers and endowed chairs for the study of business ethics have emerged around the country. These developments provide many exciting opportunities for management scholars who are interested in business ethics and want to devote some of their efforts to studying ethical issues in business.

Thus far, philosophers have provided leadership for the field and have written most of the textbooks used in teaching courses in business ethics. This is changing. More and more management scholars who are located in business schools are conducting research in the field and teaching courses in business ethics. Management scholars bring different perspectives to the issues than philosophers do and have valuable contributions to make to the field because of their more immediate acquaintance with management problems and the functioning of a business organization.

This book is written from such a managerial perspective. It is not a philosophical treatise even though the title may suggest that approach. The title is meant to indicate that there are some fundamental concepts and problems that are important to treat in classes that deal with ethical issues in business. Many management scholars who teach business ethics ignore these issues or treat them only superficially—issues such as, Why be moral? the problem of objectivity and subjectivity in ethics, the usefulness of ethical theories, and the question of moral agency. The statement is often made by management people that these issues are really not very important and are of interest only to philosophers and not to practical management scholars and students. Ethical theories can be treated quickly, if they are treated at all, to get on with the real work of dealing with cases and specific issues that have ethical dimensions.

Ignoring these questions is done at great peril to the field and to the students. Moving too quickly to issues and cases without dealing with more fundamental questions that students are sure to have about business ethics leaves many unexamined assumptions. Those assumptions pose a dilemma when it comes to resolving concrete problems in specific areas of ethical concern—employee rights, truth in advertising, conflicts of interest, and the like. What are rights, and where do they come from? What is moral truth, and how can one tell it when it appears? How can moral disagreements be resolved? These issues are basic to an intelligent discussion of cases and issues if the students are to gain an understanding of ethical analysis and arrive at justifiable ethical positions.

Perhaps a major part of the problem management scholars have in dealing with these questions is that philosophers who write about them have a tendency to be abstract and split hairs that have no practical significance. One can easily get bogged down in reading some of the philosophical literature on fact and value, for example, and quickly dismiss it as irrelevant and nonsense. Yet such is not the case, as this book hopes to show. Fundamental issues of this nature are discussed in this book in lay terms, and the philosophical jargon that is found in most of the literature has been eliminated to the greatest extent possible. Examples are used throughout the book to show the relevance of these issues to management and the teaching of business ethics.

An attempt has been made not to oversimplify the issues but to deal with them in such a way that their significance to management and the teaching of business students is readily apparent. That is what is meant by a management perspective. The issues are treated not as philosophical questions but as fundamentally important questions for management as they try to understand what business ethics is all about and how it applies to their decisions and actions on a day-to-day basis. Thus, it is hoped that this book will bridge the gap between philosophy and the practice of management and show the importance of the philosophical issues that are now dismissed as irrelevant, making them come alive for scholars who teach and conduct research in the field as well as for students and managers of business organizations.

The chapters in this book are organized around the fundamental problems that are basic to the field. They are called fundamental problems because they are prior to and more basic than issues related to whistleblowing, conflicts of interest, insider information, and other typical ethical concerns. The position one takes on these more narrow issues is very likely to be determined by the beliefs one holds about them. Each of the chapter headings is stated in the form of a question that relates to one of these fundamental problems in business ethics. The chapters and the issues they deal with can be briefly described as follows:

1. *What Is Business Ethics?* What is this field all about? How is business ethics distinguished from ethics in general, from medical ethics, legal ethics, and other kinds of ethical concerns? Where does business ethics fit into the business school curriculum, and what is the general subject matter of the field?

2. *Why Be Moral?* This is perhaps the most fundamental question of all in the field of ethics. Why should a business executive be concerned about morality? Does being ethical lead to success in business? Is it necessary that business ethics be related to corporate performance? Or is virtue its own reward in a business context as well as in a social context?

3. *What Decisions Have Ethical Dimensions?* Is every decision we make an ethical decision? If not, what differentiates an ethical decision from other kinds of decisions we make every day? What kinds of business decisions are ethical in nature? What moral factors are important to consider in an ethical decision?

4. *Are Ethical Theories Useful?* Most all of the books on business ethics make reference to and describe some of the leading ethical theories that are a part of Western philosophical thought. These theories, however, are often very abstract, and their relevance is not immediately apparent. Are they really useful in making ethical decisions, or are they merely intellectual constructs that have limited usefulness?

5. *How Can Moral Judgments Be Justified?* When we make an explicit moral judgment that a particular action is right or wrong, how can we ground this judgment and defend it to others who may be affected by our actions or guided by our recommendations? What is the basis on which we take a position with respect to an ethical prescription?

6. *Should Ethical Statements Be Taken Seriously?* Are ethical statements merely matters of opinion and thus need not be taken too seriously? Or do they have some objective basis that makes them more than just dependent on the circumstances? This chapter deals with the question of fact versus value—to use philosophical terms, the *is* versus the *ought*—or the nature of descriptive statements as distinguished from prescriptive statements.

7. *Isn't It All a Matter of Self-Interest?* The philosophical term for this problem is egoism, which has a particular relevance in a business setting. The free-enterprise system is based on self-interest, which is considered to be a universal ethical or motivating principle. How can this pursuit of self-interest be related to ethics and ethical theory? Does the pursuit of self-interest render business ethics irrelevant?

8. *Is the Corporation a Moral Agent?* Can the corporation as such be said to have moral responsibilities, or is it only the people in the corporation who are moral agents? Can anything morally relevant be said about corporate or organizational behavior?

9. *Can a Corporation Be Made Moral?* Assuming a corporation is some kind of a moral agent so that it makes sense to speak of corporations and moral responsibility, how can

a corporation be changed and directed toward more moral behavior. This chapter deals with internal and external control mechanisms that have been developed or proposed to control corporate behavior.

10.   *Does Business Ethics Have a Future?* Is business ethics becoming a permanent feature of business school curriculums and corporate organizations? Or is it just a passing fad that began because of recent corporate scandals? Is it important for business ethics to become more of an explicit consideration for management?

The organization of these problems has some logic to it, each chapter building on the preceding ones. The first chapter, describing the field, raises the question of why management should be concerned about ethics, which is the subject of the second chapter. The third chapter then deals with the ethical dimensions of management decision making in order to show more specifically where moral considerations enter into management concerns. This leads into a consideration of ethical theories and their relevance to resolving ethical questions and the problem of justifying or grounding ethical judgments, which are the subjects of the following two chapters. These considerations lead into a discussion in chapter 6 of the fact-value problem, an important problem that is basic to ethical judgments. Chapter 7 then deals with the relationship of self-interest to ethical decision making, a question that arises in any discussion of ethics and business. Following is a chapter dealing with the question of moral agency as regards the corporation and a chapter discussing the problem of making a corporation moral through internal or external regulation. The book ends with a discussion about the future of business ethics, which in some sense summarizes what has been discussed in the previous chapters.

Perhaps a diagram will help to make this logic clearer and provide a kind of conceptual road map for the reader. It should be pointed out that chapters 3 through 6 are more theoretical than the other chapters. Even though these chapters do not contain the usual philosophical jargon and provide several examples to illustrate the material, many instructors may not have the philosophical background to treat these subjects in great detail. Students should be encouraged, however, to read these chapters carefully and look at some of the supplementary reading to further their understanding of the material. The concepts presented in these chapters are essential to developing a basic understanding of business ethics that can then be applied to more practical concerns.

The cases at the end of the book illustrate these basic issues and problems in the field of business ethics. They help to show that they are not just abstractions but have concrete applications to real-world business situations. Each case is focused on one of the fundamental problems dealt with in the chapters, as the titles of the cases indicate, but each case touches on some of the other issues as well. They can thus be used in any order an instructor deems appropriate and do not have to follow the sequence indicated in the book itself.

A second book is planned that will deal with more narrow questions that relate to specific business relationships, such as relationships with employees, customers, the environment, and the general public. This second book will build on foundations laid in this current book and apply some of the theories and principles that

Outline of the Book

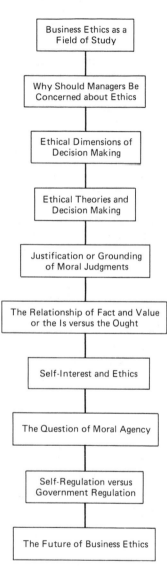

have been discussed in these pages to the major management functions, such as marketing, finance, and production.

Fundamental Concepts and Problems in Business Ethics can be used in several different approaches to the teaching of business ethics. If the primary focus of the course is on cases, this book can be used as an introductory text to deal with questions that are fundamental to the discussion of ethical issues raised by the cases. The fundamental problems discussed in this text will be reflected in the problems presented by the cases. This text can lay the groundwork for an intelligent discussion of solutions to those case problems.

This book can also be used as a primary text, which can then be supplemented by readings chosen by the instructor in the various application areas, such as advertising, conflicts of interest, and employee rights. It deals with some of the fundamental issues that need to be considered in business ethics before an intelligent discussion of concrete issues related to management practices can take place. The book can serve as an introduction to the subject of business ethics and as a springboard to a discussion of more specific issues.

Instructors who teach strategy courses and want to deal with ethical concerns might also find this book useful. In this case, the book would serve as a supplementary text to point out where it is important to consider ethical issues in formulating and implementing strategy in modern business organizations. Likewise, philosophers who teach business ethics might find the book useful in that it is more managerially oriented than some of the philosophical textbooks. Throughout the book, philosophical theories and problems have been raised in a managerial context, and their relevance to the teaching of management in business schools and the practice of management in a business organization have been demonstrated.

Corporations that have an ethical module or introduce ethical concerns into their management-training programs should find the book extremely useful. The book raises fundamental issues that are important to management ethics in a nonphilosophical manner. Thus, managers will not have to put up with philosophical jargon but will be led to see the importance of the issues that philosophers are raising. The discussion of these issues can provide a foundation for the discussion of more specific issues related to the functional areas of management.

ACKNOWLEDGMENTS

Several people and institutions must be thanked for their help in the writing of this book. My advisor at the University of Pittsburgh, where I earned my doctorate, William C. Frederick, has been a constant source of inspiration and stimulation on matters pertaining to values and ethics. His continuing work in this area has contributed considerably to my knowledge of ethics and values, and his dedication to scholarship and discussion of ethical issues has provided an example that has guided my own efforts.

The friends and acquaintances I have made over the past several years in the Society of Business Ethics have inspired me to devote more time to an explicit consideration of ethical issues and relate these issues to management practice and public-policy concerns, which have been my major interest over the years of my academic career. In particular, I would like to mention Norm Bowie, Richard DeGeorge, Tom Donaldson, and Manny Valesquez, all of whom have written extensively in the field. My personal association with them has been extremely rewarding, and I have benefited greatly from their books and articles. Many of their ideas are reflected in this book.

Many thanks go to Loyola Marymount University, and especially, Dean John Wolihan of the College of Business Administration, for naming me as the first Visiting Hilton Professor of Business Ethics in the College of Business Administration at that institution. This visit gave me the time to devote almost all my attention to business ethics, and I had the opportunity to think through the positions taken in this book. In this connection, the administration at the University of Texas at Dallas must be thanked for granting me a leave of absence so that I could take advantage of this opportunity.

While in Los Angeles, I had the privilege of meeting with Michael S. Josephson, founder of the Josephson Foundation, which was established to promote the study of ethical problems in the professions. Mr. Josephson was a source of inspiration when I first began to think about writing a book in business ethics. He had strong beliefs that people in management schools were going to have to write more about business ethics if the field was to have a significant and long-lasting impact. These beliefs encouraged me to think seriously about pursuing my own interests in business ethics along the lines of this book.

Several colleagues at Loyola Marymount provided many ideas for the book and read early drafts of some of the chapters. The many hours we spent discussing ethics and moral issues were especially stimulating and fruitful in helping to develop some of the ideas in this book. Colleagues who should be mentioned in this regard include Jeff Gale, Ed Gray, Arthur Gross-Schaefer, Mark Mendenhall, and David Mathison. Equally stimulating were the students in my M.B.A. course in business ethics, who had to put up with much fuzzy thinking, and in the course of pressing me to explain and justify my statements about business ethics, helped to clarify many of the ideas in this book. If much of my thinking is still unclear, it is certainly not their fault. They were fun to meet with each week and a constant source of inspiration.

Major Brooks and Alison Reeves of Prentice Hall were supportive in the writing of the book and had many suggestions for improvement. Thanks are also due to the reviewers who took time to read the first draft carefully and offer their suggestions: John M. Champion, University of Florida; Jeffrey R. Cornwall, University of Wisconsin at Oshkosh; and Lee G. Caldwell, University of Utah. Finally, my wife and daughter deserve thanks for putting up with my dedication to this task of writing, which took time away from family activities. There were times when I was anything but good-natured in dealing with these "weighty" matters, and yet they were understanding and sympathetic to what I was trying to do in writing this book. They also were faced with the difficult task of moving to a strange place for a semester and adjusting to a new situation.

*Fundamental Concepts
and Problems
in
Business Ethics*

1

What
Is
Business Ethics?

Some would say that there is no such thing as business ethics, either jokingly or seriously advocating the position that business and ethics don't go together. This kind of comment could be meant to imply that business is immoral, but it also could be made to suggest that moral considerations are inappropriate in business. There may be many men and women who perceive that ethics has application only to their personal life and not to their organizational life in a business institution. The business of business is to make a profit, and people who work for a business organization must concern themselves with producing goods and services to earn a profit; with buying and selling, developing new products, increasing market share, and other such business concerns rather than with morality.

The reason this view is popular in some circles may be because it is easier to deal with dollars and cents than with value judgments. People are more comfortable when discussing a business problem in terms of its bottom-line impact than in terms of its ethical impact. Most people in business are probably not very well trained in ethical analysis and are not familiar with ethical language and concepts. What they know about ethics may come from their religious background from which they have some vague notions of justice and other ethical concepts, but they have difficulty in applying them in a business context. Or their knowledge of ethics may come from some acquaintance with philosophy that they may have picked up somewhere along the way in their educational experience.

That business organizations have ethical impacts and that they are treated as moral entities should be readily apparent to anyone who reads the newspapers about business scandals and unethical practices that are exposed to the public and the appropriate authorities, who may take action against the company. Those who are concerned with the social responsibilities of business also treat business as a moral institution that has impacts on society that go beyond the production of goods and services to make a profit. Thus, the way many people treat a corporation in daily life would seem to expose as a piece of mythology the belief that business is an amoral institution.

If the problem is truly one of ethical ignorance, then some exposure to ethical concepts and problems might help to provide business managers and students with some moral sensibilities that can help them in recognizing the ethical dimensions of their activities and provide a way of thinking about these problems. Such exposure might help them to see problems that they might normally ignore, often at their peril. An exposure to concepts and problems in business ethics will not necessarily help people to be more moral, but it may help them to live more thoughtful and better-informed lives as employees in a business organization. The study of business ethics presupposes that people are moral beings who want to do the "right" thing but that there is often a great deal of confusion as to what actions and practices are morally appropriate.

DEFINITIONS AND APPROACHES

Business ethics is a subset of the study of ethics in general. Thus, a definition of what ethics in general means may be helpful in clarifying the concept of business ethics and distinguishing it from other kinds of ethical approaches. Ethics in general is concerned with actions and practices that are directed to improving the welfare of people. Ethicists explore the concepts and language that are used to direct such actions and practices to improve human welfare. "Some are primarily concerned with the justification of this concern itself, others with the delineation or justification of principles that specify appropriate welfare-meeting conduct, and others with the relationship between these principles and the rules or character traits that guide people toward specific behavior to achieve human welfare. In essence, ethics is concerned with clarifying what constitutes human welfare and the kind of conduct necessary to promote it."[1]

Ethics is the quest for an understanding of what constitutes a good life and a concern for creating the conditions for people to attain that good life. Thus, ethics deals with questions that relate to making a life worth living and helping people to achieve such a life. Ethics is largely a matter of perspective, putting every activity and goal in its place, knowing what is worth doing and not worth doing, knowing what is worth wanting and having and what is not worth wanting and having.[2]

Ethics is the study of what is good or right for human beings and what goals people ought to pursue and what actions they ought to perform. Ethics in general is

---

[1]Charles W. Powers and David Vogel, *Ethics in the Education of Business Managers* (Hastings-on-Hudson, N.Y.: Hastings Center, 1980), p. 1.

[2]Robert C. Solomon and Kristine R. Hanson, *Above the Bottom Line: An Introduction to Business Ethics* (New York: Harcourt Brace Jovanovich, 1983), p. 9.

a systematic attempt, through the use of reason, to make sense of our individual and social moral experience in such a way as to determine the rules that ought to govern human conduct and the values worth pursuing in life. Ethics concerns itself with human conduct, meaning human activity that is done knowingly and to a large extent willingly.[3]

The study of ethics is thus a philosophical inquiry into various theories of what is good for people and what is bad or evil, what constitutes right and wrong kinds of behavior with respect to human welfare and the good life, and what one ought to and ought not to do to promote human welfare and attain a life that is worth living. These ethical theories are philosophical systems that deal with the nature and justification of ethical principles, decisions, and problems.[4] This study of ethics is usually categorized into the following approaches.

Descriptive Approach

The descriptive approach consists of scientific studies or factual descriptions and explanations of moral behavior and beliefs in various societies or institutions. No attempt is made to pass judgment on the superiority or inferiority of these various ethical systems that are operative in different parts of the world or in different institutions. This approach is neutral because it does not advocate one set of values and beliefs over another but merely states that a certain set of values and ethics seems to be dominant in a society or in an institution.

Analytical Ethics

Conceptual ethics (sometimes called metaethics) consists of an analysis of the central terms in ethics in an attempt to understand the foundations of ethical systems and the functions of ethics in a social system. This approach involves clarifying and evaluating presuppositions and investigating questions of meaning and justification. Analytical ethics attempts to transcend existing ethical theories and principles, which may lead to conflicting courses of action, and judge them in light of ultimate values of human well-being and welfare to resolve such conflicts.

Prescriptive Ethics

General normative ethics is concerned with the formulation and defense of basic moral norms governing moral life. Normative ethics is concerned about presenting a particular set of principles and standards that would be best for people to follow in all areas of their lives. This approach to ethics seeks to uncover, develop, and justify the basic moral principles or the basic moral values of a moral system. Normative ethics is thus not morally neutral.

[3]Richard T. DeGeorge, *Business Ethics,* 2d ed. (New York: Macmillan Co., 1986), p. 15.

[4]Tom L. Beauchamp and Norman E. Bowie, *Ethical Theory and Business,* 2nd ed. (Englewood Cliffs, N.J.: Prentice-Hall, 1983), pp. 1, 3.

Applied normative ethics is a species of general normative ethics. It focuses the tools, concepts, and concerns of normative ethics to help specify and clarify the obligations of agents who regularly encounter ethical issues in particular sectors or spheres of activity. It is concerned about applying the principles of general normative ethics to specific moral problems that appear in certain areas of human life, such as those problems peculiar to a particular profession or to a particular institution in society.

Business ethics is concerned with the application of moral standards to the conduct of individuals involved in organizations through which modern societies produce and distribute goods and services. In business ethics an analysis of moral principles and norms is applied to the behavior of people in business institutions. It is a type of applied ethics concerned with clarifying the obligations and dilemmas of managers and other employees who make business decisions.

The terms *ethics* and *morality* are often used interchangeably in discussions about ethics, and yet it may be useful to distinguish between them to reduce confusion in certain situations. Ethics is concerned with the development and justification of principles that can be used to apply to specific situations where a decision has to be made about a particular action or practice. Ethics generally deals with the formulation of principles that can help resolve concrete ethical problems facing individuals in their daily lives. Morality, on the other hand, generally refers to traditions of belief that have evolved in societies over many years or even centuries concerning right and wrong conduct. Morality can be thought of as a social institution that has a history and a code of conduct that is implicit or explicit about how people ought to behave.[5] The two terms are very close in meaning, and this distinction does not always hold true in practice.

The terms *ethics* and *values* are also often used interchangeably. Ethics is usually considered to be the more general term, referring to conceptions of human welfare and the development of principles to attain human welfare. Values can be thought of as specific desires for concrete objects or beliefs that are held to be important. We can value specific goods and services that are available on the market or we can value more abstract concepts, such as freedom or equality. Whatever we value, however, stems from some general conceptions of a good life or a life that is worth living. We value freedom because we believe freedom is a fundamental human characteristic or need that makes for a better society. Human welfare is promoted if people are free to pursue their own interests and objectives. Ethics and values are thus closely related making them interchangeable concepts in many discussions.

THE EVOLUTION OF BUSINESS ETHICS

Tracing the development of business ethics as a field in its own right will help to understand where ethics fits into the business school curriculum and what factors have been responsible for the evolution of ethical concerns. While the subject of

[5]Ibid., pp. 1–2.

business ethics received some attention prior to the 1960s, it was with the rise of the social-responsibility debate that ethical concerns became of major importance to business organizations.[6] The years from 1960 to 1970 were years of sweeping social change that affected business organizations and the management of those organizations. The concern about civil rights for minorities, equal rights for women, protection of the physical environment, safety and health in the workplace, and a broad array of consumer issues has had far-reaching and long-lasting impacts on business organizations. The long-term effect of this social change has been a dramatic change in the "rules of the game" by which business is expected to operate.

Given this kind of social revolution, it is not surprising that the social environment of business was given increasing attention during the 1960s and 1970s by business corporations and schools of business and management. The concept of social responsibility came into its own as a response to the changing social values of society. Business executives began to talk about the social responsibilities of business and to develop specific social programs in response to problems of a social, rather than economic, nature. Schools of business and management implemented new courses in business and society or in the social responsibilities of business.

There are many definitions of social responsibility, but in general it means that a private corporation has responsibilities to society that go beyond the production of goods and services at a profit—that a corporation has a broader constituency to serve than stockholders alone. Corporations relate to society through more than just marketplace transactions and serve a wider range of values than the traditional economic ones that are prevalent in the marketplace. Corporations are more than economic institutions and have a responsibility to devote some of their resources to helping to solve some of the most pressing social problems, many of which corporations helped to cause.

The concept of social responsibility received increasing attention during the 1960s because of the need for corporations to respond to the changing social environment of business. This change was often described as a change in the terms of the contract between business and society that reflected changing expectations regarding the social performance of business.[7] The old contract between business and society was based on the view that economic growth was the source of all progress, social as well as economic. The engine providing this growth was considered to be the drive for profits by competitive private enterprise. The basic mission of business was thus to produce goods and services at a profit, and in so doing, business was making its maximum contribution to society and, in fact, being socially responsible.[8]

The new contract between business and society was based on the view that the single-minded pursuit of economic growth produced some detrimental side effects that imposed significant social costs on certain segments of society or on society as

[6]See Richard T. DeGeorge, "The Status of Business Ethics: Past and Future," Business Ethics Research Workshop, Stanford University, August 14–17, 1985.

[7]See Melvin Anshen, *Managing the Socially Responsible Corporation* (New York: Macmillan Co., 1974).

[8]See Milton Friedman, "The Social Responsibility of Business Is to Increase Its Profits," *New York Times Magazine,* September 13, 1970, pp. 122–26.

a whole. The pursuit of economic growth, it was argued, did not necessarily lead automatically to social progress. In many cases it led instead to a deteriorating physical environment, unsafe workplaces, needless exposure to toxic substances on the part of workers and consumers, discrimination against certain groups in society, urban decay, and other social problems. This new contract between business and society involved reducing these social costs of business by impressing upon business the idea that it has an obligation to work for social as well as economic betterment. This new contract did not invalidate the old contract; it simply added new terms or additional clauses to that contract.

> Today it is clear that the terms of the contract between society and business are, in fact, changing in substantial and important ways. Business is being asked to assume broader responsibilities to society than ever before and to serve a wider range of human values. Business enterprises, in effect, are being asked to contribute more to the quality of American life than just supplying quantities of goods and services.[9]

The concept of social responsibility is fundamentally an ethical concept. It involves changing notions of human welfare and emphasizes a concern with the social dimensions of business activity that have to do with improving the quality of life in society. It has provided a way for business to concern itself with these social dimensions and pay some attention to its social impacts. The word *responsibility* implies some kind of obligation to deal with social problems that business organizations were believed to have toward the society in which they functioned.

The debate about social responsibility reflected many of these ethical or moral dimensions. Proponents of the concept argued that (1) business must accommodate itself to social change if it expected to survive; (2) business must take a long-run or enlightened view of self-interest and help solve social problems in order to create a better environment for itself; (3) business could gain a better public image by being socially responsible; (4) government regulation could be avoided if business met the changing social expectations of society before the issues became politicized; (5) business had enormous resources that would be useful in solving social problems; (6) social problems could be turned into profitable business opportunities; and (7) business had a moral obligation to help solve social problems that it had created or at least perpetuated.

The opponents of social responsibility had equally formidable arguments. These arguments included the following: (1) the social-responsibility concept provides no mechanism for accountability as to the use of corporate resources; (2) managers are legally and ethically bound to earn the highest possible rate of return on the stockholder's investment in the companies they manage; (3) social responsibility poses a threat to the pluralistic nature of our society; (4) business executives have little experience and incentive to solve social problems; and (5) social responsibility is fundamentally a subversive doctrine that would undermine the foundations of a free-enterprise system if taken seriously.

---

[9]Committee for Economic Development, *Social Responsibilities of Business Corporations* (New York: CED, 1971), pp. 29–30.

After the smoke began to clear from this debate, it was obvious to many proponents and opponents of corporate social responsibility that there were several key issues in the debate that had not, and perhaps could not, be settled. One key issue concerned the operational definition of social responsibility. How shall a corporation's resources be allocated to help solve social problems? With what specific problems shall a given corporation concern itself? What priorities shall be established? Does social responsibility refer to company action taken to comply with government regulations or only to those voluntary actions that go beyond legal requirements? What goals or standards of performance shall be established? What measures shall be employed to determine if a corporation is socially responsible or socially irresponsible?

The traditional marketplace provided little or no information to the manager that would be useful in making decisions about solving social problems. But the concept of social responsibility in itself did not make up for this lack and provided no clearer guidelines for managerial behavior. Given this lack of precision, corporate executives who wanted to be socially responsible were left to follow their own values and interests or some rather vague generalizations about changing social values and public expectations. What this meant in practice, however, was often difficult to determine.

Another key problem with the concept of social responsibility was that the concept did not take into account the competitive environment in which corporations functioned. Many advocates of social responsibility treated the corporation as an isolated entity that had almost unlimited ability to engage in unilateral social action. Eventually, it came to be recognized that corporations were severely limited in their ability to respond to social problems. If a firm unilaterally engages in social action that increases its costs and prices, it will place itself at a competitive disadvantage relative to other firms in the industry that may not be concerned about being socially responsible.

The debate about social responsibility never took this institutional context of corporations seriously. Concerted action to solve social problems is not feasible in a competitive system unless all competitors pursue roughly the same policy on these problems. Since collusion among competitors is illegal, however, the only way such concerted action can occur is when some other institution, such as government, makes all competitors engage in the same activity and pursue the same policy. And that is, in fact, what happened. While the debate about social responsibility was going on and corporate executives were asking for a definition of their social responsibilities, government was rewriting the rules under which all corporations operated in society by developing a vast amount of legislation and regulation pertaining to the physical environment, occupational safety and health, equal opportunity, and consumer concerns.

The last issue that remained unresolved in the debate about social responsibility concerned the moral underpinnings of the notion. The term *responsibility* is fundamentally a moral one that implies an obligation to someone or something. It is clear to most people that business has an economic responsibility to produce goods and services efficiently and to perform other economic functions for society. These economic responsibilities constitute the reason for having something like a business organization. But why does business have social responsibilities? What are the moral foundations for a concern with its social impacts?

The proponents of social responsibility produced no clear and generally accepted moral principle that would impose upon business an obligation to work for social betterment.[10] Ascribing social responsibility to corporations does not necessarily imply that they are moral agents that are then responsible for their social impacts. But various moral strictures were used to try and impose this obligation on business, and various arguments were made to try to link moral behavior to business performance. Little was accomplished, however, by way of developing solid and acceptable moral support for the notion of social responsibility. Thus, the debate about social responsibility was very moralistic in many of its aspects, a debate that often generated a good deal of heat but very little light in most instances.

The intractability of these issues, according to one scholar, "posed the dreadful possibilities that the debate over corporate social responsibility would continue indefinitely with little prospect of final resolution or that it would simply exhaust itself and collapse as a viable legitimate question."[11] But beginning in the 1970s, a theoretical and conceptual reorientation began to take place regarding the corporation's response to the social environment. This new approach was labeled corporate social responsiveness, and while initially it appeared that only semantics was involved, it gradually became clear that the shift from responsibility to responsiveness was much more substantive. The shift represented an attempt to escape the unresolved dilemmas that emerged from the social-responsibility debate. This new concept of social responsiveness was defined by one author as follows:

> Corporate social responsiveness refers to the capacity of a corporation to respond to social pressures. The literal act of responding, or of achieving a generally responsive posture, to society is the focus of corporate social responsiveness. . . . One searches the organization for mechanisms, procedures, arrangements, and behavioral patterns that, taken collectively, would mark the organization as more or less capable of responding to social pressures. It then becomes evident that organizational design and managerial competence play important roles in how extensively and how well a company responds to social demands and needs.[12]

Thus, attention shifted from debate about a moral notion, social responsibility, to a more technical or at least morally neutral term, social responsiveness. Research in corporate responsiveness reflected this same shift and focused on internal corporate responsiveness to social problems and examined the ways in which corporations responded to such problems. Attempts were made to identify key variables within the organization that related to its responsiveness and discover structural changes that would enable a corporation to respond to social pressures

---

[10]William C. Frederick, "From CSR1 to CSR2: The Maturing of Business and Society Thought," Graduate School of Business, University of Pittsburgh, 1978, working paper no. 279, p. 5.

[11]Ibid.

[12]Ibid., p. 6.

more effectively. The important questions asked in this research were not moral, related to whether a corporation should respond to a social problem out of a sense of social responsibility, but more pragmatic and action oriented, dealing with the ability of a corporation to respond and what changes were necessary to enable it to respond more effectively.

One of the advantages of this approach is its managerial orientation. The concept ignores the philosophical debate about responsibility and obligation and focuses on the problems and prospects of making corporations more socially responsive. One of the reasons for research into response patterns is to discover those responses that have proven to be most effective in dealing with social problems. The approach also lends itself to more rigorous analytical research in examining specific techniques, such an environmental scanning and the social audit, to improve the response process. Such research can also discover how management can best institutionalize social policy throughout the organization. Such questions can be investigated as, What organizational structures are most appropriate? What role can top management play in enabling corporations to respond? What changes in the reward structure can improve the corporation's response to social problems? What role should public-affairs departments play in the response process? and How can social policy best be formulated for the organization as a whole?

Given these advantages, however, the concept of social responsiveness was still plagued with the same key problems that faced the concept of social responsibility. The concept of social responsiveness does not clarify how corporate resources shall be allocated for the solution of social problems. Companies respond to different problems in different ways and to varying degrees. But there is no clear idea as to what pattern of responsiveness will produce the greatest amount of social betterment. The philosophy of responsiveness does not help the company to decide what problems to get involved in and what priorities to establish. In the final analysis, it provides no better guidance to management than does social responsibility on the best strategies or policies to be adopted to produce social betterment. The concept seems to suggest that management itself, by determining the degree of social responsiveness and the pressures it will respond to, decides the meaning of the concept and what social goods and services will be produced.[13]

The concept of social responsiveness does not take the institutional context of business into account any more seriously than social responsibility did. Research in social responsiveness did not deal very thoroughly with the impact that government regulation was making on the corporation and with how the corporation was responding to this change in the political environment. Individual corporate institutions were again treated as rather isolated entities that could choose a response pattern irrespective of the institutional context in which a corporation operated. There was not enough concern with business-government relations and the role government played in the social-response process.

Finally, while the question of an underlying moral principle or theory is ignored in the research dealing with corporate social responsiveness in favor of

[13]Ibid., pp. 12–13.

more action-oriented concerns, this turns out to be a dubious advantage. Social pressures are assumed to exist, and it is believed as an article of faith that business must respond to them in some fashion. Consequently, business is placed more or less in a passive role of simply responding to social change. The concept of social responsiveness provides no moral basis for business to get involved in social problems. It contains no explicit moral or ethical theory and advocates no specific set of values for business to follow in making social responses.[14]

In the mid-1970s academics and business managers began to realize that a fundamental change was taking place in the political environment of business—that government was engaged in shaping business behavior and making business respond to a wide array of social problems by passing an unprecedented amount of legislation and writing new regulations pertaining to these problems. The political system responded to the social revolution of the 1960s and 1970s by enacting over a hundred new laws regulating business activity. Many new regulatory agencies were created, and new responsibilities were assigned to old agencies. These agencies issued thousands of new rules and procedural requirements that affected business decisions and operations.

This regulatory role of government continued to expand until the 1980 election of the Reagan administration. The new type of social regulation, as it came to be called, affected virtually every department or functional area within the corporation and every level of management. The growth of this new type of regulation was referred to as a second managerial revolution, involving a shift of decision-making power and control over the corporation from the managers of corporations to a vast cadre of government regulators, who were influencing, and in many cases, controlling managerial decisions in the typical business corporation.[15] The types of decisions that were becoming increasingly subject to government influence and control were basic operational decisions such as what line of business to go into, where products could be made, how they could be marketed, and what products could be produced.[16]

During the late 1970s, more and more attention was paid to the changing political environment of business. Books were written that provided a comprehensive overview of the impacts government regulation was making on business.[17] Studies were completed that attempted to measure the costs of social regulation to the private sector.[18] This activity drew attention to the political environment of business and showed that this environment had become increasingly hostile, giving

[14]Ibid., pp. 14–16.

[15]Murray L. Weidenbaum, *Business, Government, and the Public* (Englewood Cliffs, N.J.: Prentice-Hall, 1977), p. 285.

[16]Murray L. Weidenbaum, *The Future of Business Regulation* (New York: AMACOM, 1979), p. 34.

[17]Ibid.

[18]See Murray L. Weidenbaum and Robert DeFina, *The Cost of Federal Regulation of Economic Activity* (Washington, D.C.: American Enterprise Institute, 1978); and Arthur Anderson, *Cost of Government Regulation* (New York: Business Roundtable, 1979).

rise to legislation and regulation that interfered with the ability of business to perform its basic economic mission. Largely because of this activity a national debate on regulation was initiated that culminated in the election of an administration in 1980 that promised to reduce the regulatory burden on business.

Thus began a serious concern with public policy as a new dimension of management. Many business leaders recognized the importance of public policy to business and advocated that business managers become more active in the political process and work more closely with government and other groups to help shape public policy. The motivation for this concern with public policy is clear. If the rules of the game for business are being rewritten through the public-policy process and business is being forced to respond to social values through complying with laws and regulations, then business has a significant interest to learn more about the public-policy process and become involved in helping to write the rules by which it is going to have to live. These rules should not be left solely up to the public-interest groups, congressional representatives, or agency employees.

Business has since come to adopt a more sophisticated approach to public policy, an approach that has been called the proactive stance. This term means that rather than fighting change, which has often proved to be a losing battle, or simply accommodating itself to change, business attempts to influence change by becoming involved in the public-policy process. Business can attempt to influence public opinion with regard to social issues of concern to society, and it can attempt to influence the legislative and regulatory process with regard to specific laws and regulations.

The public-policy approach has some distinct advantages over the corporate social-responsibility and social-responsiveness concepts discussed earlier. For the most part, there is no question about the nature and extent of management's social responsibilities. Once regulations are approved, these responsibilities are spelled out in excruciating detail. The government gets involved in specifying technology that can be employed, publishing labeling requirements, developing safety standards for products, specifying safety equipment, and hundreds of other such management responsibilities. Where questions arise about the legality or feasibility of regulations, the court system is available to settle disputes of this nature. Management is thus told in great detail what social problems to be concerned with and to what extent it has to respond.

Obviously, the public-policy approach treats business in its institutional context and advocates that managers learn more about government and the public-policy process so that they can appropriately influence the process. Government is recognized as the appropriate body to formalize and formulate public policy for the society as a whole. Some form of response by government to most social issues is believed to be inevitable, and no amount of corporate reform along the lines of corporate social responsibility or corporate social responsiveness is going to eliminate some form of government involvement. Government has a legitimate right to formulate public policy for corporations in response to changing public expectations.

Society can choose to allocate its resources any way it wants and on the basis of any criteria it deems relevant. If society wants to enhance the quality of air and water, it can choose to allocate resources for the production of these goods and put constraints on business in the form of standards. . . . These nonmarket decisions are made by those who participate in the public policy process and represent their views of what is best for themselves and society as a whole. . . . It is up to the body politic to determine which market outcomes are and are not appropriate. If market outcomes are not to be taken as normative, a form of regulation which requires public participation is the only alternative. The social responsibility of business is not operational and certainly not to be trusted. When business acts contrary to the normal pressures of the marketplace, only public policy can replace the dictates of the market.[19]

There is also, at least on the surface, no need for a moral underpinning for a business obligation to produce social betterment. Society makes decisions about the allocations of resources through the public-policy process based on its notions about social betterment. The result is legislation and regulation that impinge on business behavior. Business, then, has a moral obligation to obey the law as a good citizen. Failure to do so subjects business and executives to all sorts of penalties. The social responsibility of business is thus to follow the directives of society at large as expressed in and through the public-policy process.

This concept of public policy, however, which at first glance seemed to eliminate many of the dilemmas and problems with social responsibility and social responsiveness, actually fares no better on closer examination. As business becomes more politically involved in writing the rules of the game or preventing new ones from being written, the question of managerial guidelines and principles again becomes relevant. What criteria, other than self-interest, are relevant to guide the corporation in the development of its political strategies? Shall these strategies be judged solely on their short-term effectiveness, say, in helping to defeat a certain bill that business didn't like? What candidates should a corporate political action committee support—only those who are judged to have the company's best interests in mind and share traditional business values? Again, the nagging question of defining social betterment, or in a public-policy context, of defining the public interest, reappears.

Regarding the institutional context, there is the question of the appropriate role for government to play in shaping business behavior. Should government continue with a command-and-control system of regulation to accomplish social objectives, or should it adopt other incentive mechanisms more consistent with market behavior? On the other side of the coin, what is the appropriate role for business to play in the political process? If business is perceived as being too influential in the political process and constituting a threat to the pluralistic nature of American society, and if its behavior is perceived as being too self-serving and not cognizant of the broader public interest, adverse public reaction can be expected.

[19]Rogene A. Buchholz, "An Alternative to Social Responsibility," *MSU Business Topics* 25, no. 3 (Summer 1977), 12, 16.

How can business avoid this kind of reaction and yet look after its own legitimate interests in the public-policy process?

And finally, the absence of a clear moral underpinning for public-policy involvement still presents a problem. Does the proactive approach simply mean that business attempts to minimize the impact of social change on itself? Does not business have more of an obligation to society than is evident in self-serving attempts to manipulate the political environment for its own advantage? Does not business have a moral obligation that goes beyond obeying the law and complying with government regulations? If business does have social and political responsibilities as well as economic responsibilities, what is the moral basis of these responsibilities?

THE ROLE OF BUSINESS ETHICS

Ethics is thus an important component of the social-political context in which public policy is formulated. The ethical standards that society holds help to shape public opinion and affect the values and attitudes that are dominant at any given time in the society at large. Ethical standards interact in a very complex fashion with other components of the social-political environment and thus help to determine which public issues are given attention by a society and the eventual outcome of the debate about issues that reach the public-policy agenda.

All of these fundamental questions about social responsibility, social responsiveness, and public policy are difficult because they are fundamentally moral and ethical questions having to do with a definition of human welfare, the meaning and purpose of life, the nature of human community, and similar questions that are basic to human existence. These questions cannot be answered by appeal to an economic calculus such as profit and loss, nor can they be answered satisfactorily through a political process. For business to be effective in responding to social and political issues, these moral and ethical dimensions of the issues must be explicitly recognized and discussed. Ethical questions are fundamental to an institution such as business because society allows institutions to be developed and continue operating based on its conceptions of human welfare and the things that make a life worth living. These institutions have to change as society's notions of these ethical concepts change.

In the early 1980s, the subject of business ethics received a great deal of increased attention in schools of business and management around the country as well as in corporations themselves. Ethical issues were given explicit attention, not subsumed under the topic of social responsibility, social responsiveness, or public policy. Several studies of business ethics were completed including the highly influential report entitled *Ethics in the Education of Business Managers,* published by the Institute of Society, Ethics and the Life Sciences at the Hastings Center. New centers for the study of business ethics and values cropped up around the country. Corporate support for research and teaching about the subject of business ethics increased as did corporate efforts to include business ethics as an important component of a management-training program. Many more conferences on various aspects of business ethics were held at locations around the country. The number of textbooks and casebooks in the field of business ethics proliferated, most being written, incidentally, by philosophers rather than the faculty in management schools.[20] Endowed chairs in business ethics were established at several schools, some on a rotating basis.[21] And finally, many more courses in business ethics were taught in schools of business and management. A survey conducted by the Center for Business Ethics at Bentley College in 1980 found that almost half of the 655 schools of business and management that responded to their survey offered a course in business ethics. Of the 338 schools that did not offer a course, 48 were planning to offer such a course, and another 144 would like to at some time in the future.[22]

There are several reasons behind this interest in business ethics, but in general, it can be said that this increased interest reflects some fundamental changes in society regarding a consensus on ethical standards and the conduct of institutions, including business organizations. The debate about business ethics reflects the confusion that has resulted from a breakup of the notions previously held about how a business ought to act in a market-oriented society. This broader view of the problem is held by Powers and Vogel writing in the Hastings Center report.

> In our view, the new concern for corporate ethics and managerial ethics is the logical culmination of a series of social transformations through which the connecting tissues that make up the "organic" connection between management, institution, and society have eroded. What constitutes "ethical custom" is evaporating. The ability of the market mechanism to carry the normative freight between corporations and society is deterioraiting as the society increasingly turns to other ways to try to connect its changing values to corporate practice.[23]

The authors go on to list four factors they believe have contributed to this erosion of a consensus about appropriate corporate and managerial practice. These factors include: (1) the growth in the size of corporate institutions has meant that the market does not govern many current corporate activities and decisions—in a sense, corporations have outgrown the market mechanism; (2) there has been a growth in the scope of legal constraints and requirements on business and of governmental involvement in corporate activities; (3) public concern has arisen about the externalities (such as pollution) that are not amenable to direct market control; and (4)

---

[20]Powers and Vogel, *Ethics*, pp. 31–34.

[21]In a novel settlement in 1983, U.S. District Judge Warren K. Urbom ordered a highway-contracting company that had pleaded guilty to bid rigging to donate $1,475,000 to endow a chair in business ethics at the University of Nebraska. The idea apparently came from a former student who said he had never heard anyone mention bid rigging while he was in school.

[22]W. Michael Hoffman and Jennifer Mills Moore, "Results of a Business Ethics Curriculum Survey Conducted by the Center for Business Ethics," *Journal of Business Ethics* 1, no. 2 (May 1982), 81–83.

[23]Powers and Vogel, *Ethics,* p. 7. Reproduced by permission. Copyright © 1980 The Hastings Center.

[24]Ibid., pp. 7–8.

"human dignity" and the "value of human life" have become new priorities in the agenda of social values.[24]

Other reasons for the interest in business ethics include the general decline of confidence in business leadership as shown by polls of public attitudes. Scandals such as illegal campaign contributions in this country and foreign payments abroad contribute to this decline of confidence and raise questions in the public mind about the degree to which corporate leaders themselves believe in and abide by the rules of the market mechanism. The growth of management as a "profession" may be another factor that carries with it a corresponding interest in developing ethical standards for management that are uniformly accepted. Finally, questions about the legitimacy of the management function as raised in the debate about corporate governance may motivate business managers to find a new ethical justification for their role in society.

The emergence of this concern about business ethics is thus consistent with the emergence of public policy as of increasing importance to business and management. As long as there is a consensus as to the appropriateness of the market mechanism in allocating all or at least the great majority of society's resources, the ethical notions embedded in the market concept are also accepted as appropriate with respect to business and managerial conduct. There is no need to raise these basic ethical assumptions to a conscious level and debate them. Concern about ethics is limited to situations where the accepted standards are violated. But as that consensus begins to crumble and public policy begins to supplant or supplement the market and increasingly shapes corporate behavior, ethical notions increasingly come to the surface and are the subject of intense and very conscious debate.

This evolution of business ethics as a legitimate object of study in and of itself is shown in figure 1.1. Business ethics offers an opportunity to confront the normative issues that were a part of the social-responsibility debate but were not handled very effectively, and that tended to be ignored by advocates of social responsiveness and public policy. These normative issues are at the heart of concerns about the future of the corporation and the appropriate roles for business to play in society. Normative concerns can provide a foundation for the continuing managerial concerns about responding to social pressures in an effective manner and learning to appropriately and effectively influence the public-policy process. Managerial activities must be based on ethical principles that are acceptable in the society at large and consistent with notions of human welfare and fulfillment that are important in Western societies.

FIGURE 1.1

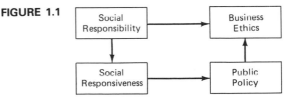

SUGGESTED READING

ACKERMAN, ROBERT W.   *The Social Challenge to Business.* Cambridge: Harvard University Press, 1975.

————, AND RAYMOND BAUER.   *Corporate Social Responsiveness: The Modern Dilemma.* Reston, Va.: Reston Publishing Co., 1976.

BOWEN, HOWARD R.   *Social Responsibilities of Businessmen.* New York: Harper & Row, Publishers, 1953.

CARROLL, ARCHIE B., ED.   *Managing Corporate Social Responsibility.* Boston: Little, Brown and Co., 1977.

CAVANAGH, GERALD F.   *American Business Values,* 2d ed. Englewood Cliffs, N.J.: Prentice-Hall, 1984.

CHAMBERLAIN, NEIL W.   *The Limits of Corporate Responsibility.* New York: Basic Books, 1973.

————.   *Remaking American Values: Challenge to a Business Society.* New York: Basic Books, 1977.

DAVIS, KEITH, AND WILLIAM C. FREDERICK.   *Business and Society: Management, Public Policy, Ethics,* 5th ed. New York: McGraw-Hill Book Co., 1984.

FRIEDMAN, MILTON.   *Capitalism and Freedom.* Chicago: University of Chicago Press, 1962.

PRESTON, LEE E., AND JAMES E. POST.   *Private Management and Public Policy.* Englewood Cliffs, N.J.: Prentice-Hall, 1975.

POWERS, CHARLES W., AND DAVID VOGEL.   *Ethics in the Education of Business Managers.* Hastings-on-Hudson, N.Y.: Hastings Center, 1980.

RESEARCH AND POLICY COMMITTEE OF THE COMMITTEE FOR ECONOMIC DEVELOPMENT.   *Social Responsibilities of Business Corporations.* New York: Committee for Economic Development, 1971.

STEINER, GEORGE A., AND JOHN F. STEINER.   *Business, Government, and Society,* 4th ed. New York: Random House, 1985.

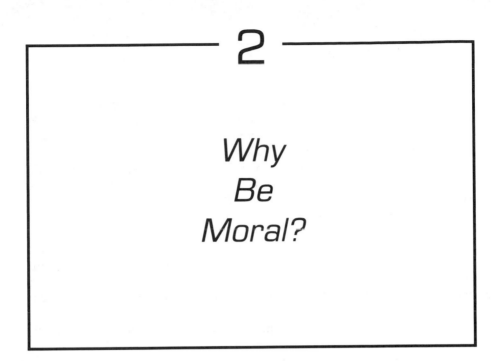

2

Why
Be
Moral?

The description in the previous chapter of the development of business ethics raises the question of why managers should be concerned about ethics and morality. Why should managers attempt to be moral and worry about ethical concerns? This question about the rationale for moral concerns is an old philosophical question that has been debated a good deal in the literature. For managers of business organizations, however, the question is critically important and not just a case of philosophical speculation. The question of, Why be moral? dealt with in this chapter has direct relevance at a practical level for business managers. Many would say that unless being ethical has something to do with business performance, ethics will have little impact on managerial behavior and action. Managers have to be concerned about the performance of their organizations, and unless ethics can somehow contribute to the goals the manager is attempting to attain, ethics will most likely remain in the area of philosophical speculation.

Another way of stating this question that has more meaning in a managerial context is to ask whether good ethics is good business. Does being ethical and following ethical principles that are important in a society or being faithful to the ethical precepts of a particular religious tradition lead to better business performance in the sense of higher profits, greater market share, or whatever other performance measure is relevant in a given situation? Or is it necessary or even desirable that ethics should contribute to performance in the marketplace? Isn't virtue its own reward even in a managerial context? There have been various ways to answer these questions that are important to consider in a discussion of this problem.

THE TRADITIONAL VIEW

The so-called traditional view on this question assumes that good ethics and good business is all part of the same question. There is and can be no divergence between the operation of a successful business organization and ethical behavior on the part of the organization. Such a divergence cannot exist because ethics is subsumed or totally contained in terms of marketplace performance. What is considered to be ethical is exactly the same as what is considered to be good business. The ethical notion that forms the basis of this view is the principle of economizing. A business organization is formed to provide goods and services that people in a society are willing to buy at prices they can afford. In order to do this successfully, business must economize in the use of resources—combine them efficiently—so that it can earn profits to continue in business and perhaps even expand into new markets.

The ethical performance of business is thus tied up with marketplace performance. If a business organization is successful and earns a satisfactory level of profits, this means that the business has economized in the use of resources, assuming that competition exists in the markets it is serving. The business has produced something people want to buy and has done so in such a way that has met the competition. Successful performance in the marketplace is ethical behavior, and there is no divergence between being ethical and being successful in the marketplace. They are believed to be one and the same thing.

The traditional view was stated some years ago by a management theorist, Oliver Sheldon, who in the closing chapter of his book on management strongly advocated the development of a professional creed for management.[1] According to Sheldon, the managerial function is a constant factor in any industrial organization no matter what external forces exist or the nature of the economic system in which the organization operates. The function of management remains much the same under any set of external conditions and is that element charged with guiding the organization through periods of change. Management is the one stable element in the process of evolution. There is no structure or system where management does not fulfill approximately the same functions as it does under the present system in this country.

Because management was such an important factor in modern societies all over the world Sheldon thought it was important to develop a managerial creed, to devise a philosophy of management or a code of principles that is "scientifically determined and generally accepted" and which will act as a guide for the daily practice of the profession. Without such a creed, says Sheldon, there can be "no guarantee of efficiency, no hope of concerted effort, and no assurance of stability."[2] Such a creed, in other words, can help to establish the legitimacy of the managerial function and assure its continuity.

Sheldon's creed links the managerial function to the well-being of the com-

---

[1]Oliver Sheldon, *The Philosophy of Management* (London: Sir Isaac Pitman & Sons, 1923), pp. 280–91.

[2]Ibid., p. 284.

munity of which it is a part and encourages management to take the initiative in raising the general ethical standards and conception of social justice in the community. The goods and services produced by a company "must be furnished at the lowest prices compatible with an adequate standard of quality, and distributed in such a way as directly or indirectly to promote the highest ends of the community."[3] Such a statement calls for management to be responsible and ethical in relation to broader community interests. Management is encouraged to look beyond the bottom line and the interests of stockholders and be concerned about what could be called the public interest. The creed recognizes that management serves at the discretion of society and derives its legitimacy from being a useful social function, a theme found in modern social-responsibility literature.

But what are the interests of the community, at least as Sheldon sees them? A close reading of the creed shows that it is based on the ethic of economizing, that the primary concern of management, according to Sheldon, is to promote the efficient use of resources, both personal, or human, resources and capital, or material, resources. The primary focus of the creed is on economic utilization of the factors of production, which can be determined by the scientific method. Thus, the community is presumably interested in an efficient use of resources in order to increase its standard of living. So management derives its legitimacy from applying scientific principles in running corporate organizations to accomplish this objective.

> Industry exists to provide the commodities and services which are necessary for the good life of the community, in whatever volume they are requested. . . . It is for Management, while maintaining industry upon an economic basis, to achieve the object for which it exists by the development of efficiency—both personal or human efficiency, in the workers, in the managerial staff, and in the relations between the two, and impersonal efficiency, in the methods and material conditions of the factory.[4]

There is no mention in the creed about what is now called the social responsibilities of management. While Sheldon recognizes the importance of certain aspects of the external environment, such as government, public attitudes, and foreign trade, social issues are not mentioned. Perhaps it is not fair to criticize Sheldon for this omission, as his creed only reflects the times in which he wrote. Social issues such as pollution, equal opportunity, and occupational safety and health were not generally recognized as serious problems that needed attention in those years. However, a more modern statement of the same view by Milton Friedman, who engages in the debate about social responsibility, argues that the social responsibility of business is to increase its profits.[5] In other words, the social and ethical responsibilities of business are exhausted in terms of marketplace performance. As long as business performs its economizing function well, it has fulfilled its social and ethical responsibilities, and nothing more need be said.

---

[3]Both quotes are from ibid., p. 285.

[4]Ibid., pp. 285, 286. Quoted by permission of Pitman Publishing, London.

[5]See Milton Friedman, "The Social Responsibility of Business Is to Increase Its Profits," *New York Times Magazine,* September 13, 1970, pp. 122–26.

Another characteristic of this view can be seen in the method Sheldon advocates to make the creed specific and to develop a set of standards to guide managerial practice. These standards, according to Sheldon, can be determined by the analytical and synthetical methods of science. The aim of those who are practicing the management profession should be to develop a "science of industrial management" that is distinct from the science it employs and the technique of any particular industry.[6] Yet if management is truly a science and the practice of management can be circumscribed by a set of scientific principles, what need is there for a philosophy of management or a professional creed for management? If management is a science, it becomes nothing more than the application of scientific principles to concrete situations. It involves no consideration of responsibilities to the larger community outside marketplace behavior nor any conscious ethical reflection that is a part of a true professional activity.

Thus, the traditional view of ethics and business subsumes ethics under marketplace performance and does not necessitate any conscious ethical considerations of business's responsibilities to society other than successful economic performance. Ethics is totally captured by the notion of economizing, which can be promoted by the development of scientific principles related to an efficient combination of resources. One advantage of this view is that it does at least place ethics at the core of managerial behavior and makes ethics central to the performance of the management function. The disadvantage of this approach is that it removes any need for conscious ethical reflection on the part of management but leaves it for the management scientists and economists to develop guidelines and principles that promote efficiency.

CHANGING VIEWS

While not everyone adhered to this view and accepted the notion that business was solely an economic institution with only economic responsibilities, it does seem that this view of ethics and business was the prevailing view in our society for several decades. And as long as the system worked well enough for most people, there were not likely to be any serious questions raised about the ethical behavior of business people outside the marketplace context. It was the concern with social responsibilities that began to raise serious questions about this view of ethics and business. The problems that social-responsibility advocates addressed, such as pollution and unsafe workplaces, were in large part created by the drive for efficiency in the marketplace. Thus, it began to be argued that there was a divergence between the performance of business in the marketplace and its performance as far as the social aspects of its behavior were concerned.

People began to believe that cleaning up pollution, providing safer workplaces, producing products that were safe to use, promoting equal opportunity, and attempting to eliminate poverty in our society had something to do with promoting

[6]Sheldon, *Philosophy of Management,* p. 290.

human welfare and creating the "good life" in our society. Yet business was causing some of these problems and perpetuating others in its quest for an efficient allocation of resources. For example, by economizing in the use of resources and disposing of its waste material as cheaply as possible by dumping it into the air or disposing of toxic material by simply dumping barrels of chemicals in some "out-of-the-way" place, business was causing some serious pollution problems regarding air quality and poisoning of drinking water. By always hiring the best-qualified person for a job opening and not having some kind of an affirmative-action program, business was helping to perpetuate the effects of discrimination against minorities and women.

It was at these points of intersection between the economic performance of business and changing social values of society that ethical questions began to arise. Business increasingly came to be viewed as a social as well as an economic institution that had social impacts that needed to be considered by management. Social-responsibility advocates strongly argued that management needed to take the social impacts of business into account when developing policies and strategies, and much effort was devoted to convincing management to take its social responsibilities seriously. A great deal of research was done to help management redesign corporate organizations and develop policies and practices that would enable corporations to respond to the social expectations of society and measure their social performance.

The deficiencies of the traditional view of ethics and business began to be exposed. It became clear that there were many points of divergence between good business performance and what society expected of its business organizations in terms of ethical behavior. An ethical creed based on this traditional view, such as the one proposed by Sheldon, doesn't include these social aspects of corporate activities and encourage management to pay attention to the social impacts of corporate operations. Thus, it provides no means or rationale for management to internalize the social costs of production and leaves this task to government regulation, a social-control mechanism that is generally unacceptable to management as well as inefficient in many of its aspects.

While Sheldon wanted to see management in a broader social and ethical context, he ended up being a victim of his own scientific outlook. Science is descriptive in nature and cannot prescribe for management or society the objectives that are worth pursuing. While the scientific method is crucially important to management, it is not sufficient in and of itself to provide an ethical or moral philosophy for management. Such a philosophy can no longer be built solely on the notion of economizing but must include the broader purposes of the community and its welfare, an ethical vision that Sheldon so eloquently stated but then failed to develop.

The problem facing modern management theorists who accept the fact that a divergence often exists between ethical behavior and marketplace behavior and one cannot be subsumed under the other is how to connect ethics with management in a way that is not peripheral to business operations. One way is simply to argue that good ethics is good business, that being ethical will lead to success in the marketplace. Ethical behavior will be rewarded by increased profits, improved performance on the stock market, and other relevant measures of business success. This view as opposed to the traditional view of business ethics, is that ethics is not subsumed under marketplace performance and the notion of economizing but has a separate grounding. Ethical considerations are not exhausted by economizing in the use of resources and deserve conscious reflection and attention. But by choosing to be ethical in all aspects of business operations and following separate ethical principles, management will be economically successful as well as ethical.

The social-responsibility advocates tried to make this argument in convincing management to take the notion seriously. They made various arguments based on the notion of long-run self-interest that by being socially responsible, business was taking account of its long-range health and survival. Business could not remain a healthy and viable organization in a society that was deteriorating. Thus it made sense for business to devote some of its resources to helping solve some of the most serious social problems of society—inferior education, discrimination, poverty—because business could function better in a society where most people enjoyed a high standard of living and an improved quality of life.

Other arguments had to do with gaining a better public image—that by being socially responsible, a business organization could improve its image in society and in this way gain more customers and provide more of an incentive for investors to put their money in the company. There are several examples of companies that have tried to present themselves as concerned about public health and the environment through their advertising program. Finally, other arguments had to do with the avoidance of government regulation, that by being socially responsible and effectively responding to changing social expectations, business might be able to eliminate the necessity of onerous government regulations that would affect its profits and other aspects of performance.

These arguments were never very convincing because they were never based on a solid moral philosophy about the nature of the corporation and its management but were more in the nature of moralizing about certain aspects of business behavior. The transparent falsity of these claims, and indeed of the general claim that good ethics is good business, was evident to many critics of this view. Being socially responsible costs money. Pollution-control equipment is expensive to buy and operate. Ventilation equipment to take toxic fumes out of the workplace is expensive. Proper disposal of toxic wastes in landfills can be very costly and time consuming. These efforts cut into profits, and in a competitive system, companies that go very far in this direction will simply price themselves out of the market. This is a fact of life for companies operating in a free-enterprise system that the social-responsibility advocates never took seriously.

> . . . every business . . . is, in effect, "trapped" in the business system it has helped to create. It is incapable, as an individual unit, of transcending that system. . . . the dream of the socially responsible corporation that, replicated over and over again can transform our society is illusory. . . . Because their aggregate power is not unified, not truly collective, not organized, they [corporations] have no way, even if they wished, of redirecting that power to meet the most pressing needs of society. . . .

Such redirection could only occur through the intermediate agency of government rewriting the rules under which all corporations operate.[7]

The argument that good ethics leads to good business also smacks of works righteousness, a criticism that has religious origins. There is no guarantee that a ''good'' person will be successful in terms of good health, material benefits, or any of the other dimensions that might be used to measure success at any given time and place. Indeed, it is often argued that virtue is its own reward and does not necessarily lead to good or bad consequences. Studies that have been done to try to demonstrate a relationship between socially responsible behavior and stock market performance or increased profitability are at best inconclusive and at worst irrelevant. Being ''good'' has no necessary connection with being successful, either on a philosophical or empirical level.

Thus, the view that good ethics is good business is subject to serious question, but if there is no close linkage between ethics and business performance, this could mean that ethics may remain peripheral to management concerns. Management has to be concerned about the economic performance of the organization. It cannot set aside these requirements to pursue some ethical or social objectives that conflict with economic performance and expect to remain in business for very long. When there is a choice to be made between an ethical ought and a technical must—something business must do to remain a viable organization within the system—it seems clear which path most managements would follow. Technical business matters are the ultimate values—a technical business necessity is a must that always takes precedence over an ethical ought that would be nice to implement but is simply not practical under most business conditions.[8]

It could be argued that ethical ideals will not provide answers to the problems of finance, personnel, production, and general management decision making. The businessperson's role is defined largely, though not exclusively, in terms of private gain and profit, and to suggest that this can be set aside for adherence to a set of ethical principles that may conflict with that role is startlingly naive and romantic. The businessperson is locked into a going system of values and ethics that largely determine the actions that can be taken. There is little question that at any given time individuals who are active within an institution are subject in large measure to its prevailing characteristics.

This divergence between good ethics and good business poses a serious problem for business ethics. For ethics to be taken seriously by business schools and by the management of business organizations, it must be related in some fashion to business performance. There must be a way to relate ethics to the core management functions, or else it will be nothing more than the liberal arts frosting on the

---

[7]Neil W. Chamberlain, *The Limits of Corporate Responsibility* (New York: Basic Books, 1973), pp. 4, 6. Copyright © 1973 by Basic Books, Inc., Publisher. Reprinted by permission of the publisher.

[8]See Benjamin and Sylvia Selekman, *Power and Morality in a Business Society* (New York: McGraw-Hill Book Co., 1956).

business school curriculum, something to be taught as long as the time and money exist but one of the first courses to go if times change and resources become scarce. The problem is one of making ethics central to the task of management and linking ethics to business performance.

A NEW VIEW

A possible way out of this problem has been suggested by Lisa Newton in an article entitled ''The Internal Morality of the Corporation.'' Newton digs beneath the surface of the good-ethics-leads-to-good-business view and finds another suggestion about the relation of ethics and business in the literature on corporate culture, particularly Peters and Waterman's best seller *In Search of Excellence,* and Deal and Kennedy's *Corporate Culture.* The suggestion made in this literature, as Newton sees it, is that the very requirements of profitable business constitute a morality and leave managers with little choice but to do good and avoid evil. Profitability requires morality, and a moral result is required by the very process by which profit is sought.[9]

> The interesting feature of the claim we are examining is its insistence that the corporation must be moral first—must treat employees as valuable and autonomous individuals, must honestly concern itself with quality of product and service, and the welfare of the customers, in order to create that institutional solidarity, ''strong culture,'' or ''corporate integrity,'' as we shall call it, from which alone long term profitability flows.[10]

Newton argues that the corporation can be seen as much more than a profit machine. It is in fact an ongoing human society, a social context in which its employees spend the greater part of their lives and energy. The manager of such an organization, who is entrusted with this valuable resource, would seem to be under a moral obligation to take very seriously its role as manager of human lives rather than just a profit-making machine. Such an understanding may begin to provide the moral basis of the corporation as an association.[11] The managers of excellent companies exemplify to some extent an understanding of this role of management.

> The excellent company concentrates not on financial goals, let alone internal political goals, but on products, services, and activities. Doing whatever you are doing very well takes first priority.
>
>   A concern to satisfy the needs of the customer, and to protect the safety and welfare of customers and employees is manifest in the ''excellent'' companies studied. The leaders in these companies endeavor to communicate that concern for welfare to each part of the company.

[9]Lisa H. Newton, ''The Internal Morality of the Corporation,'' *Journal of Business Ethics,* 5 (1986), 249.

[10]Ibid., p. 250. Copyright © 1986 by D. Reidel Publishing Company. Reprinted by permission.

[11]Ibid., p. 252.

Above all, a respect for the individual, not as recipient of the actions of others but as initiator of action, is a keystone of the operation of an excellent company. The customers are brought into the decisionmaking process. The employees are treated as autonomous adults, capable of making their own decisions, following through on them, and taking responsibility for them.[12]

How do the excellent companies view profits and the relationship between a company's pursuit of excellence and profits. Newton draws three observations or conclusions from the excellence literature related to this question. These observations include the following: (1) the excellent companies have created an integrated normative set of values in which the value of profitability has a defined place; (2) profit is not considered important enough, however, to occupy an executive to the exclusion of other, more important concerns; and (3) companies that pursue only profit do not attain their chosen goal as well as those who whole-heartedly devote themselves to some other goal or activity that can absorb the entire energies and devotion of a human being.[13]

At first glance this view appears to be simply another variation of the good-ethics-is-good-business view. But a closer look shows that what is implied here is that ethical behavior must be pursued for its own sake because that is the essential nature of the management task. Ethics cannot be pursued in the hopes that such pursuit will lead to higher profits. The empirical fact that the excellent companies were also profitable does not establish a connection between excellence and profitability or between ethics and profitability. That this is the view Newton wants to advocate becomes clear later in the article when she describes profit as largely a matter of luck, public whim, and the state of the economy.

Profit may, in the long run, be largely a matter of luck, of being in the right place at the right time, at most, of making the right guess about the future twists and turns of a chancy market in an inherently unpredictable economy in an insane world. . . . we cannot say with any assurance that corporate integrity will be profitable. . . . profit is essentially external to the enterprise, and should not . . . be taken too seriously as a day-by-day measure of the worth of corporate activity.[14]

Such a radical view of profits would probably not be acceptable to most managers let alone business schools, which would like to think that what they teach has something to do with running a more profitable organization in a competitive environment. What Newton has done is turn the question of ethics and profits around and present a radical alternative to the traditional view of the relation between ethics and business performance. In her view, good business is good ethics, not the other way around. Economic performance is largely a matter of luck and is not to be taken too seriously. What is important about management is how it treats its employees and customers and others with whom it relates, and ethical

---

[12]Ibid., p. 253. Copyright © 1986 by D. Reidel Publishing Company. Reprinted by permission.
[13]Ibid., p. 255.
[14]Ibid., p. 256. Copyright © 1986 by D. Reidel Publishing Company. Reprinted by permission.

matters are of central importance in these relationships. Thus management is ethics, the ethics of excellence if you will, and economic performance is not necessarily connected with ethical behavior. Managers should first be concerned with their ethical relationships and let profits more or less take care of themselves since they are not under control of the organization anyhow.

IMPLICATIONS

How then shall we think about the relationship between ethics and business? Perhaps Newton's view is too radical to be adopted by most managers in today's world. Surely they have to take profits seriously and cannot just set aside this concern and hope their organization survives by chance events. The argument could be made that such lack of concern would be an abdication of their role in society and their responsibilities to shareholders, creditors, and others who have a financial interest in the corporation. Thus, the relationship between good ethics and good business is still a problem, and ethics must be made central to management concerns without eliminating a concern about profits, which are in some way a measure of how well a corporation is economizing in the use of resources, a value that will always be important in a world of scarcity.

However, the comments Newton makes about management, business organizations, and ethics does lead in new directions that may be fruitful to explore further. One important implication of her ideas is that corporations can be viewed as ethical systems. They are organizations that either create or destroy values that are important to people and to the society in which corporations function. If ethics is understood as having something to do with actions that are directed to improving the welfare of people, then one primary mission of business is to enhance the economic welfare of society by producing goods and services that make people live's better and more fulfilling. In this sense, business creates economic value by taking resources and combining them in such a way as to produce something that has utility and will sell in the marketplace. Business can also destroy economic value by combining resources inefficiently or unwisely and producing something that won't sell and eventually has to be scrapped.

But business is not just an economic institution that has to do only with economic value; its activities have other dimensions. Business is also a social institution that creates or destroys social value. If business pollutes the environment in the process of creating economic value, it is destroying a social value of great significance for human life and survival. If, on the other hand, business spends money to dispose of its toxic wastes properly and protects the drinking water of a community, it is enhancing a social value of great significance to the community.

Business can also destroy or create ethical value. If business undermines the trust and confidence of the public through fraudulent and deceptive practices, it is destroying ethical value by violating ethical principles that form the basis of marketplace transactions. If it is honest and straightforward in all its transactions and fulfills its contractual obligations, however, the organization is creating ethical value by respecting the norms and standards inherent in a free-enterprise economy and a civilized society.

Business is also a human institution that creates or destroys human value. If business treats its employees with respect and as autonomous individuals with rights that should not be violated, it is creating and enhancing human value in treating people as ends in themselves and not just as a means to profits and production. If, on the other hand, business treats its employees as simply another factor of production and ignores important human needs that may not be directly related to the production of goods and services, it is destroying human value and treating people as mere things to be manipulated in the interests of higher production levels and profits.

Thinking of corporations as ethical systems that can enhance or destroy various kinds of value that relate to the welfare of society means that the management task is primarily ethical in nature. Management becomes the management of values in this perspective, rather than the management of people, machines, money, or other more traditional elements of productive activity. The management of values implies that the basic management task is to create values that enhance the well-being of society and of the people in that society. The traditional function of management is to manage resources efficiently to create as much economic value as possible and in this way make a significant contribution to society. But management can also create social, ethical, and human values that enhance the welfare of people just as the creation of economic value does.

The obvious question to ask about this view of management is, What rewards or incentives exist for management to be concerned about creating social and other kinds of values? Why should management be socially responsible and concerned about pollution? Why should it be concerned about enhancing the quality of the workplace so employees' lives can be enriched in more than monetary terms? Why should management be concerned about adhering to ethical standards if more money can be made by engaging in bribery or other fraudulent practices? Profits are a reward for creating economic value. What rewards exist for creating other kinds of values? Are the only incentives negative in the sense that government regulations are the likely result if business isn't responsive to social concerns or that the corporation may be fined and receive a great deal of negative publicity if fraudulent practices are discovered and disclosed?

Here again Newton is helpful. The pursuit of profit or the creation of economic value is simply not important enough to absorb all of a manager's time and effort and all of the energies and devotion managers bring to the organization. Managers are encouraged to think more highly of their own task and recognize that they can contribute much more to society than the creation of economic value. This is not to suggest that economic value isn't important, only to say that it is not enough. Managers are encouraged to accept the challenge that a broader view of the corporation entails, to think of corporate performance in broader terms than mere economic performance, and to develop an awareness of the manifold impacts they can have on an economy and a society through their decisions and actions. The managerial task is an incredibly significant role in our society and in the world, as

Sheldon points out, but its significance cannot begin to be captured by focusing only on the notion of economizing and marketplace transactions.

Are these ideas suggesting that virtue is its own reward? In some sense, that is probably true. Managers cannot expect to receive economic rewards that are directly tied to good performance along social and other value dimensions. It could be argued that if we expect to receive economic rewards for everything we do, these other values are denigrated and reduced solely to economic values. Managers must find intrinsic rewards in creating other kinds of values, rewards that come from the satisfaction of having made something useful out of one's life and from having made the maximum possible contribution to society. Human beings want to feel good about themselves and feel their lives have counted for something important. Managers, with their expertise, are in a unique position to develop this sense of significance because of the resources under their command that society has entrusted to them.

Is there then no connection between being ethical in the sense just described and good business? The excellence literature to which Newton refers would suggest otherwise. If management has taken great pains to produce a good product that is safe to use and will enhance people's lives, there should be a confidence that it can be sold at a profit in the marketplace without bribery or dishonest advertising. If a company treats its employees well and gains a reputation as a good place to work, it should have no trouble finding good employees who are willing to devote their energies to the production of goods and services in that company. If the company becomes known throughout the investment community as a well-run company, it should have no trouble attracting investors who are willing to put their money into its stock in good and bad times.

This situation is analogous to the writing of a paper in the academic world. If a scholar has done an excellent job of research and has written a topnotch paper, he or she should have the confidence that this excellence will be recognized and that the paper will eventually be published in a respectable journal. Pursuit of excellence, in this sense, is its own reward, but writing because one wants to make a contribution to knowledge and advance our understanding of a particular phenomenon will more likely lead to publication than will writing solely for the sake of publication itself in order to gain tenure or a promotion.

The final implication of this view is that not only is good ethics good business but the fundamental business of business is ethical, the creation of values that enhance the welfare of communities, societies, and the world. Thus, ethics is central to the managerial task; in fact, it is the task of management. Good ethics and good business are all part of the same question, as the traditional view held, but the economic performance of business is subsumed under the ethical notion of business as an organization that creates or destroys different kinds of values that are of great moral significance. The notion of business performance must be broadened to include the social, ethical, and human aspects of business activities. A managerial philosophy that takes this view seriously cannot, then, be built on scientific principles related only to efficiency but must be built on ethical principles related to the way human beings treat each other, the relationship of business to the physical environment, the use of resources to create economic value, and other principles related to a host of relationships and activities of management that have moral significance.

SUGGESTED READING

BAIER, KURT. *The Moral Point of View: A Rational Basis of Ethics.* Ithaca, N.Y.: Cornell University Press, 1958.

FRANKENA, WILLIAM K. *Thinking about Morality.* Ann Arbor: University of Michigan Press, 1980.

GAUTHIER, DAVID P., ED. *Morality and Rational Self-Interest.* Englewood Cliffs, N.J.: Prentice-Hall, 1970.

GERT, BERNARD. *The Moral Rules: A New Rational Foundation for Morality.* New York: Harper Torchbooks, 1973.

RICHARDS, DAVID A. *A Theory of Reasons for Action.* New York: Oxford University Press, 1971.

SCRIVEN, MICHAEL. *Primary Philosophy.* New York: McGraw-Hill Book Co., 1966.

SINGER, MARCUS G. *Generalization in Ethics.* New York: Atheneum Publishers, 1971.

TAYLOR, PAUL W. *Normative Discourse.* Englewood Cliffs, N.J.: Prentice-Hall, 1961.

3

What Decisions Have Ethical Dimensions?

If management is basically an ethical task, as was argued in the last chapter, then the next problem is one of addressing more specifically the ethical dimensions of management decisions. Since business ethics is primarily concerned to clarify the moral obligations and ethical responsibilities of managers who make business decisions, it is necessary to discuss the nature of decision making in relation to ethical concerns. The problem to be addressed is not one of distinguishing between an ethical decision and an unethical decision but of distinguishing an ethical decision from a nonethical decision. In other words, the problem is one of identifying the ethical dimensions of a decision. Are ethical dimensions present in every decision made by a manager or only in certain decisions? What are the important ethical dimensions to consider in analyzing managerial decisions?

In general, it could be said that an ethical decision as distinguished from a nonethical decision is one that affects human welfare or human fulfillment in some significant manner. An ethical decision is one where somebody's welfare is at stake, where somebody will be positively or negatively affected by the decision. According to this definition, some ethicists would argue that every decision one makes throughout his or her life has an ethical dimension. There are no decisions that do not affect human welfare in some sense and that do not have some kind of ethical implications. Even such a trivial decision as which tie to wear in the morning can have ethical implications. If the tie is made in Korea, for example, the decision to wear it affects the welfare of the textile industry in this country and the people who work in that industry and are dependent on it for an income. Perhaps one should have bought American if one lives in the United States and promoted the welfare of the country one lives in rather than that of a foreign country. This action might have been the ethical thing to do since one benefits from living in the United States and thus has a moral obligation to promote its welfare.

Such a view, however, loses practical significance when the multitude of decisions one makes every day are considered. There are a host of daily decisions that are best considered matters of personal preference. What color socks to wear or which shirt to put on in the morning are more matters of personal preference or good taste than of ethics. The choice of a route to get to work in the morning is more likely a question of efficiency than one of ethics. To see ethical implications in all these decisions is to trivialize the whole notion of ethics and is likely to lead to ethical exhaustion. It would seem best to reserve ethical analysis to decisions where the moral significance of the decision is greater than in the foregoing examples.

Thus, the definition of an ethical decision still needs further clarification. To speak of human welfare or human fulfillment is too vague and abstract to be of much help in clarifying the nature of an ethical decision and analyzing its components. Few decisions promote the welfare of everyone affected. Most managerial decisions benefit some people and groups, within or without the organization, and hurt others. Even where a decision seems to benefit everybody, a win-win type of situation, not all people and all groups are benefited to the same extent. There are usually questions of trade-offs involved in most management decisions, and the distribution of benefits and burdens is a relevant consideration.

So an ethical decision can be further defined as a decision where questions of justice and rights are serious and relevant moral considerations. These concepts are central ethical considerations in human affairs, and an ethical decision is one where a consideration of them is an important dimension of the decision. Can the decision be defended on grounds of justice? Is it fair and equitable in some sense to all the parties affected? Does the decision violate some basic human rights, such that it could be labeled an immoral decision? These are the kinds of questions that must be asked.

Perhaps this definition can be clarified by specifying certain levels of ethical decision making in a corporate context and illustrating ethical issues at these levels with specific examples. Kenneth Goodpaster has identified three such levels of ethical issues, which vary in scope or coverage. These levels are the individual level, organizational level, and system level.[1]

At the individual level, the manager is making personal, day-to-day decisions that mostly involve the application of corporate policy to specific concrete situations. Judgments have to be made when the policy isn't clear or when exceptional circumstances arise. It is at these points that ethical issues arise and the personal judgment of managers on a day-to-day basis have important ethical dimensions.

The organizational level involves decisions about corporate policy, decisions that are not merely personal but are made for and in the name of the corporation that will guide the behavior of all, or at least significant numbers of, employees. Thus,

---

[1]Kenneth E. Goodpaster, "The Concept of Corporate Responsibility," *Journal of Business Ethics* 2, no. 1 (February 1983), 2–3. See also Kirk O. Hanson, "Ethics and Business: A Progress Report," Stanford GSB (Spring 1983), 10–14.

these decisions are broader in scope than those made at the individual level and involve more people and resources. It is at this level, Goodpaster argues, that questions of corporate social responsibility are relevant.[2]

At the system level, broad questions are raised about the ethical foundations of capitalism and whether the system as presently constituted is fair, equitable, and just, and provides for and promotes human welfare better than some alternative system. Thus, questions are raised about the legitimacy of the fundamental components of capitalism, such as private property and competition. Should property rights be overridden in the interest of the general welfare? What is the proper role of government in a capitalistic society? Questions at this level are obviously the most comprehensive in scope and the most difficult to resolve. They are public-policy questions, by and large, where the corporate manager is only one actor in a very complex and political decision-making process.

The specific nature of the decisions involved at each of these levels can be seen if a concrete example is used. Personnel decisions about hiring, firing, and promotions are fraught with ethical dimensions and provide a useful vehicle to illustrate ethical dilemmas at each of these levels. Let us assume that the basic corporate policy or decision rule in regard to personnel decisions is one of hiring, promoting, or retaining the best qualified people. The criteria related to who is best qualified is most likely determined by testing procedures, interviews, performance evaluations, and other methods, all related to helping a decision maker judge the merit of the individual or individuals involved.

Ethics enters into these decisions at the individual level in borderline or exceptional cases that corporate policy does not cover. There may be situations where two candidates are equally qualified for only one position or where an individual is in a gray area when it comes to meeting the criteria. These become difficult personal decisions as far as a manager is concerned. Corporate policy usually isn't a great deal of help, even where numerical scores are involved. Policy may state that a person has to receive a certain minimum score in order to be employed. But given the subjective and uncertain nature of the whole testing process, it hardly seems fair to apply this policy mechanically and exclude people who score one point below the minimum without considering other factors. Then there are exceptional cases where a person may be clearly less qualified for a job or promotion but where something like need may be so great as to make a manager deviate from corporate policy in the interests of justice or rights.

At the organizational level, the ethical dimensions of decision making come into play when corporate policy is determined. Managers must make certain that the criteria and procedures that are established to determine who is best qualified do not discriminate against certain individuals or groups on the basis of irrelevant factors such as race, sex, religion, creed, or national origin. Such systemic discrimination not only is considered to be an injustice in our society, it is also illegal at this point. If the company has had discriminatory personnel policies in the past, then it is faced with a decision about establishing an affirmative-action program where the decision

[2]Ibid.

rule of hiring the best-qualified person may be set aside in some cases in order to give groups who have suffered injustices in the past preferential treatment. There are complex and difficult questions of justice and rights involved in these kinds of policy decisions.

At the system level, the ethical question concerns merit itself, which is one of the ethical pillars of a free-enterprise system. Is merit the appropriate principle to use in distributing the benefits of society? Do those who merit rewards in the sense of better qualifications and job performance merit the better and higher-paying jobs society has to offer? Egalitarians question the justice of this arrangement, arguing that merit, which is not earned and for which no individual can take credit, cannot be ethically justified as a valid distribution principle. They would advocate that benefits be distributed equally across all members of society. Others would argue that need is the appropriate and fair way to distribute benefits. These kinds of questions are settled through the public-policy process, and the eventual outcome is reflected in laws related to employment practices, such as the Civil Rights Act, and through the establishment and continuation of welfare or entitlement programs that transfer resources between groups in society.

Exhibit 3.1 shows these various levels of decision making and the ethical issues that are relevant to each level. There are obviously conflicts between these various levels of decision making. Corporate policy may require that a corporate manager go against his or her personal ethical standards, causing a very agonizing dilemma for individual managers. And corporate policy may not always reflect the ethical standards of the society at large so that new laws must be passed to force a change in corporate policy and behavior.

Another example can be taken from the admissions process for an M.B.A. program in a public university or college, something that will be closer to home for business students. Most business schools that are accredited by the American Assembly of Collegiate Schools of Business (AACSB) use a combination of the grade point average (GPA) a student has attained in undergraduate studies and his or her performance on the Graduate Management Admissions Test (GMAT). A typical formula combining these two indicators is that 200 times the GPA plus the GMAT score must equal 1100 ($200 \times GPA + GMAT = 1100$). Student applicants who do not meet this minimum index score are rejected. By using such a cut-off point, schools hope to assure themselves of a high-quality student body.

Ethics enters into this decision at the individual level (exhibit 3.2) in borderline or exceptional cases where applying the policy in mechanical fashion does

EXHIBIT 3.1 Personnel Decisions

Decision rule: Hire the best-qualified person.

Individual level:	Borderline and extraordinary situations.
Policy level:	Are criteria discriminatory? Is some kind of affirmative-action program just and equitable?
Social level:	Is making decisions on the basis of merit just and equitable?

not seem just or equitable. For example, if a student scores 1099, should he or she be automatically rejected without looking at other information such as where the student attended school and what kind of recommendations he or she has? Such a decision hardly seems fair given the subjective and uncertain nature of the grading and testing process and seems to violate even rudimentary conceptions of justice and the basic right to be treated fairly. Suppose a student is narrowly rejected who attended Stanford University, and another is narrowly accepted who attended East Podunk University. Is that fair, given that grade point averages are hardly comparable between these two schools? And then what about exceptional cases where students have had to overcome severe handicaps in their undergraduate careers? Should they be mechanically rejected without some special consideration?

At the organizational, or policy, level, ethical considerations come into play when one considers justice and rights in relation to the policy itself. Does the policy discriminate unjustly on the basis of race or sex, or can it be defended as fair and equitable? Some foreign students, for example, have complained that the GMAT is biased in favor of American students because of the concepts and language used in the examination. Is their right to equal treatment violated by the use of this exam? And given the fact that grade point averages mean different things depending on the school one attended, is it fair that the GPA be used to determine admission to a graduate program?

At the level of the social system, questions could be asked about the justice of public institutions having admission standards that may exclude certain residents of the state from attending. Do not any taxpayers in the state who support the school have a right to send their children to a public school? Should those children not have the right to be admitted and at least have a chance to get graduate degrees? Questions could also be raised about the way public institutions are supported. They depend on some kind of tax, usually property taxes, for their support. Is this arrangement fair to the people who don't have children to send to these schools? Do renters actually pay their fair share of property taxes? These are serious ethical questions that often come up for debate when elections of state officials are held.

These examples serve to illustrate where questions of justice and rights are relevant at different levels of decision making in organizations. The decisions that are made at all these levels distribute benefits and burdens in different ways and affect individuals and groups differently. Their welfare is enhanced, or it is affected adversely, thus making questions of justice and rights important. Since these con-

---

EXHIBIT 3.2   Admission Decisions

Decision Rule: Reject students who do not meet the index.

Individual level:	Borderline and extraordinary situations.
Policy level:	Is the cut-off point of 1100 fair and equitable to all groups, including all races and both sexes?
Social system:	Is it fair and just for public institutions to have admissions standards? Do public educational institutions supported by property taxes respect the rights of all taxpayers?

---

cepts are central to making ethical decisions, some discussion of these concepts and the different meanings they have been given would seem to be in order.

JUSTICE

There are several kinds of justice that need to be mentioned at the outset of this discussion. Distributive justice is concerned with a fair distribution of society's benefits and burdens. This type of justice is concerned with the proper distribution of the goods and services society has available through its major institutions including business organizations and governmental institutions. Distributive justice poses a special problem for business, which relies on inequalities as incentives to induce people to be more productive. How can these inequalities be morally justified?

Compensatory justice is concerned with finding a just way of compensating people for what they lost when they were wronged by others. The amount of compensation should be somehow proportional to the loss suffered by the person being compensated. This type of justice is of particular relevance to business organizations facing huge lawsuits involving products that are alleged to have caused harm to human health. What is a just compensation for the loss of a loved one or the loss of one's health if, indeed, the product was the causal agent and the manufacturer was at fault? Theories of strict liability assign more of the responsibility to the manufacturer and make it easier for complaints about defective products to be brought against companies.

Retributive justice has to do with just imposition of punishments and penalties upon those who do wrong. The wrongdoer needs to be punished, especially if the wrong was done intentionally, so that justice is served and the wrongdoer's behavior is changed or he or she is removed from society. Business is affected by this type of justice in the area of punitive damages, which some juries have been prone to award in damage cases. Punitive damages are awarded over and above compensatory damages and have no limit in most cases, although they should be consistent and proportional to the wrong committed.

Justice is often expressed in terms of fairness or what is deserved. People have been treated justly when they have been given what is due or owed them, what they deserve or can legitimately claim. The so-called formal principle of justice states that like cases should be treated alike—equals ought to be treated equally and unequals unequally. This is called the formal principle of justice because it states no particular respects in which equals ought to be treated the same or unequals unequally. The principle merely states that whatever particulars are under consideration, if persons are equal in those respects, they should be treated alike. Individuals who are similar in all respects relevant to the kind of treatment in question should be given similar benefits and burdens. even if they are dissimilar in other irrelevant respects; and individuals who are dissimilar in a relevant respect ought to be treated dissimilarly, in proportion to their dissimilarity.[3]

---

[3]Tom L. Beauchamp, *Philosophical Ethics: An Introduction to Moral Philosophy* (New York McGraw-Hill Book Co., 1982), p. 223.

This formal principle of justice can be considered to be a minimal moral rule. It does not tell us how to determine equality or proportion and therefore lacks substance as a specific guide to conduct. Material principles of justice, on the other hand, specify in detail what counts as a relevant property in terms of which people are to be compared, what it means to give people their due, and what are legitimate claims. These theories put material content into a theory of justice and identify relevant properties on the basis of which burdens and benefits should be distributed. Some of the most difficult questions about the nature of justice arise over the specification of the relevant respects in terms of which people are to be treated equally or unequally.[4]

> Each material principle of justice identifies a relevant property on the basis of which burdens and benefits should be distributed. The following is a sample list of major candidates for the position of valid principles of distributive justice: (1) to each person an equal share; (2) to each person according to individual need; (3) to each person according to the person's rights; (4) to each person according to individual effort; (5) to each person according to societal contribution; (6) to each person according to merit. There is no obvious barrier to acceptance of more than one of these principles, and some theories of justice accept all six as valid. Most societies use several in the belief that different rules are appropriate to different situations.[5]

Conflicts between these properties come up in the typical classroom situation, particularly when it comes time for grading. Most of us try to assign grades on the basis of merit and accept this as the relevant principle for distributing grades. We try to develop tests, papers, and other exercises that will determine merit so that we can be just and fair in our allocation of grades. But students will attempt to make a need a relevant property: they should be given a higher grade than they deserve on the basis of merit because they need it in order to graduate or receive an honors award. Other students will be offended by a merit-based approach because they feel they have worked harder and put more effort into the class than someone who received a higher grade. They believe they should be rewarded for their effort and that this is a relevant property to be considered.

Theories of justice have been developed to provide general guidelines in determining what justice requires in a given situation. These theories systematically elaborate one or more of these material principles of justice and show how they are relevant properties on which to distribute burdens and benefits. Three such theories will be discussed here that have relevance to management decision making. These theories are egalitarian theories, which emphasize equal access to primary goods and services; libertarian theories, which emphasize rights to liberty; and Marxist theories, which emphasize need as a relevant property. The acceptability of any of these theories depends on the quality of the moral argument they contain as to whether one or more of the material properties they advocate ought to be given priority.[6]

[4]Ibid., pp. 225–29.
[5]Ibid., p. 229.
[6]Ibid., p. 230.

Egalitarian Theories

Egalitarians base their view of justice on the proposition that all human beings are equal in some fundamental respect, and in virtue of this equality, each person has an equal claim to society's goods and services. The theory implies that goods and services should be allocated in equal portions regardless of people's individual differences. In its radical form, distributions of burdens and benefits are considered just to the extent they are equal, and deviations from absolute equality are considered to be unjust without respect for other properties in which members of the society may differ. The only relevant property in radical egalitarian theory is the simple possession of humanity, which is the sole property to be used in determining the justice of distributions.

Such a radical view overlooks the fact that there is no quality that all human beings possess in precisely the same degree. Human beings are unequal in most respects, and some of these differences are relevant properties in determining what people deserve. Radical egalitarianism ignores some characteristics that should be taken into account, such as need, ability, and effort. The theory stated in this form also ignores the absence of incentive effects when benefits and burdens are distributed solely on the basis of the possession of humanity. Why should anyone produce more than another if both are going to get the same amount in return?

Most egalitarian theories of justice are qualified in some respects so that they are not this radical, even though they still hold to a central egalitarian thrust. One of the most influential egalitarian theories of recent years, for example, was developed by John Rawls, who was concerned about the lack of just distributions that could result from utilitarian theory. His objection to utilitarianism is that the social distributions produced by maximizing utility could entail violation of basic individual liberties and rights expressive of human equality and deserving protection as a matter of social justice. Utilitarianism is indifferent, he argued, as to the distribution of satisfactions among individuals and would permit infringement of some people's rights and liberties if such infringement genuinely promised to produce a proportionately greater utility for others.[7]

Rawls's theory is based on a hypothetical social contract that people would agree to behind a so-called veil of ignorance, the principles that free and rational persons concerned to further their own interests would accept in an initial position of equality. Valid principles of justice are those people would agree on if they could freely and impartially consider the social situation from a standpoint outside any actual society behind a veil of ignorance. This veil of ignorance prevents people from promoting principles of justice that are biased toward their own combinations of fortuitous talents and characteristics. No one knows his or her place in society, status, fortune in distribution of natural assets and abilities, intelligence, or strength. Thus no one is advantaged or disadvantaged in the choice of principles.[8]

The initial situation is thus symmetrical, and parties are forced to be fair and impartial and show no favoritism toward any special group. Everyone will want to

---

[7]Ibid., pp. 243–44.

[8]John Rawls, *A Theory of Justice* (Cambridge: Harvard University Press, 1971), pp. 136–42.

secure a maximum amount of freedom so he or she can pursue whatever interests he or she has on entering society. All parties will want to protect themselves against the possibility of ending up in the worst position in society. Under these conditions, according to Rawls, people would unanimously agree on two fundamental principles of justice:

1. Each person is to have an equal right to the most extensive basic liberty compatible with a similar liberty for others.
2. Social and economic inequalities are to be arranged so that they are both (a) reasonably expected to be to everyone's advantage and (b) attached to positions and offices open to all (difference principle).[9]

The first principle requires equality in the assignment of basic rights and duties. Each person is permitted the maximum amount of equal basic liberty compatible with a similar liberty for others. This principle defines and secures equal liberties of citizenship, such as political liberty, freedom of speech and assembly, liberty of conscience, freedom of thought, the right to hold personal property, and freedom from arbitrary arrest and seizure. The second principle says that inequalities in wealth and authority are just only if they result in compensating benefits for everyone and, in particular, for the least-advantaged members of society. The hardship of some being offset by a greater good in the aggregate cannot be justified.

This division of advantages, it is argued, should draw forth the willing cooperation of everyone, including those less well situated. Everyone should benefit from social and economic inequalities. Inequalities of birth, historical circumstances, and natural endowment are undeserved. Persons in a cooperative society should correct them by making more equal the unequal situation of naturally disadvantaged members. Society must give more attention to those with fewer native assets and correct for arbitrariness of nature. In justice as fairness, people agree to share one another's fate and avail themselves of the accidents of nature and social circumstance only when doing so is for the common benefit. Such accidents are not relevant moral properties for the distribution of burdens and benefits in society.[10]

In criticism of Rawls's theory, some have argued that it is not clear exactly what principles people would agree to behind a so-called veil of ignorance. People might agree to a riskier system of basic rules that permitted more dramatic wins as well as losses. The way people have responded to the lotteries sponsored by some states would suggest that this is a real possibility. The difference principle has been attacked by both sides in the debate as being at once too weak and too strong. Some claim it would still allow for unjust inequalities, and others claim that it would deny justice to those who have worker harder or been more innovative and thus deserve greater benefits.[11] This theory has caused a good deal of controversy because of its implications for the distributions of goods and services in our society.

[9]Ibid., p. 60.
[10]Ibid., pp. 175–83.
[11]Richard DeGeorge, *Business Ethics*, 2d ed. (New York: Macmillan Co., 1986), p. 78.

Another kind of egalitarian theory of justice has been proposed by William K. Frankena, who argues that if people who compete for the goods and positions that society has to offer have not had a chance to achieve all the virtue they are capable of achieving, then virtue is not a fair basis of distribution. If virtue is to be adopted as a relevant property for distribution, there must be a prior equal distribution of the conditions for achieving virtue. Thus, equality of opportunity, equality before the law, and equal access to the means of education are important considerations. Recognition of virtue as a basis of distribution is reasonable only against background conditions that acknowledge the principle of equality. The primary criterion of distributive justice is thus equality rather than merit in the form of some kind of virtue. [12]

The basic standard of distributive justice should be equality of treatment, according to Frankena. Justice requires that we give extra attention to people with certain kinds of handicaps, for example, because only with such extra attention do they have something approaching an equal chance to compete with others in enjoying a fulfilling life. Helping them in proportion to their needs is necessary for making an equal contribution to their lives. Treating people equally in this sense, however, does not mean making their lives equally good or maintaining everyone's life at the same level of goodness. In other words, equality of results is not a requirement of justice as equal treatment. Justice in this sense does, however, mean "making the same relative contribution to the goodness of their lives (this is equal help or helping according to need) or asking the same relative sacrifice (this is asking in accordance with ability)." [13]

Libertarian Theories

Libertarian theories of justice emphasize rights to social and economic liberty. These theories advocate distinctive processes, procedures, or mechanisms for insuring that liberty rights are recognized in economic practice. Because the contributions people make to the economic system are freely chosen, they can be considered morally relevant bases on which to discriminate among individuals in distributing econmic burdens and benefits. People are not deserving of equal economic returns because they do not make the same contribution to the production of economic goods and services. People are free to choose the kind of contribution they want to make; they have a fundamental right to own and dispense with their labor as they choose. This right must be respected even if its unrestricted exercise leads to greater inequalities of wealth in a given society. [14] Human agents are considered to be ends in themselves, free to act according to their own purposes. This basic liberty should not be interfered with in order to achieve a more equitable distribution of the benefits and burdens in society.

Robert Nozick has developed what has been called an entitlement theory of justice, that there are certain basic rights to liberty people are entitled to that should

[12]William K. Frankena, *Ethics,* 2d ed. (Englewood Cliffs, N.J.: Prentice-Hall, 1973), p. 50.
[13]Ibid., p. 51.
[14]Beauchamp, *Philosophical Ethics,* pp. 231–32.

not be interfered with by government or any other groups or institution in society. Government action is permissible only to the extent it protects these fundamental rights or entitlements. This entitlement theory holds that whether a distribution is just depends upon how it came about. The set of holdings people end up with is not or should not be patterned, according to some notions of equality. Whoever makes something, having bought or contracted for all other held resources used in the process, is entitled to it regardless of the inequality that may result. According to Nozick, there are three fundamental principles that society needs to concern itself with in order to assure justice in the distribution of benefits and burdens:

1. Principle of justice in acquisition: the process by which things come to be held. This principle refers to the original acquisition.
2. Principle of justice in transfer: the process of acquiring things from another or of divestiture.
3. Rectification of justice in holdings: what, if anything, ought to be done to correct injustices.[15]

A person who acquires a holding in accordance with the principle of justice in acquisition is entitled to that holding. A person who acquires a holding in accordance with the principle of justice in transfer, from someone else entitled to the holding, is entitled to the holding. And finally, no one is entitled to a holding except by repeated applications of the first two principles. Any outcome is just as long as it results from consistent operation of these specified procedures. To maintain a pattern of equality, one must continually interfere to stop people from transferring resources as they wish or continually interfering to take from some persons resources that others for some reason choose to transfer to themselves. This is a violation of people's basic rights and entitlements.[16]

Libertarianism has been criticized as passing too quickly over the fact that the freedom of one person necessarily imposes constraints upon other persons. If constraints require justification, so does freedom. There are many different kinds of freedom. The freedom of one group to pursue its interests restricts the freedom of other agents to pursue their interests. Arguments for a specific freedom must show that the interests that can be satisfied by that kind of freedom are somehow better or more worth satisfying than the interests that other opposing kinds of freedom could satisfy.[17]

Libertarianism also enshrines a certain kind of value—freedom from the coercion of others—and sacrifices all other rights and values to it without persuasive reasons why this should be done. Other forms of freedom must also be secured, such as freedom from ignorance and freedom from hunger. These other forms of freedom may in some instances override freedom from coercion. Those with surplus money may have to be taxed to provide for those who are starving.[18]

---

[15]Robert Nozick, *Anarchy, State, and Utopia* (New York: Basic Books, 1974), pp. 150–53.

[16]Ibid., p. 151.

[17]Manuel G. Velasquez, *Business Ethics: Concepts and Cases* (Englewood Cliffs, N.J.: Prentice-Hall, 1982), p. 73.

[18]Ibid., p. 84.

The theory has also been criticized as generating unjust treatment of the disadvantaged. Under libertarianism, a person's share of goods depends wholly on what the person can produce or what other persons choose to give out of charity. But people have vastly unequal opportunities to make a contribution to the economy and be productive. People born into favorable circumstances have the chance to attend good educational institutions to develop their native abilities and talents. Thus, they can attain better positions and be rewarded for being more productive. People born into unfavorable circumstances may have just as much innate ability but never have the chance to develop those abilities. The conditions necessary to be productive may be unavailable through no fault of the person. If people through no fault of their own are unable to care for themselves, their survival should not depend on the outside chance that others will provide them with what they need. They should have these needs attended to as a basic right of humanity.[19]

Marxist Theories

Marxist theories of justice hold that free-market exchange based on private property rights corrupts a worker's relation both to his or her own product and to fellow workers. Workers are alienated from their product because they work simply to acquire products produced by others. The creation of a product has no intrinsic value but is purely a means to the end of exchange. People are naive in assuming that true freedom of choice in economic matters is compatible with systems of private property and capitalist exchange.

Marxist theory thus rejects free-market conceptions of justice and would substitute some material principle of specifying need as the relevant respect in which people are to be compared for purposes of determining the justice of economic distributions. Justice requires satisfaction of fundamental human needs that have a higher social priority than the protection of economic freedom or rights. Work burdens should be distributed according to people's abilities, and benefits should be distributed according to people's needs.

The socialist principle is based on the conception that people realize their human potential by exercising their abilities in productive work. Since the realization of one's full potentiality is a value, work should be distributed in such a way that a person can be as productive as possible. This means that work should be distributed according to ability. The benefits produced through work should be used to promote human happiness and well-being. This implies that goods should be distributed so that people's basic biological and health needs are met, and then what is left over is used to meet people's other, nonbasic, needs. But perhaps most fundamental to the socialist view of economic life is the notion that societies should be communities in which benefits and burdens are distributed on the model of a family. Just as able family members are expected to support the family, and just as needy family members expect to be supported by the family, so also the able members of a society should contribute their abilities to society by taking up its

[19]Ibid.

burdens while the needy should be allowed to share in the benefits that are produced.[20]

Marxist theories have been criticized for not recognizing a relation between the amount of effort a worker puts forth and the amount of remuneration he or she receives. If human nature is essentially self-interested and competitive, workers require an incentive to be productive. Entire societies cannot be modeled on familial relationships. Marxists, however reply that human beings are taught to be self-interested and competitive by modern social and economic institutions that inculcate and encourage competitive and self-interested behavior.[21]

It is also argued that if the socialist principle were enforced, it would obliterate individual freedom. The occupation each person entered would be determined by abilities, not by free choice. The goods a person gets would be determined by needs and not by free choice. Thus, the socialist principle substitutes paternalism for freedom and does not recognize the basic right of people to determine their own destinies. The basic right of people to make choices and take responsibility for their own actions would be overridden by a principle based on abilities and needs. Someone would have to decide which of the abilities a person had should be put to productive use and which of the multiple needs a person had should be satisfied.[22]

RIGHTS

The notion of rights has received a great deal of attention in our society in the last several decades. Various movements have appeared to press for the rights of specific groups, such as the civil-rights movement concerned about fundamental rights for blacks and other minorities, women's-rights movements developed to press for equal treatment of women in our society, and more recently, right-to-life movements that attempt to protect the rights of unborn children and oppose abortion. Where do these rights come from and what gives rise to these kinds of movements that support certain kinds of rights?

People have used the notion of rights throughout history to overthrow systems of governance and establish new forms of social and economic power. In the Middle Ages kings claimed a divine right to govern in order to throw off the shackles of the Church, and they went on to claim ever more extensive powers over the subjects they came to dominate. Fledgling democracies claimed a natural right to liberty in order to overthrow kings and establish a new system of government. Rights seem to emerge as a significant force in history when there are enough people who feel a basic injustice is being perpetuated and are able to organize or be led to force a basic change of some kind in the society.

Our Declaration of Independence refers to certain basic rights that are believed to be self-evident; they stem from the nature of things. Such rights can be

---

[20]Ibid., p. 82.
[21]Ibid., pp. 82–83.
[22]Ibid., p. 83.

based on some kind of a natural-law concept, that there is an ideal standard of justice fixed by nature that is binding on all persons. This standard takes precedence over the particular laws and standards created by social convention. It provides absolute criteria against which the laws and policies of particular states and institutions are to be measured.

This notion of natural rights may be seen to arise out of a need to check the sovereign power of kings, as was the case in the establishment of our country. Such rights can also be used to put a check on the sovereign power of the state as do the rights contained in the Bill of Rights in the Constitution. These are considered to be fundamental rights irrespective of merit, due to be respected because they are rooted in a knowledge of certain universal regularities in nature. The concept of nature refers to a proper ordering of the universe, and knowledge of this structure was believed to be accessible to all men by virtue of the reason they possessed.[23]

Today we speak more about human rights than natural rights and attempt to promote such human rights throughout the world. (See box.) Rights are no longer derived from the operations of natural reason, but rather from ideas of what it means to be human. It is assumed that human beings have some kind of an essential nature that determines the fundamental obligations and rights that are to be respected by other people and social institutions. The rights that are asserted as fundamental to the development of humanity are believed to stem from knowledge of these essential properties of human nature.

United Nations Universal Declaration of Human Rights

The right to own property alone as well as in association with others.

The right to work, to free choice of employment, to just and favorable conditions of work, and to protection against unemployment.

The right to just and favorable renumeration ensuring for the worker and his family an existence worthy of human dignity.

The right to form and join trade unions.

The right to rest and leisure, including reasonable limitation of working hours and periodic holidays with pay.

A person can exercise a right to something only if sufficient justification exists, and a right has overriding status. Moral rights are important, normative, justifiable claims or entitlements. Basic human rights cannot be overriden by considerations of utility. Rights can be overridden only by another, more basic right of some kind. Property rights, for example, can be overridden by a program of affirmative action to promote equal opportunity, on the basis that equality of opportunity

---

[23]Kenneth Minogue, "The History of the Idea of Human Rights," *The Human Rights Reader,* Walter Laqueur and Barry Rubin, eds. (Philadelphia: Temple University Press, 1979), pp. 14–15.

is a more basic human right, not because it promotes social welfare. The right to liberty on the part of employers can be overridden in the interests of the rights of workers to a safe workplace. In this respect, certain rights can be considered as fundamental because (1) other rights are derived from them while they are not derived from any more basic rights, and (2) they are preconditions or necessary conditions of all other rights.[24]

There is a difference between moral and legal rights. One may have a legal right to do something immoral, or a moral right without any corresponding legal guarantee. Legal rights are derived from political constitutions, legislative enactments, case law, and executive orders of the highest state official. Moral rights exist independently of, and form a basis for, criticizing or justifying legal rights. Legal rights can be eliminated by lawful amendments or by a coup d'état, but moral rights cannot be eroded or banished by political votes, powers, or amendments.[25]

A right is an individual's entitlement to something. A person has a right when that person is entitled to act in a certain way or is entitled to have others act in a certain way toward him or her. These entitlements may derive from a legal system that permits or empowers the person to act in a specified way or that requires others to act in certain ways toward the person. Legal rights are limited to the particular jurisdiction within which the legal system is in force.[26]

Entitlements can also be derived from a system of moral standards independent of any particular legal system. They can be based on moral norms or principles that specify that all human beings are permitted or empowered to do something or are entitled to have something done for them. In this case, rights are not limited to a particular jurisdiction. The most important moral rights are those that impose prohibitions or requirements on others and enable individuals to pursue their own interests.[27]

There are negative rights, which can be considered to be duties others have not to interfere in certain activities of the person. A negative right is a right to be free to hold and practice a belief, to pursue an action, or to enjoy a state of affairs without outside interference. Negative rights protect an individual from interference from the government and from other people. Government is to protect this basic right to be left alone and is not to encroach on this right itself. Libertarian theories of justice emphasize negative rights because human beings are viewed as ends in themselves, free to act according to their own purposes, and this right is to be respected by other people as well as by the institutions of society.

Positive rights, on the other hand, mean some other agents have a positive duty of providing the holder of a right with whatever he or she needs to freely pursue his or her interests. Positive rights are rights to obtain goods and services, opportunities, or certain kinds of equal treatment. Egalitarian theories of justice emphasize more positive rights in that society should correct for the arbitrariness of

[24]Beauchamp, *Philosophical Ethics*, p. 194.
[25]Ibid., p. 189.
[26]Valesquez, *Business Ethics*, p. 59.
[27]Ibid., pp. 59–60.

nature by providing goods and services to its least advantaged members and assuring them equal opportunities. These are fundamental rights that require an obligation on the part of people and institutions to respect.

Moral rights of either kind, however, are tightly correlated with duties. Rights can be defined in terms of moral duties other people have toward that person. Even negative rights imply a duty on the part of other people to respect the right to be left alone. Negative rights imply a duty on the part of government to protect these rights. These correlative duties may fall not on any specific individual but on all members of a group or society.[28]

Moral rights provide individuals with autonomy and equality in the free pursuit of their interests. These rights identify activities or interests that people must be left free to pursue or not pursue as they themselves choose and whose pursuit must not be subordinated to the interests of others except for special and exceptionally weighty reasons. Moral rights provide a basis for justifying one's actions and for invoking the protection or aid of others. They express the requirements of morality from the point of view of the individual instead of society as a whole and promote individual welfare and protect individual choices against encroachment by society.[29]

Utilitarian standards promote society's aggregate utility and are indifferent to individual welfare except insofar as it affects this social aggregate. Moral rights, however, limit the validity of appeals to social benefits and to numbers. If a person has a right to do something, then it is wrong for anyone or any institution to interfere, even though a large number of people might gain much more utility from such interference. If utilitarian benefits or losses imposed on society become great enough, they may be sufficient, in some cases, to breach the walls of rights set to protect a person's freedom to pursue his or her interests.[30]

The Manville case at the end of the book provides a useful vehicle to illustrate applications of these concepts about justice and rights to a concrete situation. The case is permeated with ethical questions related to these concepts. It is important to discuss the issues in the case with regard to the theories of justice described in this chapter. The discussion can center on which theory of justice seemed to prevail in the final settlement. The rights of the various stakeholders also are important to consider. How were these rights of stockholders, management, claimants, creditors, and consumers treated in the outcome of the case? How were property rights balanced against the rights of those who were harmed by the product?

Concepts of justice and rights are related. Rights most often stem from some basic feelings of injustice, and assertion of rights is meant to correct these injustices. Rights are meant to serve justice, and justice should take rights into account. The question for the manager to answer is, Whose rights should be respected and what concept of justice is appropriate? Libertarian theories of justice that emphasize liberty and negative rights would seem to be more consistent with a

[28]Ibid., p. 60.
[29]Ibid., p. 61.
[30]Ibid., p. 62.

free-enterprise system. In the last several decades in our country, with the rise of a welfare system, government has emphasized more of an egalitarian concept of justice to correct for some of the inequalities produced by capitalism and has emphasized positive rights to goods and services, opportunities, and health and safety.

Some kind of balance between these approaches would seem to be a reasonable solution to disagreements that arise over them. Our market economy and the government act as counterweights to each other. The market gives priority to property rights and economic concerns such as efficiency and growth and is concerned about getting the economic job done in a manner that obtains the most useful output from labor, capital, and natural resources. The government is concerned with egalitarian and humanitarian values related to justice and respect for certain basic human rights related to equal opportunity and protection from fraud and abuse in the marketplace as well as from harm in the workplace.

Throughout our history, we have been able to reach compromises between these two sets of values and have reached different conclusions on particular policy issues that define the scope of the marketplace and scope of governmental responsibility. We have traveled a road between a strictly laissez-faire type of economy with severely limited government intervention and outright government ownership of the means of production and central planning. We have largely avoided polarizing ideological debates that threaten compromise and have been able to veer to the right or left of center as economic and social conditions necessitated but never to the extremes. The vital center in American political and social attitudes generally prevails and keeps us somewhere near the middle of the road as regards rights to liberty and equality. It is within this political and economic context that the manager of today's corporation must operate.

SUGGESTED READING

BEDAU, HUGO A., ED. *Justice and Equality*. Englewood Cliffs, N.J.: Prentice-Hall, 1971.

BLACKSTONE, WILLIAM T., ED. *The Concept of Equality*. Minneapolis: Burgess Publishing Co., 1969.

BOWIE, NORMAN E. *Towards a New Theory of Distributive Justice*. Amherst: University of Massachusetts Press. 1971.

CRANSTON, MAURICE. *What Are Human Rights?* New York: Taplinger Publishing Co., 1973.

DWORKIN, RONALD. *Taking Rights Seriously*. Cambridge: Harvard University Press, 1977.

FLATHMAN, RICHARD E. *The Practice of Rights*. Cambridge: Cambridge University Press, 1977.

FRANKENA, WILLIAM K. *Thinking about Morality*. Ann Arbor: University of Michigan Press, 1980.

FRIEDMAN, MILTON. *Capitalism and Freedom*. Chicago: University of Chicago Press, 1962.

HARRINGTON, MICHAEL. *Socialism*. New York: Bantam Books, 1973.

HARTLAND-SWANN, JOHN. *An Analysis of Morals*. London: George Allen & Unwin, 1960.

HAYEK, FRIEDRICH. *Individualism and Economic Order*. Chicago: University of Chicago Press, 1948.

HEILBRONER, ROBERT. *Between Capitalism and Socialism*. New York: Random House, 1970.

LADD, JOHN. *The Structure of a Moral Code*. Cambridge: Harvard University Press, 1957.

LYONS, DAVID. *Rights*. Belmont, Calif.: Wadsworth Publishing Co., 1979.

MELDEN, ABRAHAM I. *Human Rights*. Belmont, Calif.: Wadsworth Publishing Co., 1970.

MILLER, DAVID. *Social Justice*. Oxford: Clarendon Press, 1976.

NOZICK, ROBERT. *Anarchy, State, and Utopia*. New York: Basic Books, 1974.

RAWLS, JOHN. *A Theory of Justice*. Cambridge: Harvard University Press, 1971.

RESCHER, NICHOLAS. *Distributive Justice*. Indianapolis: Bobbs-Merrill Co., 1966.

STERBA, JAMES. *The Demands of Justice*. Notre Dame, Ind.: University of Notre Dame Press, 1980.

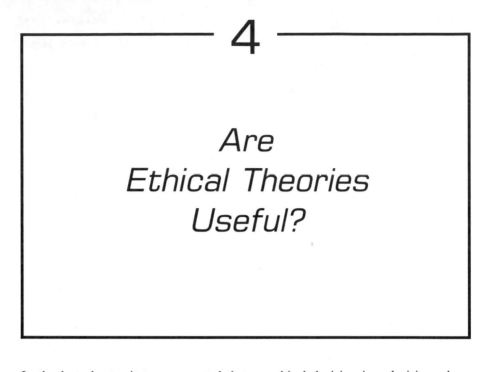

4

Are
Ethical Theories
Useful?

In the last chapter it was suggested that an ethical decision is a decision where questions of justice and rights are involved. Various theories of justice were then described, and the concept of rights was discussed to better understand the nature of an ethical decision. These considerations lead to a quest for theories and techniques that may prove useful in helping to analyze ethical decisions and think about them rationally. What does moral philosophy have to offer by way of theories that can help to clarify ethical questions related to justice and rights and provide a way of making a decision that is morally defensible.

Like any good intellectual activity, ethics proceeds from theory to practice in terms of analyzing decision making. There are some very general ethical theories or approaches to moral problems that appear in all the business-ethics literature and are generally held to be the major theories that relate to ethical decisions. These theories are meant to help us arrive at an ethical decision that can then be defended on some rational basis or to reflect on a decision we made to determine what assumptions were operative and whether the decision can be justified. From these more general theories, different levels of principles or rules can be developed to apply to specific problem areas or issues. As one moves down the hierarchy of principles and rules, one moves from theory to practice, and the principles and rules become more specific and concrete.

TELEOLOGICAL THEORIES

Teleological theories of ethics, sometimes called consequentialist theories, hold that the moral worth of an action or practice is determined solely by the consequences of

48

the action or practice. The rightness or wrongness of actions and practices are determined by the results that these actions and practices produce. What makes an action right or wrong is the good or evil that is produced by the act, not the act itself. Thus teleological theories do not hold that an act has intrinsic value in and of itself, but all acts and practices must be evaluated in terms of the good and bad consequences they produce.

There are several different kinds of teleological theories that can be mentioned. Ethical egoism holds that whether an act is morally right or wrong depends solely on how good or bad the consequences of the action are for oneself. How others are affected is irrelevant to the decision unless the way in which others are affected somehow alters the consequences for oneself. Ethical altruism, on the other hand, holds that whether an action is right or wrong depends solely on the good and bad consequences produced by the action for everyone except oneself. How the initiator of the action is affected is irrelevant to the decision unless how one is affected somehow alters the consequences for everyone else affected by the action.[1]

Regarding ethical egoism, a legitimate question can be raised as to whether most acts and practices can be evaluated solely in terms of their effect on oneself. Most every action we take does affect other people or our environment in some fashion, and thus our actions have consequences beyond their effect on oneself. These external consequences may, in turn, have further consequences for oneself, as the theory suggests, but it would seem difficult, even for the most diehard individualist, to deny that consequences for others are not taken into account in many, if not most, decisions. On the other hand, it is also hard to maintain that one can be totally uninterested in the effect of a decision on oneself. Even the most heroic act that on the surface may seem to be done totally without interest in the effects on oneself may have elements of self-interest that are not readily apparent.

Thus, a teleological theory that combines both of these elements may be most realistic. Such a theory is utilitarianism, which holds that whether an action is right or wrong depends on the good or bad consequences produced for everyone affected by the action. So the way the action affects oneself is relevant, as is how the action affects all others. Thus, utilitarian theory is more universal or comprehensive than the others and considers the consequences for all the parties affected by the act. Utilitarianism involves the consideration of alternatives, as an action or practice is judged to be correct if it leads to the greatest possible balance of good consequences or the least possible balance of bad consequences for everyone affected by the action or practices when compared with alternative actions or practices that are available. Utilitarianism thus promotes human welfare by minimizing harms and/or maximizing benefits.

Making a utilitarian decision, then, involves the following steps: (1) determining what alternative actions are available regarding any specific decision, (2) estimating the costs and benefits that a given action would produce for each and every person affected by the action, and (3) choosing the alternative that produces

[1]Tom Regan, ed. *Earthbound: New Introductory Essays in Environmental Ethics* (New York: Random House, 1984), p. 24.

the greatest sum of utility or the least amount of disutility.[2] If these steps are followed, the action chosen can then be defended as a morally correct action. Thus, utilitarianism advocates a specific method to arrive at a correct decision and grounds that method in a conception of the greatest good that can be produced for the greatest number of people who are affected by the decision.

Utilitarianism involves some conception of the "good" or ultimate utility in terms of which the effects of all the alternatives are to be evaluated. In this regard, there are hedonistic utilitarians who argue that the ultimate "good," or utility, is pleasure and the ultimate "bad," or disutility, is pain, and all actions or practices ought to be evaluated in terms of how much pleasure or pain they produce for all the people affected. Pluralistic utilitarians, on the other hand, argue that there is no single "good" that people pursue in an ultimate sense but that friendship, knowledge, courage, beauty, and health are also "goods" worth pursuing and a utilitarian decision ought to take account of the effects of an action or practice on all these values.

Philosophers also make a distinction between act and rule utilitarianism. The former holds that in all situations one ought to perform the act that maximizes utility for all the persons affected by the action. What utility means is different in different situations, and these different situations vary enough to justify separate analysis. Thus, in every situation one needs to make a utilitarian analysis to determine the right action or practice. Rule utilitarianism, on the other hand, holds that utility can be applied to classes of actions rather than to each individual action. Rules can be developed that when followed will tend to maximize utility in situations that are similar or where similar actions are relevant.

Thus, an act utilitarian, when faced with the temptation to break a promise, would have to evaluate the consequences of breaking a promise in every situation where the question arose. The concept of utility would have to be applied to the breaking of a promise in a particular situation under a particular set of circumstances. A rule utilitarian, on the other hand, would look at the general consequences of breaking promises in any situation and might develop a rule that it is immoral to break promises because, in general, keeping promises produces more good than breaking them. The advantage of having rules is that one does not have to take time to think through the consequences of alternatives in every situation but can use rules as guidelines to determine the right action. This is a particular advantage when time pressures are involved, and one does not have the time to perform a thoroughgoing utilitarian analysis. The disadvantage is that rules can become inflexible and be applied to situations that are truly unique and deserve new thinking.

Utilitarianism is obviously committed to the good and asserts that we ought always to choose that action which produces the greatest possible balance of good for all persons affected by the action. Concepts of duty and rights, which will be discussed later, are subordinated to, or determined by, such action, which maximizes the good or promises the best outcome for all affected parties. Thus a

---

[2]Manuel Velasquez, *Business Ethics: Concepts and Cases* (Englewood Cliffs, N.J.: Prentice-Hall, 1982), p. 47.

utilitarian decision could bring about harm or disutility to a minority group and violate basic rights they believe they possess, in the interests of producing the greatest good for the greatest number. Some philosophers hold that there are basic human rights that ought not to be violated in the interests of the general welfare.

A related criticism points out that utilitarianism considers only how much total utility is produced by an action and fails to take into account how that utility is distributed. Various distributional patterns can result from different actions, and yet utilitarianism is indifferent between different distributions as long as they produce the same amount of total utility. Thus, philosophers argue that justice, which is a basic concept of morality, cannot be derived from a utilitarian analysis, and they question the moral validity of utilitarian theory. Some ways of distributing benefits and burdens are believed to be unjust, regardless of how great a store of benefits such distributions produce.[3]

Utilitarianism is also committed to the measurement and comparison of goods and assumes that all benefits and costs of an action can be measured on a common numerical scale and then added or subtracted from each other. In our modern economic society, the hedonistic calculus advocated by Jeremy Bentham has been replaced by the price mechanism. Utility is measured by the price people are willing to pay for something in the market. Thus, benefits and costs of alternative courses of action can be measured by determining a market price that will express the positive benefits or negative impacts of a particular action on the people affected.

Criticisms are leveled at this process and questions raised about the possibility of quantifying goodness or badness in this or any other manner. Philosophers argue that attempts to quantify utility and measure benefits and costs of alternative actions involve arbitrary and subjective assessments of value. It is difficult in many cases to determine what is a benefit and what is a cost, let alone trying to place some dollar value on them that is realistic and acceptable to all the parties concerned. When we get into the problem of valuing the benefits of pleasure, health, knowledge, and happiness or measuring the costs of pain, suffering, sickness, death, and ignorance, we are faced with an apples-and-oranges problem, and it is impossible to find a common denominator that will do justice to valuing all these goods and bads appropriately and uniformly.[4]

Finally, critics argue that it is impossible to determine all the consequences of alternative actions, or at least that some important consequences will most likely be ignored because of the limitations of the decision situation. How far into the future can we see when we try to determine the consequences of our actions that we perform today? Even obtaining knowledge of those consequences we can determine may take so much time and effort that we will not be able to discover what to do in a given situation. Thus, the theory is believed to be impractical because of the uncertainty involved in determining the consequences and the time pressures that are generally present when a decision is to be made.

---

[3]Tom L. Beauchamp, *Philosophical Ethics: An Introduction to Moral Philosophy* (New York: McGraw-Hill Book Co., 1982), p. 99.

[4]Ibid., pp. 97–98.

The approach of utilitarianism is universalistic. Utilitarian calculations are made from an impersonal point of view in that what is weighed is the good or bad produced for each person affected by the action. This is believed to be an objective state of affairs that should come out the same for every rational person.[5] However, the difficulty of arriving at objective judgments about benefits and costs calls this view into question. Nonetheless, the utilitarian method may have some value as a way of thinking, even if it cannot be strictly followed in a quantitative sense. Thinking about alternatives and arriving at some rough estimates of their consequences may still be a useful method for a decision maker who is faced with making an ethical judgment.

DEONTOLOGICAL THEORIES

The deontological approach to ethical decisions maintains that actions are not justified by their consequences, that factors other than good or bad outcomes determine the rightness or wrongness of actions and practices. Thus, actions or practices themselves have intrinsic value apart from their consequences. The value of actions lies in motives rather than consequences. It makes a difference to deontologists whether one's motive is based on duty or on self-interest. Doing one's duty is a matter of satisfying the legitimate claims or needs of others as determined by applicable moral principles. The sources of duty can be a divine command, reason, or intuition or a social contract arrived at by the members of a society.

For example, promises ought to be kept and debts paid because of one's duty to keep promises and pay debts, not because of the good or bad consequences of such actions. If a person borrows money from someone with a promise to pay the debt at a later date with interest, this payment should be made because of the moral obligation inherent in the agreement. Not to pay the debt would violate a principle of great moral significance. From a utilitarian perspective, however, the debt should be paid because of the consequences involved. The debt should be paid because the debtor may go to jail if it is not paid or be subjected to other adverse actions.

The theories of Immanuel Kant are most often cited in further explanation of deontological theory. According to Kant, the ultimate basis of morality is to be found in pure practical reason, not in intuition, conscience, or production of utility. By analyzing reason as applied to action (practical reason), the key to morality can be found. Since reason is assumed to be the same in each individual, what is rational and moral should be the same for each individual. Thus, morality has an objective basis that is independent of our own personal goals and preferences. The ultimate basis of morality must be founded on principles of reason that all rational agents possess in common. Individuals act morally when they willingly choose to act the way reason demands.[6]

[5]Richard T. DeGeorge, *Business Ethics,* 2d ed. (New York: Macmillan Co., 1986), p. 47.
[6]Ibid., p. 67.

This demand to be moral comes to us in the form of a categorical imperative, something that everyone must do because it is a command of reason. These moral commands are categorical, not hypothetical, because they admit of no exceptions and are absolutely binding. They are imperative because they give instructions about how one must act in all circumstances. A categorical imperative tells us what must be done, whether or not we wish to perform the action, and prescribes maxims that are binding regardless of the circumstances and consequences. If one wants to be a rational human being, one is duty bound to obey these categorical imperatives.

How does one tell a valid moral principle from one that is not morally valid? Kant's theory has been called ethical formalism because Kant holds that an action or principle is right if it has a certain form and is morally wrong if it does not have that form. Thus, the moral law at its most general level states the form an action must have to be moral; it does not state the content an action must have to be a right action. Kant provides us with certain criteria that we can use to judge whether an action or a lower-level moral principle is indeed moral. For an action or principle to be moral, (1) it must be possible for it to be made consistently universal, (2) it must respect rational beings as ends in themselves, and (3) it must stem from and respect the autonomy of rational beings.[7]

Universalizability

An action is morally right for a person in a given situation if and only if the person's reason for carrying out the action is a reason that he or she would be willing to have every person act on in any similar situation. If an action is moral for one person, it must be accepted as moral for everyone. Can dishonesty, for example, be justified as a valid moral principle on these grounds? Not according to Kant because the principle cannot be applied universally. If dishonesty were the rule, nobody could believe a statement made by anyone, including a statement that one was being dishonest. One would have no way to sort out claims to truth. Thus, the principle cannot be applied consistently across all people and has no meaning in and of itself. Dishonesty has meaning only against a general presumption of honesty, which can be advocated as a valid moral principle because it can be applied consistently in all situations.[8]

Respect for Rational Beings

An action is morally right if and only if in performing the action, the person does not use others merely as means for advancing his or her own interests but respects people as ends in themselves. To treat people as means is to exploit them or otherwise use them without regard to their interests, needs, and concerns. People should be treated with dignity and have rights that should not be violated in pursuit

[7]Ibid., p. 69.
[8]Ibid., pp. 69–70.

of the general welfare or a so-called social good. People are not to be sacrificed on the altar of a utilitarian approach to morality that defines some general good as the ultimate end of human existence.[9]

Autonomy

An action is morally right if and only if the action respects people's capacity to choose freely for themselves. People are to treat each other as free and equal in the pursuit of their interests. Deception, force, and coercion fail to respect a person's freedom to choose and are therefore immoral. The moral law is self-imposed and self-recognized; people determine its content for themselves in accordance with reason. Each person imposes the law upon himself or herself and accepts its demands. Those who possess moral dignity are the determiners of their own destinies and are self-governing beings. The autonomous person is both free of external control and in control of his or her own affairs.[10]

Actions and principles must meet all three of these tests to be a valid moral action or principle. Actions and principles such as truth telling and keeping promises must be subjected to these criteria, and if they pass they then have the status of a categorical imperative. Thus, the right action to perform in a given situation is determined by these formal criteria rather than by an appeal to consequences. An action has moral worth when performed by an agent who possesses a good will, defined as a person whose sole motive for action is performance of a moral duty based on a valid moral principle.

As in utilitarianism, there are act and rule deontologists. According to act deontology, individuals in a decision situation must grasp immediately what ought to be done without relying on rules or guidelines. Each situation is unique and is not subsumable under general rules of moral behavior. This view emphasizes the particular and changing features of moral experience and relies on individual intuition, conscience, faith, or love as the basis for moral judgments. Kant's theory would seem to rule out this kind of deontology as it provides a weak basis for moral action. Rule deontology, on the other hand, is consistent with Kant's theory, as it states that acts are right or wrong because of their conformity or nonconformity to one or more moral principles. Such rules facilitate decision making and are binding on individuals.

There are also monistic deontological theories, which advocate a general rule, such as the Golden Rule, as the supreme moral principle from which all other moral rules and principles are derived, and pluralistic deontological theories, such as the Ten Commandments, which hold that there are a number of moral principles that have more or less equal validity. Ross, for example, lists a number of moral maxims, such as faithfulness, promise keeping, justice, beneficence. nonmalevolence, and gratitude, that are prima-facie moral duties. They are always to be acted

[9]Ibid., pp. 70–71.
[10]Ibid., pp. 71–72.

on unless they conflict on particular occasions with equal or stronger duties. Prima-facie duties are thus not absolute and can be overridden under some conditions.[11]

Deontologists have been accused of making a covert appeal to consequences to demonstrate the rightness of actions. It is often argued that the consequences of an action cannot be separated from the action itself. Even Kant's theory is said to rely on a covert appeal to the utilitarian principle. If the consequences of the universal performance of a certain type of action can be shown to be undesirable overall, then the action is wrong. However, Kant never advocated that consequences be disregarded entirely, only that the judgment about the morality of a particular act does not rely on consequences.[12]

There is something of a problem of imprecision with regard to deontological theories. How can you tell if people are being treated as ends or means? How can you determine if a person has a good will and is acting on a motive of duty based on the demands of reason? How can you tell if people are autonomous and that this autonomy is being respected? And what if people don't want to be autonomous and self-governing but would rather leave the governing up to some philosopher king? Thus, deontological theory is too imprecise to be used to prescribe normative behavior, and there can be legitimate disagreement as to exactly what action reason demands in a given situation.

Finally, what happens when moral rules conflict. Which one should be overridden in favor of the other? How should conflicting rights and principles be adjusted to each other? If one rule demands truth telling while another rule demands the protection of a person from serious harm, what are we to do when asked to disclose a piece of information that will bring serious harm to someone? Should one tell the truth and disclose the damaging information or lie to protect a person from being harmed?[13]

Neither theory is free from problems, but deontology is again valuable as a way of thinking about ethical problems and arriving at valid moral actions and principles. Even if the categorical imperative can't be applied to all actions, thinking about one's duty and examining motives are important elements of ethical decision making. There are instances where doing one's duty is of overriding importance, even if adverse consequences for oneself and others is the result. Doing one's duty is an important motive that is emphasized at various times by every society and constitutes an important part of morality.

APPLICATIONS

Applying these theories to specific events that have recently happened or are still going on may help to determine their usefulness in analyzing decisions already made from an ethical point of view or in arriving at a decision that can be ethically

[11]William David Ross, *The Right and the Good* (Oxford: Clarendon Press, 1930).
[12]Beauchamp, *Philosophical Ethics,* pp. 138–39.
[13]DeGeorge, *Business Ethics,* pp. 74–76.

justified. An example presented itself at the time this chapter was being written. Readers will probably remember the hijacking of a Pan American 747 aircraft in Karachi, Pakistan, in the fall of 1986, an event that was a grim reminder that terrorism was alive and well despite several months of relative quiet.

The hijackers boarded the aircraft while it was still on the ground and demanded to be flown to Cyprus. The crew, however, managed to escape by climbing down a rope ladder extended from the cockpit. The aircraft was thus immobilized and couldn't be flown anywhere. Eventually, the hijackers panicked when the lights in the aircraft went out, and they began to fire their guns and explode grenades more or less at random. Several people were killed in the melee, but the hijackers were finally abducted and the rest of the passengers released and taken to the hospital if they were injured.

One of the most important questions to be asked that has moral significance is, Did the crew act ethically in leaving the aircraft and essentially leaving the passengers to fend for themselves? If their motive was solely one of saving their own skins and they evaluated the consequences of their action solely in terms of its effect on themselves—in other words, acted as ethical egoists—most people would probably have a hard time justifying their action as an ethical and moral action. They may, however, have adopted some other form of consequentialism, such as utilitarianism, to justify their behavior. In fact, the company claimed the crew was following company policy in leaving the aircraft if possible and thereby preventing it from being flown elsewhere.

This policy and the crew's action could be justified on the basis of utilitarianism, that in examining all the alternatives available to the crew, leaving the aircraft produced the greatest amount of good for all the parties affected as compared to any of the alternatives available, including staying with the aircraft. Perhaps it would be more accurate in this situation to say that such an action produced the least amount of bad for all the parties concerned. Immobilizing the aircraft forced the situation to be resolved at that point rather than postponing it until the plane landed at another airport where conditions would be different. More people eventually might have been killed if they had flown to Cyprus or elsewhere, and the anxiety and uncertainty facing both crew and passengers would certainly have been prolonged.

On the other hand, a strong argument could be made that the crew had a moral duty to stay with the aircraft, that they had a responsibility to the passengers that was categorically binding, and that their continued presence in the cockpit was morally required in spite of the possible consequences. One of the reasons the crew does not wear parachutes in commercial aircraft as they do in military aircraft is so they cannot bail out when the aircraft develops a problem in midair. It would not be feasible for all the passengers to be given parachutes; thus, the crew doesn't have any either. There was a moral duty then, it could be argued, for the crew to stay with the passengers, and they acted immorally by leaving at the first available opportunity.

Another example is provided by the debate about imposing economic sanctions on the country of South Africa to force it to change its system of apartheid. Economic sanctions are usually imposed in order to accomplish political objectives.

It is hoped that if a country is damaged economically, it can be forced to adopt new policies that are more acceptable to the country or countries imposing the sanctions. In South Africa's case, by cutting off trade with other nations and other such measures, it is hoped that the South African economy will be significantly affected so that the government will abandon its system that keeps the races separate and adopt policies more in line with those of other Western nations.[14]

A utilitarian argument against economic sanctions would be based on the consequences of particular sanctions on all the parties involved. In the case of economic sanctions in general, there is a considerable body of evidence to suggest that economic sanctions rarely, if ever, accomplish their political objectives. In most cases, they are not successful in an economic sense. Nations can find ways to circumvent the sanctions and obtain the goods they need elsewhere. It is impossible to get all the countries of the world to agree on a particular sanction and impose it uniformly. But even if the sanctions are economically successful, evidence suggests they still do not accomplish the intended political objectives. Sovereign nations resent being coerced into changing their behavior and will resist change all the more if pressured to alter their institutions or way of life. They will learn to live with less, if necessary, and accept the suffering sanctions may produce in order to preserve their autonomy and freedom.[15]

Thus, economic sanctions could be rejected on utilitarian grounds as producing more bad consequences than good for all the parties affected. They may adversely affect blacks in South Africa more than the white community. Sanctions may also have adverse effects on other African nations that trade with the country of South Africa for some essential goods and services. And they often have bad consequences for the countries imposing them as well as for the target nation. The grain embargo imposed on shipments to the Soviet Union, for example, hurt the American farmer, perhaps more so than the Soviet Union, which was able to obtain grain elsewhere. The embargo on supplying equipment to help the Soviets build the Western European pipeline hurt companies like Caterpillar Tractor, which had a contract for pipe-laying equipment, while the Soviet Union was able to obtain the equipment from a Japanese firm. Thus, the pipeline may have been delayed for a time, but it was not stopped. The political objectives of changing the Soviet Union's immigration policies or of forcing it to reduce its pressure on the Polish government to take strong steps against Solidarity were not accomplished to any significant degree.

It would seem, then, that taking the consequences into account, economic sanctions against South Africa or any other nation, for that matter, cannot be morally justified. However, one could also make a case for sanctions on deontological grounds, that we have a moral duty to oppose apartheid by any means possible regardless of the consequences, that economic sanctions are a way of

---

[14]See S. Prakash Sethi, ed. "South Africa: Is There a Peaceful Path to Pluralism?" *Business and Society Review*, no. 57 (Spring 1986), pp. 4–128.

[15]See Donald J. Losman, *International Economic Sanctions* (Albuquerque: University of New Mexico Press, 1979).

making a moral statement of great significance and of putting ourselves on the side of justice. Such sanctions and other actions are in the nature of a categorical imperative to have nothing to do with such a system and make this known by our actions. Apartheid is immoral; it is not universalizable; it does not treat people as ends; and it does not respect the autonomy and freedom of people.

Other examples where these theories could be applied abound. The issue of plant closings can be analyzed from a utilitarian perspective and the benefits and costs for all the parties concerned estimated and weighed against other alternatives. Or one could argue that management has a duty to the community and employees to keep a plant open and modernize it despite the fact that this action may not be as profitable as some other alternatives. Management and regulators can adopt a cost-benefit approach to pollution control or argue that they have a moral duty to clean up the environment and protect human health regardless of the costs involved.

The cases dealing with Ford Motor Company and South Africa at the end of the book can be used to illustrate the application of these theories. Ford Motor Company performed a cost-benefit analysis in the decision about the Pinto and thus attempted to apply utilitarian concepts to decision making. But questions can be raised about the way they did this analysis and whether they were truly following utilitarian principles. Questions can also be asked about the duties they had to consumers in this case and whether these duties overrode any utilitarian considerations. The South African case can be subjected to the same kind of discussion. Is a utilitarian analysis helpful in this situation or are there overridding duties that take precedence over all other considerations?

The important question as far as management is concerned is, Which theory is the correct one to follow and will lead to a morally justifiable and acceptable action or practice? Is one of these theories the right one to apply in all times and places, or are there situations where one of these approaches is better to use and other times and places where the other approach is more useful? The answer to this question, if there is one, is terribly important to a management that wants to do the right thing because the approach that is chosen will often lead to different answers. Where both approaches lead to the same action or practice, or where an action already taken can be justified by both approaches, management would seem to be on firm ground. But when these theories lead to different actions, as the above examples show is often possible, then management is presented with a dilemma, and the problem of relativism and subjectivity again appears.

Adopting a posture of both/and rather than either/or leads one to state that both theories are applicable to all ethical questions. Consequences and motives both have moral significance and should be taken into account in making moral decisions. The consequences of an action can benefit and harm people, and it is important to have some idea of who is benefited and who is harmed and to what degree. Thus, some objective analysis of the consequences of different actions and practices would seem to be a categorical imperative in and of itself. Human beings have a duty to take consequences into account in making ethical decisions. That is a universalizable principle; it treats people as ends rather than means, and it respects the autonomy of individuals in giving them a choice rather than a binding command to be followed regardless of the consequences.

On the other hand, motives are important to examine in making an ethical decision. Motives can lead us to skew the results of a utilitarian analysis to come up with a predetermined answer. If we have a strong motive to deregulate the economy, we are very likely to evaluate benefits and costs of a proposed regulation in such a way as to always show that regulations are not justifiable on utilitarian grounds. That is why the objectivity and accuracy of people who do these calculations who are also on record as being strong advocates of deregulation are open to serious question. Some objective way of examining our motives and some criteria that can help us to determine our duties is crucial to making a moral decision.

Human beings actually operate this way in their ordinary or common-sense notions related to making ethical judgments. We take both motives and consequences into account in making judgments about the morality of an action or practice. If a robbery is committed and the robber is caught, we punish the robber regardless of the fact that the robbery may have led to tightened security procedures that will prevent an even greater robbery from being committed in the future. Robbery is wrong regardless of the consequences, and people have a moral and legal duty not to steal from each other. On the other hand, the actions of an average citizen to help victims of a car crash can lead to serious consequences if one of the victims is moved and further injury results. The appropriate action would have been to wait for medical personnel who knew what they were doing. However, we do not lock such a person in jail because we judge his or her motives to have been good and the intent was to help the victims, not harm them.

Thus, immoral motives can lead to good consequences, and bad consequences can be the result of good motives. In making a moral decision, it is important to take both consequences and motives into account. The robber should consider the inherent immorality of his action, and the citizen should consider the possible harm that can result from moving an injured person if it is not necessary for other reasons. The same thing holds true for managers. They must consider the consequences of an act like closing a plant on all the affected parties and must also consider their motives and duties in considering alternative courses of action. Motives and consequences then begin to merge into each other and become part of the same decision-making process.

VIRTUE THEORY

This merging of consequences and motives brings us to a third body of ethical theory, sometimes called virtue theory. In the final analysis, it could be argued, ethics boils down to individual action. Ethics does not consist of a set of rules or prescriptions that determine how people ought to act, it consists of the actions and motives of ethical people who are concerned to do the right thing in all the situations they face. Ethical actions stem from virtuous people who are concerned about doing the good and are not slavishly following a set of rules that are thought to be connected with the good in some fashion.

> An ethical rule never actually resolves an ethical dilemma. For the good, which is the central concern of ethics, is finally what a good man does. Being ethical is, after all, just that: a matter of being. The problem before the businessman who aspires to be ethical is not that of doing, but of becoming and being. . . . An ethical decision will be made only by an ethical man who knows the situation, discerns what ought to be done, and does it. Those who persist in the belief that if only certain rules are obeyed, we shall have ethical conduct in business are much too abstract about ethics, far too disrespectful toward the particular and the concrete, naive in the failure to recognize the rationalizing talent with which each of us can escape an onerous rule, and doomed to continual frustration of their expectations.[16]

The former theories of teological and deontological ethics dealt with principles and rules that prescribed what we ought to do, not what kind of persons we ought to be or strive to become. The task of ethics is to provide guides to action that are consistent with general notions of what it means to be ethical or moral. Yet in our everyday judgments about ethics and morals we not only judge actions as being right or wrong, we also make character-centered judgments that describe a person or character as being good or bad, praiseworthy or blameworthy, admirable or reprehensible. We give people credit or criticism not only for what they do but also for what they are and the kind of inward character they exemplify.

An example is the man who passed the rope to others so they could be saved in the accident involving an Air Florida Boeing 737 several years ago. The plane crashed into the Potomac River on takeoff from Washington's National Airport. There were a few survivors, some of whom were standing on pieces of the plane that were floating in the icy river. There were several people standing on one such part of the plane who were being rescued one at a time by a rope dropped from a bridge overhead. One of the men on the piece of the plane kept passing the rope to other people who were waiting to be rescued along with him, and they were pulled to safety. By the time it came to his turn, the piece of the aircraft on which he was standing had sunk beneath the river, and the man himself disappeared beneath the icy waters. We admire him not only for the actions he took but also for the kind of person he was in displaying the virtue of complete unselfishness and the willingness to sacrifice his life so that others might be saved.

Thus, virtue ethics deals with the cultivation of virtuous traits of character as among the primary functions of morality. Correct choices that are made out of a sense of duty do not necessarily signify that a person is virtuous. People who act only out of a sense of duty can sometimes despise and grudgingly fulfill their moral obligations. We would tend not to describe such persons as virtuous and possessed of a good and moral character. We might admire their actions and decisions but not the individuals themselves.[17]

---

[16]Paul T. Heyne, *Private Keepers of the Public Interest* (New York: McGraw-Hill Book Co., 1968), pp. 111–13.

[17]Beauchamp, *Philosophical Ethics*, p. 149.

An ethics based on virtues depends on an assessment of selected traits of character and should not be confused with principles or statements of what ought to be done. Virtue ethics deals with dispositions, habits, or traits a person possesses or aspires to possess. Moral virtues can be defined as "a fixed disposition, habit, or trait to do what is morally commendable."[18] Thus, virtues deal with the kind of person one is, the qualities he or she possesses internally that are exemplified in daily activities. Virtue ethics is based on being rather than doing.

Philosophers differ as to which virtues are central to the moral life. The Christian religion mentions the virtues of faith, hope, and love as central traits of a moral character. To these could be added the virtues of wisdom, courage, temperance, and justice, which were advocated by classical philosophy. They were held to be cardinal virtues in that they could not be derived from each other, and all other moral virtues were believed to stem from them. The virtues of fairness, faithfulness, and gratefulness are also believed to be qualities that a moral person should possess and exemplify.

Aristotle held that moral virtues are universally praiseworthy features of human character that have been fixed by human habituation. The virtuous person is one who aims at moderation between extremes, who avoids the vice of excess (too much) and the vice of defect (too little). The proper balance between these extremes is best determined by persons of practical wisdom who have experience and great skill of judgment to face new situations. A person possessed of practical wisdom knows which goals are worth attaining and knows how to achieve them, keeping emotions within proper bounds and thus exhibiting a proper balance between reason, feeling, and desire.[19]

An ethics of virtue is therefore quite different from an ethics of principle. Virtue ethics focuses on character traits that a good person should possess and holds that what we need to direct us toward ethical behavior is fundamental directives about the kinds of persons we should strive to become. Those who believe virtue ethics should be primary in ethical theory believe that "morality does not consist in obedience to Kant's categorical imperative; rather, it is the expression of a virtuous character internal to the person—a character needing no external rules specifying right conduct."[20] The good is what the virtuous person does, not some abstractly defined notion of human welfare.

Moral ideals can be a part of virtue ethics because they are directed at the kind of person it is commendable to become, but they do not state specifically what that person ought to do in any given circumstance. One can pursue moral ideals and aspire to certain actions apart from belief in a morality of obligations. Saints and heroes are often used as role models and examples of what a moral person should be like and the virtues that are worth attaining. These people help us to learn to be virtuous and show us what a moral life looks like in the contemporary world. Their actions often go beyond what duty alone would seem to require and stem from an

[18]Ibid., p. 150.
[19]Ibid., pp. 158–59.
[20]Ibid., p. 163.

Aristotle's Virtues

Courage: particularly courage in battle.

Temperance: which includes the enjoyment of pleasure as well as moderation; a man who abstained from sex, food, and drinking would not be considered virtuous by the Greeks, as he might be by some people today.

Liberty: what we would call charity.

Magnificence: spending lavishly and doing great deeds.

Pride: appreciation of one's own worth (humility was a vice).

Good temper: but it is important to get angry when appropriate.

Friendliness: a very important virtue for the Greeks, not just a personal pleasure or necessity.

Truthfulness

Wittiness: people who can't tell or take a joke aren't virtuous. Aristotle would not equate ''seriousness'' with being moral, as some people do.

Shame: being sensitive to one's honor and feeling appropriately bad when it is besmirched. ''Feeling guilty,'' on the other hand, did not even seem to be worth talking about.

Justice: the sense of fair treatment of others.

Source: Robert C. Solomon and Dristine R. Hanson, *Above the Bottom Line: An Introduction to Business Ethics* (New York: Harcourt Brace Jovanovich, 1983), p. 8.

---

inward commitment to live a virtuous and good life rather than a commitment to implement a set of principles. They are attractive individuals because they seem to have their act together and are moderate in all things. They provide a concrete example of ideals that we may deem important and show that in actuality these ideals can be lived out and become reality.[21]

There are several questions that can be raised about an ethics of virtue. One concerns the motivation to live a virtuous life and follow the example of those saints and heroes we admire. Does virtue ethics actually contain a subtle form of obligation, in that if we know what it means to live a virtuous life, is there not some kind of a demand or imperative that we should so live our own lives? The presumption behind virtue ethics is that we ought to be virtuous, and does not this presumption entail an obligation? If such an obligation is not a part of virtue ethics, then how do the moral ideals that we admire in heroes and saints become a reality for the vast majority of people, particularly when these ideals may conflict with living a pros-

[21]Ibid., pp. 170–73.

perous and rewarding life in terms other than feeling good about being virtuous? Can virtue indeed be its own reward for people in a society like ours that is success oriented?[22]

Since virtue theory does not focus on actions, how can such a theory be used to determine the rightness or wrongness of actions? Supposing two people whom we regard as virtuous in all of their daily activities have two different opinions as to the appropriateness of economic sanctions on South Africa. This is not just an abstract example because there are instances every day where people we admire and regard as virtuous often hold different opinions as to what course of action to take with regard to specific situations. Which action, then, is the right one, and how are we to decide between two different actions on the basis of virtue theory alone?[23]

Likewise, the fact that a virtuous person chooses a certain action does not in itself make that action moral. Actions may be misguided and still be done with the best of intentions by virtuous people. The virtuous person may not know what should be done in certain circumstances because he or she is not aware of all the alternatives and does not have enough information. Judging the moral quality of an action solely by judging the moral quality of the person does not seem to be completely satisfactory. Even saints and heroes are fallible and may need rules to follow in very morally ambiguous situations. They may need obligations to rely on when the will is weakened. Even virtuous people can act out of character and commit moral wrongs. The fact that they are usually virtuous does not make a wrong a right, but if we rely solely on virtue ethics, we have no way of knowing when an act is wrong and deciding when they may be acting out of character.

An ethics of virtue and an ethics of principle thus complement each other. An adequate theory of ethics needs to include principles that can be used to judge the morality of actions and emphasize those virtues that are deemed to characterize the moral person. In practice, these two approaches are linked, as the way we come to know a virtuous person is largely through his or her actions. If virtues are to have any meaning they must be implemented through actions that people take toward each other and the world in which they live.

Most of us do not know anything at all about the man who passed the rope along apart from that action. Yet we judge him to be a virtuous person exemplifying unselfishness and courage because of the actions he took. Whether he did those things out of a sense of obligation we don't know, and it probably wouldn't make any difference in our judgment. We think of him as a hero because of the actions he took and assume that he possessed the character traits that are consistent with the action. We believe in this case that there is a correspondence between the action taken, which we could argue was a moral action, and the person himself. Rather than saying that ethics is what a good person does, perhaps we should say that ethics consists of moral actions taken by moral people. A morality of duty and principles and a morality of virtues or traits of character are not rival kinds of morality between which we must choose but are complementary aspects of the same morality.

[22]Ibid., pp. 174–75.
[23]Ibid., pp. 177–79.

SUGGESTED READING

ARISTOTLE. *The Nicomachean Ethics*. Trans. by Sir David Ross. London: Oxford University Press, 1961.

BAYLES, MICHAEL D., ED. *Contemporary Utilitarianism*. Garden City, N.Y.: Doubleday & Co., 1968.

BENTHAM, JEREMY. *An Introduction to the Principles of Morals and Legislation*. London: Athlone Press, 1970.

BLANSHARD, BRAND. *Reason and Goodness*. London: George Allen & Unwin, 1961.

FOOT, PHILIPPA. *Virtues and Vices*. Oxford: Basil Blackwell, 1978.

GEACH, PETER. *The Virtues*. Cambridge: Cambridge University Press, 1977.

GERT, BERNARD. *The Moral Rules: A New Rational Foundation for Morality*. New York: Harper & Row, 1970.

GRICE, GEOFFREY RUSSELL. *The Grounds of Moral Judgment*. Cambridge: Cambridge University Press, 1967.

HARE, R. M. *Moral Thinking*. Oxford: Clarendon Press, 1981.

KANT, IMMANUEL. *Foundations of the Metaphysics of Morals: Text and Critical Essays*. Indianapolis: Bobbs-Merrill, 1969.

————. *Lectures on Ethics*. New York: Harper Torchbooks, 1963.

MAYO, BERNARD. *Ethics and the Moral Life*. London: Macmillan Co., 1958.

MILL, JOHN STUART. *Utilitarianism*. New York: Liberal Arts Press, 1957.

MOORE, GEORGE E. *Ethics*. New York: Oxford University Press, 1965.

PATON, H. J. *The Categorical Imperative*. Chicago: University of Chicago Press, 1948.

ROSS, WILLIAM D. *Foundations of Ethics*. Oxford: Clarendon Press, 1939.

SIDGWICK, H. *The Methods of Ethics*. Indianapolis: Hackett Publishing Company, 1981.

SMART, J. J. C. *An Outline of a System of Utilitarian Ethics*. Melbourne: Melbourne University Press, 1961.

WALLACE, JAMES D. *Virtues and Vices*. Ithaca, N.Y.: Cornell University Press, 1978.

WARNOCK, GEOFFREY J. *The Object of Morality*. London: Methuen & Co., 1971.

5

How
Can Moral Judgments
Be Justified?

If theories are useful in helping us analyze moral problems and make decisions about the morality or immorality of certain actions or practices, and if both consequences and motives have moral significance, the question of grounding or justifying the ethical judgments one makes is still of crucial importance. Presumably, normative or prescriptive statements are made to change the behavior of people and institutions, to convince them that certain actions are better than in others in terms of contributing to human welfare. Normative statements are not normally made solely for intellectual reasons. They are meant to direct human behavior toward goals and objectives that have to do with human well-being.

How does one justify the selection of certain ethical principles over others to prescribe behavior, and how does one ground the selection of these principles, which will often lead to different actions and practices from other principles? How does one justify the use of utilitarian analysis or the deontological approach to develop moral principles or rules on which to base moral decisions? Justification has to do with providing some basis for our moral prescriptions so that others can examine what we prescribe and be persuaded or convinced that what we say has merit and deserves serious consideration. The goal of moral justification is to provide such a convincing argument in support of certain normative principles that people will actually change their behavior to conform with these prescriptions.

INTERNAL JUSTIFICATION

Moral judgments can be justified by an appeal to ethical standards that are considered applicable within a system of ethical theory. In other words, moral judgments can be justified by an appeal to the theories that have just been discussed. From these general ethical theories, moral principles can be derived that support the development of moral rules. These rules are more specific guidelines for human behavior indicating that actions of a certain kind ought or ought not to be performed. Thus moral judgments, which are decisions about a particular action, could be shown to be consistent with certain moral rules that are derived from moral principles that are ultimately developed from general moral theories. Different levels of generality and specificity are involved with this kind of justification where the particular or less general moral statement is justified by an appeal to the more general.[1] This idea can be diagrammed as in Figure 5.1.

Perhaps an example will help to illustrate this process of justification. Suppose a company is attempting to decide whether to require mandatory testing of employees for AIDS and is trying to justify its decision on moral grounds. One possible argument for deciding against AIDS testing could be justified by the following line of reasoning. Testing for AIDS is wrong because an employee's right to privacy is of fundamental importance, and such testing violates this right. This rule is derived from the more general principle of respect for persons and ultimately comes from deontological theory, which advocates treating people as ends in themselves rather than as means. Thus, the decision not to engage in AIDS testing is justified by an appeal to a moral rule related to privacy, which in turn is justified by a principle that is ultimately derived from a deontological moral theory.

Successful justification of an action thereby occurs when there is successful grounding of the action in a standard that is independent of the action itself. Each level is justified by an appeal to the next higher level of moral reasoning and must be consistent with this level. Correct inferences must be made that follow the rules of logic in order for the justification process to be rational. Otherwise one could be accused of being arbitrary in the selection of rules and principles that will make the action itself weakly supported.

An internal justification process thus has to assume the legitimacy of the next higher level, which is a necessary condition for its acceptability. An appeal is made to more fundamental principles or theories of morality. However, this process cannot go on forever, and at some point one reaches the highest or most general theoretical level that is required for the correctness of all the other principles. This level cannot be justified by further appeal. If moral disagreement still exists when the final level is reached, one must step outside the system of morality itself for further justification.[2]

EXTERNAL JUSTIFICATION

External justification deals with justifying an entire system of moral beliefs and reasoning. An appeal to an internal principle will not suffice, as the entire system of

---

[1]Tom L. Beauchamp, *Philosophical Ethics: An Introduction to Moral Philosophy* (New York: McGraw-Hill Book Co., 1982), p. 308.

[2]Ibid., p. 311.

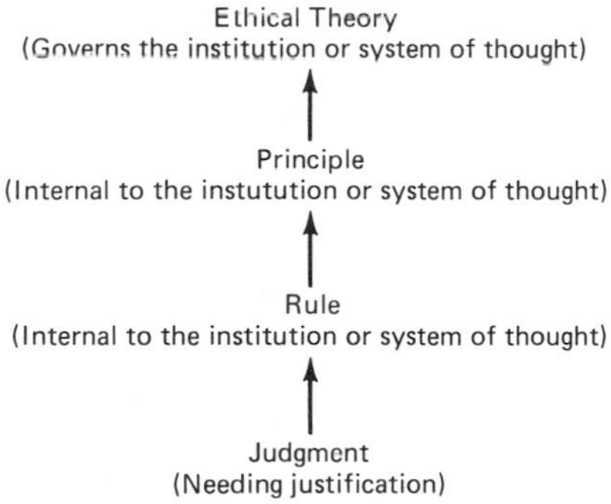

Ethical Theory
(Governs the institution or system of thought)

↑

Principle
(Internal to the instutution or system of thought)

↑

Rule
(Internal to the institution or system of thought)

↑

Judgment
(Needing justification)

FIGURE 5.1 SOURCE: Tom L. Beauchamp, *Philosophical Ethics: An Introduction to Moral Philosophy* (New York: McGraw-Hill Book Company, 1982) pp. 308 and 311.

thought must be justified. This kind of justification is necessary when moral disagreement exists at the most fundamental level of ethical reasoning. Why should one accept the consequentalist approach to ethical reasoning or the deontological approach? Perhaps virtue theory is the right way to think about ethical problems. When ethical theories lead to different actions, which system is the correct one to apply in a given situation. External justification is necessary to ground the entire system of thought including theory, principles, and the rules that are part of a particular system. One cannot appeal to the system itself because it is precisely the entire system of thought that is in question.[3]

Perhaps the difference between an internal and external justification process can be further explained by noting the difference between validation and vindication. Validation applies to internal justification and concerns whether appeals to higher and higher standards have been made correctly within an accepted system of thought. Questions can be asked whether correct inferences have been made and whether the rules of logic have been consistently followed. Vindication, however, is concerned with a justification of the entire approach, the entire set of internal principles and rules that are unique to a system of thought. Without such an external justification, moral principles could be said to be arbitrary and rationally indefensible.[4] There are several ways to justify ethical principles and theories by appeals to external sources of vindication.

Moral or Natural Law

Appeals can be made to the moral law or natural law as a basis for justifying ethical prescriptions, that there exists a basic set of moral principles that ultimately govern the universe. There is a natural order of things that we can seek to understand and work toward in the development of moral prescriptions. The expression natural law refers to fundamental norms that come before all moral principles and

[3]Ibid.
[4]Ibid., p. 316.

theoretical formulations. This law is binding on all human beings; it is universal, everlasting, and unchangeable. Moral values belong to the very nature of things and are not superimposed on an amoral reality by the human mind. They are not social conventions invented by humans to create a functional society as in social contract theory.

This idea of a moral or natural law is analogous to the physical sciences, which proceed on the basis of empirical investigation to discover the physical laws governing the universe to improve our understanding and control over the world in which we live. These moral laws can be discovered by the use of reason, the same as physical laws, proceeding in a rational manner to discover the nature of moral reality and prescribe universal moral behavior for humans to follow. Natural law is based on the idea that there are fundamental structures governing the universe from which human beings cannot be released. There is a moral order, which humans did not create, that lays a demand or obligation on them. There is a kind of fundamental moral knowledge that is given within human existence itself.

> Natural law is, as it were, the pointer within us that orients us to the goal of human existence. Actual rules, laws, and prohibitions are judged by this "unwritten law" in accordance with whether they promote or impede the movement toward fuller existence. Natural law changes, in the sense that the precepts we may derive from it change as human nature itself changes, and also in the sense that man's self-understanding changes as he sharpens his image of mature manhood. But through the changes there remains the constancy of direction.[5]

There are thus basic moral laws that should be followed, and deviations from them lead to all sorts of adverse consequences for the human race. For example, managers may believe that workers who are treated as ends in themselves and not just as means to greater productivity will actually be more productive in the long run, that workers who are treated with respect and as autonomous human beings will be naturally disposed to work harder and be loyal to company goals and objectives. Workers who are treated as means will be hostile and uncooperative and will see management as adversaries rather than as mutual employees to be trusted and respected. These attitudes will lead to a disfunctional organization that will not be as productive as one that adheres to the moral law in its treatment of employees.

Another example could be drawn from the environment where treating the environment solely as a means to dispose of waste leads to all sorts of adverse consequences that pose threats to human health. Treating the environment with respect as an end in itself means disposing of wastes properly so as not to damage the ecological structures or at least so as to affect them to the least extent possible. Violation of the moral law with respect to the environment will ultimately lead to destruction of the human race itself because the moral law cannot be transcended in the course of history. It is up to reason to discover these relationships and implement them in our society with respect to individual and institutional behavior.

[5]John Macquarrie, *Three Issues in Ethics* (New York: Harper & Row, Publishers, 1970), p. 108.

Ethical formalism is an attempt to describe the form these moral laws take and help us recognize one when we see it, but these laws are not considered apart from their consequences. If what we believe to be a valid moral law consistently produces more bad consequences than good consequences, we will certainly go back to the drawing board and take another look at what we believe about moral reality. Thus the notion of a natural or moral law is an ideal toward which we can work, but what constitutes ultimate reality will never be known by any human being. The ideal itself is important and is used to judge all our prescriptions of a more transitory nature.

The Use of Reason

While the use of reason is basic to most, if not all, attempts at justification, it can become the ultimate means by which justification is attempted. Reason can be considered to be the same in all rational beings, and thus if people use reason to approach moral problems instead of letting emotion and interests get in the way, they will arrive at the same position with regard to moral principles and judgments. The assumption is made that people are basically rational beings who have the possibility of reasoning their way to moral standards that are universally acceptable. The process of moral reasoning has been described as follows.

> First, we must take the moral point of view . . . not that of self-love or aesthetic judgment, nor the more general point of view involved in judgments of intrinsic value. We must also be free, impartial, willing to universalize, conceptually clear, and informed about all possible relevant facts. Then we are justified in judging that a certain act or kind of action is right, wrong, or obligatory, and in claiming that our judgment is objectively valid, at least as long as no one who is doing likewise disagrees. Our judgment or principle is really justified if it holds up under sustained scrutiny of this sort from the moral point of view on the part of everyone. . . . If this line of thought is acceptable, then we may say that a basic moral judgment, principle, or code is justified or "true" if it is or will be agreed to by everyone who takes the moral point of view and is clearheaded and logical and knows all that is relevant about himself, mankind, and the universe.[6]

Because morality consists in acting rationally the source or morality is to be found in ourselves and our reason and not in anything external. We act morally when we willingly choose to act in the way reason demands. And since the basic structures of reason are the same in all human beings, what is ultimately rational and moral is the same for all human beings. If a rule, principle, or action is to be judged as moral or immoral, the question will have to be asked whether the rule, principle, or action in question would be morally acceptable to all rational beings acting rationally. The final test of a moral judgment is whether all rational beings acting

[6]William K. Frankena, *Ethics*, 2d ed. (Englewood Cliffs, N.J.: Prentice-Hall, 1973), p. 112. Reprinted by permission of Prentice-Hall, Inc., Englewood Cliffs, New Jersey.

rationally would accept the action as moral regardless of whether they were the agents or the recipients of the action.[7]

An attempt at moral justification is successful if reasons are supplied to show a judgment is morally right or at least defensible by an appeal to reason. Reasoning is not the same as logic although logic is relevant to reasoning. Logic is concerned with argument and proof, and these are often relevant to reasoning. But reasoning is concerned with more than logic; reasoning involves inferences and assumptions that cannot be proved but that can be justified by an appeal to reason itself. The task of reason is to discover those universal moral principles that would be agreed to by all rational beings.

Reason involves a certain degree of moral autonomy in the sense that people must have reached a stage of moral development where they do not blindly accept moral principles on the basis of authority but are rational beings who have the capability of thinking about morality and adopting those principles they have reason to believe are correct and appropriate. People must be willing to think for themselves. They must also be free from coercion, either internal compulsions or external threats, so that reason can be used to arrive at an acceptable justification. Thus, people must also be free to think for themselves.

What happens, however, when people still disagree about moral judgments but claim to be rational beings who are using their free and unfettered reason to justify their positions? Who can make the final judgment as to which person is rational or more rational than the other. An appeal to reason itself would seem to be begging the question in settling this kind of difference. It seems reasonable to assume that there will be differences of this kind that appear from time to time. People can support or oppose economic sanctions against South Africa and have good reasons for supporting either course of action. Who is being more rational?

> Suppose we encounter someone who claims to be doing this but comes to a different conclusion. Then we must do our best, through reconsideration and discussion, to see if one of us is failing to meet the conditions in some way. If we can detect no failing on either side and still disagree, we may and I think still must each claim to be correct, for the conditions never are perfectly fulfilled by both of us and one of us may turn out to be mistaken after all. If what was said about relativism is true, we cannot both be correct. But both of us must be open-minded and tolerant if we are to go on living within the moral institution of life and not resort to force or other immoral or nonmoral devices.[8]

So we must not try to coerce others who disagree with us to adopt our point of view. We must continue to use reason to discover the nature of the disagreement and uncover hidden assumptions or faulty inferences that may make a difference. We must continue to engage in dialogue with each other and not retreat into irrational means to justify our positions. If we really believe that moral judgments can be justified by the use of reason, then we have to continue to operate on this

[7]Richard T. DeGeorge, *Business Ethics,* 2d ed. (New York: Macmillan Co., 1986), pp. 67–72.
[8]Frankena, *Ethics,* p. 112.

basis, recognizing the fallibility of any particular human being but not giving up on the principle of rationality itself.

Special Revelation

This type of justification is most often religious in nature, at least those religions that depend on revelation for their source of ultimate truth. The revelatory justification claims that moral truth comes to us from outside ourselves; it is revealed by a deity through some kind of special event or events, which are usually recorded in a document called the scripture. What is morally required of us is thus contained in this scripture or some other record of divine intervention. The task of theology is to restate this truth in modern categories so that the demands of the moral law are clear in contemporary situations.

This approach holds that there is no moral law as such contained in the universe in some natural manner, at least that can be known by human beings using reason alone, but moral prescriptions must be based on the divine law as revealed to humankind. This divine law is the ultimate basis on which all human law must be judged. Using reason alone to discover or develop moral prescriptions is not possible because reason itself is distorted and needs to be set aright by the revealed truth of the ultimate reality. Reason alone cannot be relied on to decide the ultimate ends of life that are worth pursuing nor in deciding on the appropriate means to attain these objectives. Those means are given through divine revelation, which contains an imperative to follow the commands of the divine being.

The revelatory approach argues that men legitimately disagree on ethical prescriptions because of the finiteness of human nature. Where disagreement exists, however, there is no way of settling differences because reason is relative and subjective in each individual. To settle these differences, an appeal should be made to the ultimate reality either directly or to the scriptures as a revelation of such truth or reality. Usually some religious institution develops to continually restate and interpret this ultimate truth to the followers of the religion. These institutions make attempts to extend their influence and gain more adherents to their interpretation of moral reality.

The problem this approach to justification faces is one of establishing such a claim to ultimate truth and expecing others to accept this claim. How can one claim to have a direct pipeline to a divine being so that one can be a spokesperson with authority or interpret scriptures correctly so that one's authority is accepted. People use reason in deciding who has religious authority that should be obeyed, and they use reason in interpreting scriptures and applying moral precepts to current situations.

Thus, reason cannot be totally excluded even from a revelatory situation, as the claim of truth is most often evaluated on some basis outside the revelation itself. There must be some independent way of knowing what judgments are true and reasonable in order to test for the authority of another's moral judgments when they are based on revelation. The revelatory event or events have to be interpreted and applied to contemporary situations and are not immediately self-evident to all the parties concerned. Perhaps one could argue that there has to be some correspondence between the revealed moral law that supposedly breaks in upon us from outside and an inner moral law that is rooted in the nature of things in order for a revealed truth to be acceptable.

In other words, nothing is ever completely external nor is anything completely internal. The moral law may have to be thought of as coming from a divine source in order for us to transcend our immediate situation and see things from a different perspective, but it also must reside in the nature of things in order to make sense and be acceptable to our reason. There must be a correspondence of internal and external sources of morality in order for normative prescriptions to have force that can lead to changes of behavior. Revelation alone may be a weak support for morality as is reason alone, but if both can be used to support a moral judgment, that judgment would seem to have greater justification.

The Social Contract

Moral prescriptions can also be grounded or justified in terms of social-contract theory, the principles people would agree to live by under normal conditions. The social contract can be based on a Hobbesian view of the human condition where morality becomes a necessary evil to hold society together. Without a minimum morality, society is impossible. Hobbes believed that human beings were created equal in the sense that they had an equal ability to do each other in if given the chance. Human nature knows no limits to greed and the quest for more and more of the limited resources society has available. Thus in a state of nature, there is no security, no common ways of life, and no reliable expectations about other people's behavior except that they will follow their own inclinations and perceived interests, tending to be arbitrary, violent, and capricious.[9]

This kind of equality creates a constant state of insecurity as people are a continual threat to one another. The natural state of affairs is a war of all against all, and individual life is solitary, poor, nasty, and brutish. Such a constant state of war and chaotic anarchy is really in no one's interest; therefore it would be better for all people individually and collectively to adopt certain minimal rules that would override immediate self-interest whenever a threat to the other was created. People must adopt such minimal rules to preserve human life and have some kind of society. Without such a social contract, no one can attain his or her objectives.

Hobbes thought that such a minimal morality could be only enforced by the creation of a Leviathan, an absolute ruler with power to enforce the rules and make people adhere to them. People would have to choose a sovereign to enforce the social contract and give up some short-term interests in the interests of long-term survival. It would be better to have a despot than total anarchy. But implementation of the social contract might also be achieved democratically if all members of the society agreed to common rules for their behavior that were taught to all members of the society and enforced by the group. The members who agreed to the social

[9]See Thomas Hobbes, *Leviathan* (Indianapolis: Bobbs-Merrill, 1958).

contract would have a right to expect the other members to obey the rules even when it was not in their immediate self-interest.

In any event, morality can be grounded in certain minimal moral rules that people agree is necessary to have a society where everyone can have a chance to accomplish his or her life objectives. Normative prescriptions can then be justified if they contribute to stability and continuity in the society and promote the freedom of human beings to pursue their own goals and objectives. Such a social contract is based on the assumption that people do not want to continue in a state of constant war but are rational creatures who prefer peace and stability to a state of chaos and anarchy.

Another kind of social contract was advocated by John Rawls in his theory of justice. This contract was based not on anarchy as a state of nature but on a so-called original position where human beings had no knowledge of their intelligence, status, power, wealth, or any other element that might define their position in society. One had to imagine being behind a veil of ignorance where none of these things, including one's race and sex, were known. Based on this original position where all people were in theory equal, people would agree to certain principles to govern their life in society and the distribution of benefits and burdens.[10]

The principles that constituted the social contract would be operative once people left the original position and stepped into society to assume their rightful place. But in formulating the principles, the rational thing to assume is that one might end up being one of the most disadvantaged people in society, with little or no wealth and education or any of the other amenities that make life worthwhile. Thus, one would want to design principles that would work to the advantage of those in the worst positions in society and give them something approaching an equal opportunity with those more fortunate and provide for some distribution of benefits to correct for some of the inequalities that might be present in actual society.

The social-contract notion thus provides a basis for morality rooted in the use of reason to design rules that everyone would agree to because it is in their long-run self-interest to do so or because it is necessary for society to function. The social contract assumes that rationality is the same in every human being so that people can arrive at a consensus regarding the rules they will agree to and adopt. It is assumed that through the use of reason and moral imagination people can arrive at such an objective state of affairs, where they will set aside their immediate self-interest for the long-run interests of the whole of which they are a part. People thus create the kind of world in which they want to live and agree on laws and structures to attain a decent life for themselves.

Moral Authority

Appeals can also be made to a moral authority to justify normative claims. Such appeals can be made to a religious figure, for example, who claims to speak for God or has been given an institutional role as a moral authority. What this

[10]See John Rawls, *A Theory of Justice* (Cambridge: Harvard University Press, 1971).

person says is right and wrong is thus right and wrong, provided his or her authority is accepted. However, it would seem that for rational people, at least, acceptance of a moral authority depends on the reliability and credibility of the authority, something that has been earned over time. Autonomous individuals will not simply accept authority in any area without good reasons. There is no good reason for accepting someone's moral authority unless the judgments of the authority have been checked for their truth value and reasonableness by using some independent source and not relying on the judgments of the authority themselves as their own grounds for truth and reasonableness. Therefore, the credentials of a moral authority can be established only if there are independent ways of establishing their validity.

Appeals can also be made to a document or set of scriptures as a source of moral authority, and therefore, what is contained in the scriptures is the ultimate justification for moral statements. The problem here is that the scriptures are ambiguous on many moral questions and need interpretation and application to the modern world. Many difficulties arise, for example, when Christians consult the Bible for direction and justification of moral statements. Many find justification for treating blacks as inferior and maintaining slavery as a legitimate social institution. Others think this is absurd. Many find ample justification for a pacifist position with respect to war and argue that it is in fact the only legitimate position for a Christian to take. Others find justification to go to war and engage in taking the life of other people under wartime conditions. In other areas, the Bible makes no reference at all, such as the issue of whether animals have rights that should be respected. Thus, consulting the scriptures for ultimate justification is fraught with problems, and again rational people will use some independent source to judge whether moral commands in the scriptures are credible and reasonable and so ought to be followed.

Power

Closely related to this justification is the use of power to establish one's authority in moral matters. If one has political power to command the loyalty of subjects, as did kings in times past, then this power can be used to establish standards of moral behavior that can be implemented throughout the realm where the person or party in power has control. In other words, might makes right. Power can be used to impose a moral authority on people and give them essentially no choice as to the standards of behavior that are acceptable and appropriate in the society. The justification for these standards lies in the power that has been given to or taken by the commander, and to change the standards means the one in power must usually be overthrown or persuaded that change is needed.

Power need not be political, however, to be effective. Power can also take the form of persuasion. Some people have the ability, primarily through appeal to the emotions, to persuade others that their authority or views on a moral issue ought to be accepted and followed. If enough people can be persuaded, then the strength of numbers is also added to the persuasive power of the individual. One thinks of evangelical preachers who are able to be very persuasive in convincing people to follow their version of the truth and are very effective in using modern communication techniques to play on people's emotions to elicit commitment to their interpretation of what is right and wrong with respect to human behavior.

There are then several forms power can take in terms of justifying normative statements, from the overt use of power to command people's commitment to more subtle forms of persuasion. The use of power is prevalent in any society as there are those who believe they have some connection with the truth that ordinary people lack or that they have been chosen for a leadership position. Power is used to impose standards of right and wrong on other people who may be all too willing to sacrifice their autonomy and their thinking processes to someone else and be relieved of the burden that goes with thinking about moral issues and arriving at decisions that are at best ambiguous. Making moral decisions is not an easy task, and some people are able to accumulate power and become moral authorities because they have the ability to command or persuade people to give up their moral autonomy to an authority.

Intuitionism

Normative prescriptions can also be justified by an appeal to intuition. An intuitionist believes that ethical concepts such as good, right, and courage do not refer to something that can be known through sense experience or through the empirical methods of the social sciences. Value judgments about the good and right cannot be justified by an appeal to empiricism but are known to be true or false by intuition. They are self-evident to all right-thinking people. Intuitionists believe that human beings can directly apprehend the presence of a value property without the aid of any form of direct empirical evidence to support the rightness or wrongness of the proposition. In some sense, this view is contained in the United States Declaration of Independence, which states, "We hold these truths to be self-evident." These truths need no outside support, in other words, but any right-thinking American should be able to recognize the truth value of the claims about human rights made in that document.[11]

Intuitionists hold that directly apprehending the truth of moral statements is a method unto itself. Moral principles and value judgments are intuitive or self-evident and do not need to be justified by any kind of argument since they are self-justifying. Analogies have been made to mathematical thinking where certain fundamental truths are said to be self-evident to any person who has the appropriate mathematical background and development. Likewise in the moral realm, certain truths are self-evident to people who have achieved an appropriate stage of moral development or maturity. Where there are moral conflicts that appear to be unresolvable, the problem may be that the parties to the conflict are simply at different stages of moral development.

The problem of moral disagreement cannot, however, be so easily dismissed. Pure intuition is difficult to distinguish from a strongly held belief, and if this is so, then how does intuition make a claim to knowledge that is critical to the acceptance

[11]Beauchamp, *Philosophical Ethics,* pp. 352–54.

of a normative statement? If intuition is nothing more than belief, then claims to truth can be challenged on the basis of evidence that shows the belief to be false. But if empirical evidence is not accepted, then what could be appealed to when two people have different intuitions and arrive at different conclusions about a moral judgment? What is self-evident to one person may not be self-evident to another. When these conflicts appear, there seems no way to resolve these differences by an appeal to intuitionism itself.[12]

Cultural Justification

Moral judgments can also be grounded in deeply held cultural values that have withstood the test of time and are in the nature of basic beliefs as to what human welfare is all about. These cultural values are widely shared and are passed on from generation to generation. They are what makes the culture distinct and provides meaning and identity to the members of that culture. There are basic notions of right and wrong in a culture that can be appealed to in order to justify moral judgments. These core values are said to compose the bedrock upon which valid moral principles can be established and justified.

> Embedded within humankind are moral meanings and conceptions of what is felt to be ethical. Great systems of thought, whether Christian, Marxist, or humanist, have captured portions of these moral meanings. These moral notions—they could be called moral archetypes—comprise the most fundamental, deeply felt value orientations of humankind generally. Each society varies its emphasis upon the rudimentary moral meanings but each returns over and over again to the basic structure of morality inherent in human interactions. Human behavior occurs within a web of such moral meanings and cannot escape being judged in terms of such a culture of ethics.[13]

Even in a society as pluralistic as the United States, certain core moral values can be discovered. A belief in certain fundamental human rights is part of the American tradition, including the right of free speech, the right to freedom of religion, and other such rights. Respect for private property is another such core value that can be appealed to if the government begins to interfere in business to an extent that violates this fundamental notion. Many of these basic moral notions are contained in our Constitution, which forms the ultimate basis of legal appeal. Laws that are found unconstitutional have no chance of being accepted and implemented short of an overthrow of the government itself.

The obvious problem with this approach to justification is, of course, cultural relativism. Anthropologists have shown that cultures differ in their basic moral values and have different moral beliefs about right and wrong behavior. Grounding moral judgments in culture opens up the problem of cultural relativism. In an age of multinational business and increasing internationalization of economic activity, this

---

[12]Ibid., p. 358.

[13]William C. Frederick, "Toward CSR3: The Normative Factor in Corporate Social Analysis" (invited paper presented at the Social Issues in Management Division, Academy of Management, Forty-fifth Annual Meeting, San Diego, Calif.), August 13, 1985, pp. 16–17.

presents a serious problem. This problem appears in questions of bribery, which may be an acceptable cultural practice in some societies even though it is not in our country. Which cultural norms shall a business follow, and whose culture is right on this question? Making moral judgments on the basis of certain core values in a culture provides no guidelines when cultures differ on certain practices.

Another problem with this approach is one of defining the concept of culture. Where are the boundaries of a culture such that it can be determined where one culture ends and another begins? The United States might be considered a culture with certain core values. But within the United States there are several subcultures, such as the Amish, with radically different values from the majority. Are their values to be ignored in the interests of the larger whole? There are various ethnic and racial groups in the United States that have beliefs different from Anglo-Saxon Protestants, and some of these ethnic groups are becoming dominant in certain regions of the country. Whose values are the core values of the culture? Does the kind of melting pot that characterizes a society like ours render the concept of culture meaningless?

Procedural Justification

Moral statements can also be justified by procedural means, by following proper procedures in arriving at a moral judgment. If proper procedures have been followed in making a moral judgment, then that judgment, more or less by definition, is justified. This approach involves the determination of the correct procedure to follow, or in other words, the definition of a so-called ideal moral judgment. What would such a judgment look like, and what steps constitute such a judgment? Such an ideal moral judgment could include the following stages or steps.[14]

Clarity.   When we engage in moral reasoning to arrive at a judgment and use concepts such as rights and justice, we must be as clear as possible as to what we mean by these concepts. If we talk about the rights of future generations, for example, we must be clear as to what we mean by a right in this context. If we say that a particular act or practice is unjust, we must describe in detail what kind of practice we are talking about and what we mean by justice in this context. This kind of conceptual clarity is important in resolving moral conflicts and in arriving at a justification for moral judgments. Quite often parties to a dispute argue past each other because they have not taken time to be clear about the issues involved and thus are not really arguing about the same thing.

Information.   Moral judgments take place in the real world, not in the abstract world of philosophical speculation. Therefore, a knowledge of how the world works and how variables relate to each other is important in order to make judgments about the morality or immorality of particular actions and practices. If,

---

[14]See for example Tom Regan, "Introduction," *Earthbound: New Introductory Ethics in Environmental Ethics* (New York: Random House, 1984), pp. 19–21.

for example, we argue that employers ought to do something to reduce accidents in the workplace, that this would be an ethical action in treating employees with respect and ends in themselves, then what exactly is it that employers ought to do with respect to accidents and injuries in the workplace? In order to answer this question we must have some information about those aspects of the workplace that contribute to accidents and injuries and that need attention. If overtime and turnover are highly correlated with accidents and injuries, as some studies indicate, then controlling these aspects of the workplace may do more to reduce accidents and injuries than more immediately obvious things such as guard rails and machine guards.

Rationality.   Rationality is often defined as logical thinking, rules that specify when valid conclusions can be drawn from certain premises and that certain statements are logically true and others false based upon these premises. In proceeding to apply logic to our justification of moral principles, then, we must be careful to show how our beliefs about morality are logically related to other things we do or do not believe. Suppose we strongly believe in the sanctity of private property and support the libertarian notion that people should be free to use property in their own self-interest free of government restrictions. But suppose we also support government legislation to clean up the environment in the interests of human health and welfare. These two beliefs, on the surface at least, would seem to be inconsistent and a contradiction that does not follow the rules of logic. For discussion and analysis to take place, it would seem that such inconsistencies constitute a major, if not insurmountable, hurdle.

Impartiality.   For a moral judgment to be valid, it must be impartial and not favor someone or something above others. In order to reach a defensible answer to moral questions, we must strive to guard against partiality; otherwise we run the risk of being accused of bigotry and prejudice, elements that make our judgment and justification suspect. We must treat similar cases alike regardless of who is involved. If we argue that blacks and other minorities do not deserve preferential treatment because of past wrongs but then support preferential treatment for veterans, we must explain how these two groups are different, how they are morally differentiated so that the one group deserves preferential treatment and the other does not. If there are no legitimate moral differences between these two groups, then we must treat them the same and not let prejudices enter into our justification.

Levelheadedness.   In this scheme of things, levelheadedness could be defined as being in a emotionally calm state of mind. Supposedly if we are calm, then we have a better chance of arriving at a defensible moral judgment than if we are excited and emotionally charged. While emotions are critical to life in other circumstances, strong and volatile passions are not necessarily a reliable guide to doing what is the right thing. People who are in an emotional state may not be able to be rational or make an impartial decision. If people are excited enough, they may not even care about what happens or why something is done. Shoot first and ask questions later is an example of emotion-based action. But you can't bring back to life a person who was wrongfully killed because someone waited until later to ask questions.

Consideration.   In dialogue about ethical questions, consideration of other points of view is important. No one has a corner on moral truth, and therefore the contributions that others have to make to a discussion, no matter how silly they appear on the surface, must be recognized. Parties to a discussion should not engage in tactics designed to intimidate others or to shame them in front of their peers. Such tactics do nothing to promote discussion and serve only to alienate people from each other. Discussion about ethics should not be a shouting match where the loudest person tries to impose his or her view on others. People should be treated as ends in the best sense of the word and all views respected and given a fair hearing.

There are therefore several ways to attempt to justify normative statements. The methods mentioned here are not necessarily mutually exclusive; any single moral judgment can have elements from a number of these methods. The use of divine revelation and the use of moral authority are closely related. Moral authority and power are also closely related, as are reason and an appeal to moral or natural law as justification. The existence of different methods of justifying moral judgments, however, does not mean that we are back in a relativistic position, anymore than the existence of different statistical methods to establish the truth of empirical statements means we are victims of relativity. No one knows absolute truth; in fact, in some systems of thought there is no absolute truth. But we can continue the search for knowledge about the world we live in and about the values that are worth pursuing. In doing so we are working toward advancing human welfare and achieving a more rewarding and satisfying life.

If one adopts either one of the extreme positions—that normative statements have no truth value so there is nothing to justify or argue about or if one claims to have a lock on truth—then dialogue is impossible. Yet it is in dialogue that progress is made toward greater understanding, and we can hope to increase our knowledge of human welfare and our ability to build a better world in which to live. Justification of moral judgments must be seen in this light, that there may be no ultimate justification but by being accountable to each other in providing the best justification we can for normative statements, we can progress in our ability to reason about ethics and the behavior that is deemed to be appropriate in any given circumstance.

SUGGESTED READING

Aiken, Henry David.   *Reason and Conduct: New Bearings in Moral Philosophy.* New York: Alfred A. Knopf, 1962.

Becker, Lawrence C.   *On Justifying Moral Judgments.* New York: Humanities Press, 1973.

Beehler, Rodger.   *Moral Life.* Totowa, N.J.: Rowman & Littlefield, 1978.

BRENNAN, JOHN M.   *The Open-Texture of Moral Concepts.* New York: Barnes & Noble, 1977.

EWING, ALFRED C.   *The Definition of Good.* New York: Macmillan Co., 1947.

HUDSON, W. D.   *Ethical Intuition.* New York: St. Martin's Press, 1967.

PHILLIPS, D. Z., AND H. O. MOUNCE.   *Moral Practices. New York: Schocken Books, 1970.*

RAZ, JOSEPH.   *Practical Reason and Norms.* London: Hutchinson Publishing Group, 1975.

ROSS, WILLIAM DAVID.   *Foundations of Ethics.* Oxford: Clarendon Press, 1939.

6

Should Ethical Statements Be Taken Seriously?

Regardless of the manner in which ethical prescriptions or ought statements are justified, there is a more fundamental question that needs to be asked. Should any kind of ethical statements be taken seriously whether they are grounded in revelation, reason, authority, intuition, or whatever? Are ethical oughts in any way scientific or empirical propositions that say something significant about the world in which we live or are they merely matters of opinion? Do ought statements relate in any significant way to factual statements that are the subject matter of scientific endeavors?

In philosophical terms, these questions relate to the problem of objective versus subjective morality. While on the surface this problem may not seem very important in a business school context, on closer examination it is actually of crucial importance. Instructors who argue that this kind of problem is best left to the philosophers who are trained to debate this kind of question may be doing their students as well as themselves a great disservice. This question of objective versus subjective morality has to do with the way in which ethical issues are approached and analyzed in a classroom and the acceptance of ethical questions as legitimate objects of study in a business school setting.

Briefly, the question of objective and subjective morality boils down to the difference between descriptive and prescriptive statements. Descriptive statements deal with matters of "fact" and attempt to make clear to people the way things are or the nature of reality. Such statements are the purview of science, an activity that attempts to analyze real-world problems and establish relationships between variables to understand the way the world works. Prescriptive statements, on the other hand, deal with questions of value and attempt to prescribe the way things should be in order to obtain the ''good'' life or be consistent with notions of human welfare and fulfillment. Thus, the problem of objective and subjective morality can also be stated as matters of fact versus questions of value or as the is versus the ought.

Perhaps describing the extreme positions on this issue will help to understand its importance. At the one extreme are those who claim moral philosophy is not a body of genuine knowledge, that judgments of value or prescriptive statements about what ought or ought not to be done are neither true nor false. They express nothing but our personal preferences, our likes and dislikes—in other words, our subjective feelings about the objects or actions in question. Thus, moral judgments are mere opinion, concerning which there is no point in arguing and certainly no way of investigating a proposition to determine its validity. Descriptive statements are the only kind of statements that can be examined by a scientific method to determine their so-called truth value.

At the opposite extreme are those who believe that there are absolute and universal standards of right and wrong and of what ought to be done or ought not to be done in specific circumstances. They believe there is a universal morality that applies to all people at all times and places and feel secure in a dogmatic assertion that the existence of objective moral standards and values is incontrovertible. People who enunciate this view claim an authority to make moral judgments and expect them to be accepted by others on the basis of this claimed authority. Again, there is nothing to argue about or examine as far as prescriptive statements are concerned, as adherents to this view claim to be speaking absolute truth that need not be validated by external criteria.

Most of us probably fall somewhere in between these extreme positions, but in a business school or business organization that adheres to a positivistic orientation toward reality—where empirical data are gathered to analyze and solve problems—the first view is likely to be more strongly held. This poses a special problem for moral philosophers who want to make normative statements about what business ought to be doing or what it ought not to be doing. How can the validity of these statements be established, and how can they be seen as anything other than mere opinion, which can then be easily dismissed?

If this question isn't dealt with, and an instructor plunges right in to deal with cases and issues without examining the ethical assumptions people are making, arguments about what is right and wrong are very likely to be a my-opinion versus your-opinion type of argument. This may be satisfactory for some people but certainly very frustrating to those who are trying to learn something of a more objective nature that can be applied to real-world situations. It would seem that for business ethics to establish itself as a legitimate subject for study in a business school and not be just a passing fad, it must establish that ethical theories and principles are more than opinion and convince the business community that prescriptive statements about the way things ought to be done have some objectivity about them that can be examined and argued about the same way one can argue about and examine descriptive statements. Students need to be challenged to examine their own assumptions about ethics and look at the foundations of their ethical judgments in order for ethics to be internalized and have a lasting effect.

THE PHILOSOPHICAL DEBATE

The question is whether moral values and prescriptive judgments about what ought to be are subjective and relative or whether they are objective and absolute in some fashion. The subjective can be understood as that which differs between people, and the objective is that which is the same for everyone. The relative is that which varies from time to time and changes with alterations in the circumstances, while the absolute is that which does not vary from time to time and does not change with alterations in the circumstances.[1] Nothing much can be said about the subjective and relative other than it all depends on the circumstances, a statement that is often hard in relation to judgments about ethical behavior.

The philosophical literature usually deals with two kinds of relativism, cultural relativism and normative relativism. According to cultural relativism, moral beliefs and principles that prescribe acceptable forms of human behavior are closely connected in a culture to other cultural characteristics, such as language and political institutions. Anthropological studies show that moral beliefs—the particular actions and motives that are deemed worthy of approval or disapproval—differ greatly from culture to culture. Thus, moral standards are held to be simply a historical product sanctioned by customs that have developed over a long period of time in response to conditions in which the society functions. Moral beliefs and principles are relative to groups and individuals that make up a culture, and consequently there are no universal norms that apply to all people and all cultures.[2]

Normative relativism, on the other hand, holds that when any two cultures or individuals have differences regarding the morality of a particular action or practice, both can be right because morality is relative. An action may be right for one culture and one individual under certain circumstances and wrong for another culture and individual under other circumstances. In other words, morality does depend on the circumstances. Moral statements are simply statements of opinion or feeling; they have no objective basis where their truth value can be determined. People can never really disagree about the morality of an action, nor can they be mistaken in their moral judgments. Statements of opinion or feeling are relative; one cannot in any real way show an opinion about a moral action to be false or invalidate a particular feeling about morality.[3]

According to Mortimer Adler, ancient philosophy had to deal with this problem in the form of the hedonist view of reality. The hedonists identified the good with pleasure and argued that pleasure was the ultimate end in life and the ultimate value worth pursuing. Everything else was an instrumental value in relation to the ultimate value of pleasure. However, if pleasure is the ultimate end of life, one can conclude that what is deemed good by one individual because it gives pleasure may not be deemed good by another. The pleasures human beings experience vary from

[1]Mortimer J. Adler, *Ten Philosophical Mistakes*, pp. 110–11.

[2]Tom L. Beauchamp, *Philosophical Ethics: An Introduction to Moral Philosophy* (New York: McGraw-Hill Book Co., 1982), pp. 34–35.

[3]Richard T. DeGeorge, *Business Ethics*, 2d ed. (New York: Macmillan Co., 1986), pp. 34–38.

person to person, from time to time, and with variations in circumstances. Thus, hedonism leads its exponents to be subjectivists and relativists about moral judgments and values.[4]

Philosophers attempted to deal with this problem by adopting a more pluralistic approach to ultimate moral values and redefining pleasure as the satisfaction of any desire, rather than as mere sensual pleasure. Things worth pursuing in life or the "good" could be wealth, health, friends, knowledge, wisdom, or even sensual pleasure. When one or more of these "goods" is desired by people, and they succeed in obtaining the object of their desire, they experience the pleasure that consists in having their desires fulfilled.

However, according to Adler, such an approach did not solve the problem of moral values that we are considering. Identifying the good with the desirable rather than with sensual pleasure still leads to subjectivism and relativism. Individuals may legitimately differ in their desires, and who can say that one desire is better than another? What is desired by one individual may not be desired by another for very good reasons. What is desired at one time under certain circumstances may not be desired at another time under other circumstances.[5]

A more modern problem for prescriptive statements was formulated by David Hume, who argued that descriptive statements cannot provide adequate grounds for validly and cogently reaching prescriptive statements. A prescriptive conclusion cannot be validly drawn from premises that are entirely descriptive.[6] Medical science, for example, can establish grounds for believing that cigarette smoke harms people who breathe in the smoke, whether they are actually smoking themselves or sitting in a smoke-filled room. But such a "factual" statement does not lead to the conclusion that nonsmoking areas ought to be established in all public places to protect the health of people. This prescriptive statement would have to be established on other grounds.

Apparently, Hume could not resolve this problem and thus is held to be responsible for much of the skepticism about the objective truth of moral philosophy that is prevalent in the twentieth century. Some philosophers also give G. E. Moore credit for developing this argument, which is sometimes called in philosophy the naturalistic fallacy. Moore argued that it is fallacious to deduce value statements from factual statements because value predicates are not identical in meaning with factual predicates. No list of facts or descriptions of what is the case could ever determine what ought to be the case or what is good. Therefore, no factual term entails a value term, and no factual judgment entails a value judgment. Naturalism, which holds that value judgments are a species of factual judgments, is mistaken.[7]

This separation of fact and value that Hume and Moore advocate can lead one to hold a view that ethics is noncognitive in nature, that neither ethics nor moral philosophy has the status of genuine knowledge. Ethics consists solely of opinions

[4]Adler, *Ten Philosophical Mistakes*, p. 112.

[5]Ibid., pp. 115–16.

[6]Ibid., p. 117.

[7]Beauchamp, *Philosophical Ethics*, pp. 345–52.

that express our likes and dislikes, our preferences or predilections, our wishes and aversions.[8] It is this complete separation that constitutes a serious problem for moral philosophy in a world that is scientifically and empirically oriented.

Another problem for moral philosophy appeared in the thinking of A. J. Ayer, who formulated the so-called correspondence theory of truth. This theory is based on an agreement of the mind with reality, that we are in contact with truth when what we think agrees with the way things are in the world. Obviously this theory applies only to descriptive statements—statements that involve assertions about what is or is not reality. Prescriptive statements cannot be either true or false. Sentences that express moral judgments do not say anything, but they are purely expressions of feeling and do not come under the category of truth and falsehood. Statements about what ought to be are unverifiable because they do not express genuine propositions about the world.[9]

Kant tried to solve this problem by making moral duty or obligation, expressed in prescriptive, or *ought,* judgments, totally independent of our desires and totally devoid of any reference to facts, especially the facts of human nature. The categorical imperative is a prescriptive statement that is regarded as a moral law by which our reason must be bound because it is self-evidently and universally true for all human beings in all circumstances. Kant asserts that the only thing that is really good is a good will, a will that obeys the categorical imperative and that discharges its moral obligations accordingly. These moral obligations can be known by all rational beings simply by thinking and reasoning without appeal to knowledge acquired through observation. Reason alone is the source of morality.[10]

Adler's solution is to distinguish between natural desires and acquired desires. Natural desires are those inherent in our nature and consequently are the same in all members of the human species, all of whom have the same nature. Acquired desires differ from individual to individual, according to differences in temperament, upbringing, and different conditions that affect their development. Whatever we need to fulfill our natural desires is really good for us, and in this sense there are no wrong needs. The needs inherent in our nature are all right desires. So a prescriptive judgment has practical truth if it expresses a desire for a good that we need because it is based on a natural desire.[11]

The moral principle Adler advocates is that we ought to desire whatever is really good for us and nothing else. It is impossible for us to think that we ought to desire what is really bad for us or ought not to desire what is really good for us. An understanding of the "really good" carries with it the prescriptive note that we "ought to desire" it; thus there is a link between the descriptive and prescriptive. The *ought* and the *really good* are related. Natural needs are the basis of natural rights—rights to the things we need in order to discharge our moral obligation to

[8]Adler, *Ten Philosophical Mistakes,* p. 118.

[9]Ibid., pp. 119–20.

[10]Gilbert Harman, *The Nature of Morality: An Introduction to Ethics* (New York: Oxford University Press, 1977), pp. 66–67.

[11]Adler, *Ten Philosophical Mistakes,* p. 124.

seek everything that is really good for us in order to lead good human lives. Natural needs are the same for all human beings everywhere, at all times and under all circumstances.[12]

APPLICATION

These solutions to the fact versus value problem seem less than satisfactory. It is difficult to be specific about a good will and how such a good will can be determined or developed. Many people can claim to be acting out of a good will and following the categorical imperative and yet do totally opposite things. The problem is objectively deciding which has the valid claim to morality. Likewise, it is problematical to be specific about the needs that are natural to all human beings beyond a few fundamental items like food and shelter. Even food and shelter come in many different packages, and what is adequate for one person under certain circumstances may not at all be adequate and acceptable under other circumstances. What is a basic need and what is an acquired want varies with people in different cultures and at different times and places.

The solution to this problem must be found elsewhere. Perhaps the best place to start is to attack the sharp dichotomy that often is claimed to exist between fact and value or between descriptive and prescriptive statements. Facts have been defined as descriptions and causal explanations of human or natural phenomena. Facts are not action guiding in the sense of indicating that something ought to be done. Value judgments, on the other hand, do have an action-guiding function and commend or condemn particular courses of action.[13] Such a definition makes a rather clear separation between facts and values and opens up the problem with which we have been trying to deal. Facts and values do not seem to be related.

But is this definition of a fact or a descriptive statement realistic? Do such statements come to us labeled ''I am a fact,'' or ''I describe the real world.'' Many such factual statements are made all the time but we do not accept all of them. Instead, we try to sort them out testing them with scientific methods we believe in or using our experience and our own sense of reason to judge their truth claims. Eventually, human beings have to decide what they accept as a fact and what they believe to be the nature of reality. They have to decide what constitutes adequate evidence and what are valid methodologies so that they will be persuaded that a descriptive statement deserves to be accepted as true and thus labeled as fact.

These judgments about what the facts are, are influenced by our values. Our values enter into our judgments about what facts are acceptable, what evidence we will believe, and what methodology is appropriate to answer questions about a particular part of reality. Values also enter into an interpretation of the facts, in describing what the facts mean. Scholars can arrive at two different conclusions from looking at the same set of facts. Thus, reality isn't only a given that we can

[12]Ibid., pp. 125–27.
[13]Beauchamp, *Philosophical Ethics*, p. 366.

reach out and touch but is partly defined by us as we progress in knowledge and understanding. This progression is influenced by our values as we make judgments about the facts in building a store of knowledge.

Perhaps this relationship between fact and value can be illustrated by some examples. One of the most frustrating areas of controversy affecting business these days is the attempts of medical science to establish the truth of claims about human health. Does smoking cause cancer or not? Are certain substances used in the workplace dangerous to workers' health? Did the Rely tampon cause toxic shock syndrome? The examples are endless, as debates about health matters and what causes certain illnesses continue. (See the appendix to this chapter.) The outcome of these debates are crucial to business because of the liability involved.

One would think that science could answer these questions conclusively to the satisfaction of all parties, particularly in a society where the scientific method is so dominant. But in most of these situations, the facts are never conclusively established, and the debate continues. Business comes up with its studies that show no linkage between a substance and human health, and government comes up with other studies that show such a linkage. Who is right, and which studies should be accepted as the basis of policy?

Could it be that such debates are not really about the facts at all but are really questions of value? This possibility is well illustrated in the case about smoking, at the end of the book. The values we hold about smoking as a human activity enter into our judgments about the validity of scientific evidence and influence what we accept as the facts about this question. These values reflect our interests, financial and nonfinancial, that we have in the question of smoking. Do we own stock in a tobacco company? Do we work for such a company? Are we concerned abour our health? Has one of our relatives died of cancer? All such interests are reflected in our values as they relate to a specific activity such as smoking.

Most of the facts about our complex world are disputable and relative; they change as we discover new things about the world. They are no more objective and absolute than values. Perhaps it would be safe to say that there are no indisputable facts in existence. Even so clear a fact as our birth date may be disputable under certain circumstances. If I tell someone that I was born on a certain day, should this be accepted as an indisputable fact? For ordinary human discourse the date I enunciate will be accepted. But when some significant interests are involved, I may have to prove with some objective evidence that the date I state is in fact true. Thus, I may have to produce a birth certificate to establish the truth value of my claim.

Perhaps a clever lawyer will find a way to question the validity of this birth certificate. He may discover in the course of an investigation that the county court house where my birth was registered burned down after I was born and that the records had to be reconstructed. The lawyer may find good reason to question the accuracy of this reconstruction. If he can question the accuracy of the records, he may then find reasons to dismiss my own claim on the basis of my interests in being born at a certain time, which may give me certain rights to benefits that I would not otherwise have. The point is that under certain circumstances any fact is disputable.

The final establishment of a fact depends on what authority is accepted: the records in the county court house, expert testimony, scientific studies, or whatever.

Why isn't science accepted as the final authority in questions of health effects? Why can't science give a definitive answer to questions about the effects of a proposed merger on the competitive conditions in an industry? The problem is that there is no such thing as science. There are various sciences, and there are various scientific methodologies that can be employed to answer a question. The sciences provide different answers to questions. They use different methodologies to answer these questions and come up with conflicting conclusions. The interpretation of these conclusions differs among scientists. Thus, managers who establish policies have to make decisions about the facts; facts are not self-evident. Managers have to decide whom to accept as the final authority and what methodology is appropriate. These decisions are influenced by the values they hold and the interests they have in the outcome of the decision. Facts are thus not the objective and absolute entities we thought they were; they are largely matters of decision.

Facts, of course, also influence values. For years we did not pay much conscious attention to our environment and used it as a gigantic waste dump for disposing of our waste material. We did not value our environment very highly and polluted it so badly that our quality of life was affected. Then we began to learn how important our environment was to us; we began to learn about ecosystems and how our pollution was disrupting such systems on which human life depended. In a matter of a few short years, our values relative to the environment changed dramatically, and the nation began to devote a great deal of attention to cleaning up pollution. When we began to learn more of the facts about our environment and the nature of ecosystems, we changed our values and believed the environment was worth spending some money on in order to preserve human life and promote a higher quality of life in the world.

All of this is meant to suggest that facts and values are related to each other. They come at us intertwined and cannot be so neatly separated as philosophers and scientists would have us believe. What we often think of as a question of fact that can be answered by scientific means is often a question of value. A particular chemical or substance is believed to be harmful or dangerous to human health or the environment only because of the way in which health and the environment are valued. And questions of value that we believe can be settled by argumentation often turn out to be questions that can be settled by a closer examination of the facts. On closer examination, it may indeed turn out that certain substances have no adverse affect on human health. So we need to be aware of this relationship and not kid ourselves that facts and values can be neatly separated, and one realm is objective and absolute and the other subjective and relative.

Does this mean that facts and values are one and the same thing? There are some philosophers who would go so far as to claim that there is no distinction between facts and values. However, in practice it seems useful to maintain some degree of distinction. Facts cannot be totally reduced to values any more than values can be totally reduced to facts. Nonetheless, these concepts are complex structures that are integrally related to each other. They are not separate so that facts are objective and absolute, and values are subjective and relative. Both facts and values have objective and subjective components; they both are absolute and relative in some aspects.[14]

What implications does this view have for business schools and the business community? Most people in business are trained in some elements of the scientific method or at least have adopted the scientific outlook on reality. This means that we are comfortable with empiricism, with gathering data and analyzing data to arrive at some conclusions about relationships between variables. We are more sure of ourselves when we make what we consider to be descriptive statements and are careful, if we want to be good scientists, about overgeneralizing from the relationships we have discovered to other circumstances.

We are not nearly so comfortable when it comes to dealing with questions of values or ethics. While we recognize the necessity of making prescriptive statements from time to time, we have trouble justifying them or arguing about them intelligently. This is so because we are not trained to carry on philosophical discourse and argue about ethics and values in some reasonable fashion rather than just as matters of opinion. We have trouble justifying what we take to be prescriptive statements and establishing their validity.

Because of this problem we often don't recognize a value question when we see it. We are likely to spend a lot of time and effort in more studies to settle what we perceive to be a question of fact when it is really a question of value that could be better settled by philosophical examination. This gives a role for business ethics to play in business schools as well as in the business community. That role is to equip ourselves with the tools and language of philosophical analysis so as to be able to recognize and analyze questions of value as we do questions of fact. The fact that they are so intertwined in most circumstances makes this task vitally important. We must recognize how values influence our acceptance and interpretation of the facts and how facts influence and change our values.

This interaction is the crucial point to be made about facts and values, or about descriptive and prescriptive statements. They both have elements of subjectivity and objectivity; they are both relative and absolute. These categories are not mutually exclusive and are not sharply dichotomized. We need to be better aware of where facts are relevant to advance our knowledge and enlighten our discussion and where the facts are well enough known to be able to focus our efforts on value and ethical questions and make a decision on the basis of what we believe promotes human welfare and human fulfillment.

The problem for most of us is not that we are unethical but that we are ethically ignorant. We don't know the categories of ethical thought to be able to argue value questions intelligently. So we hide our ignorance behind more empirical studies that actually further confuse the issues. If a decision is necessary, we eventually make it but probably on grounds that are more political in nature than on a conscious view of the "good" in relation to the particular area under consideration. We avoid stating what we think "ought to be" because it is hard to justify

---

[14]Ibid., p. 372.

such statements and have them accepted as more than just mere opinion. Using statistical techniques, however, we can establish scientific validity for our descriptive statements and hope to convince others of their validity. We are victims of our narrow scientific and empirical outlook.

Moral disagreements can be resolved only by engaging in open and honest dialogue about what kind of world we want to live in and what we believe constitutes human fulfillment. Hiding behind either a bogus scientific or religious authority does nothing to promote this dialogue. No one knows absolute truth, but we can search for better versions of the truth if we engage in human discourse with our fellow human beings. We should not let scientific and technical people resolve questions of value under the guise of dealing with "factual" information and making decisions to maximize or optimize something or other and choose the objectives for society. We must deal with value and ethical questions explicitly and debate them on philosophical grounds. We need to learn more about ethics so that we are as comfortable in searching for moral truth as we are in searching for empirical truth. We need to know how to recognize a moral problem and how to apply moral theories and arguments to the solution of these problems.

As one moves higher in the management hierarchy, facts become more complex and disputable and problems become more comprehensive in nature. The managerial task also becomes more philosophical and ethical as managers make judgments about the future of their company and the future of our society. Ethics becomes more relevant and important as managers make decisions that affect human welfare in a significant manner. By dealing explicitly with ethical questions related to their everyday decisions and actions, managers can truly implement ethical concerns throughout their organizations and give recognition to the fact that their task is fundamentally ethical in nature.

APPENDIX   Testing for Health Effects

The process of testing substances for possible adverse health effects is extremely complicated. Epidemiology is a science that examines the patterns of occurrence of human disease and of human exposure to suspect causative agents. Epidemiological studies directly identify human risk factors and thus do not suffer from the uncertainties associated with animal testing. Many substances have been found through these studies to cause adverse health effects, including cancer and other serious illnesses.

Epidemiological testing, however, suffers from several inherent defects. One problem is the difficulty of finding reliable information on a large number of people

SOURCE: See the American Council on Science and Health, *Of Mice and Men: The Benefits and Limitations of Animal Cancer Tests,* March 1984, pp. 1–22; Michael Shodell, "Risky Business," *Science* (October 1985), 43–47.

by means of interviews or an examination of medical records. Another problem is the difficulty of finding groups of people to compare who differ only on the single factor being studied. If they differ in other ways, which is most likely, these other differences might generate a spurious relationship.

Another problem is the difficulty of finding a group of people to act as a control group who have never been exposed to the factor being studied. Finally, the long latency periods of some diseases, such as cancer, means that one must wait for decades to establish that a substance being used today will not result in a serious adverse health effect in the future. If the purpose of testing is to identify the adverse health effects of new substances before significant human exposure is allowed, such a procedure is not acceptable.

Thus animal testing, where laboratory animals serve as proxies for humans, is used as an alternative to epidemiological studies. Chemicals are introduced into animals by every orifice, by various types of injection, by skin painting, surgery, and other methods. Large doses of the chemical are used in order not to miss even a weak carcinogen. These doses are also used to speed up the process and see the effects more readily. Animals usually receive thousands of times the dosage that people could possibly receive even if they made a conscious effort to increase their exposure. Thus, extrapolating the results of these tests to human beings is extremely uncertain.

Human beings, for one thing, are a lot bigger that the rats or mice normally used in testing. Human beings have about two thousand times the number of cells found in a mouse, live about thirty-five times longer, have lower metabolic and respiratory rates, and have different surface areas because of their different shapes. Animals used in tests are exposed to one substance under carefully controlled conditions. This situation hardly compares to our relatively haphazard environment and sundry genetic backgrounds. Therefore, major questions can be raised about using data from a high level of exposure in animal testing to estimate the cancer risk of humans at real exposure levels, often thousands of times lower.

Another problem is the assumptions made about the relationship between risk and exposure. The position of industry is that there are safe levels that can be established for most substances, below which exposure causes no harm; so standards ought to be set at this level. Government agencies often argue that the law requires them to set health standards so as to ensure ''to the extent feasible'' that ''no citizen will suffer material impairment of health.'' If the best available evidence suggests there isn't any ''safe level,'' then it must set the standard at the lowest feasible level.

The Occupational Safety and Health Administration (OSHA), for example, agrees that for particular individuals there may be thresholds of safe exposure for certain carcinogens. But the thresholds vary from person to person, OSHA argues, so that it is impossible to identify a safe threshold for entire populations. Research also indicates, OSHA says, that carcinogens may act in combination with each other to increase risk, and thus proper threshold levels cannot be set for any given substance. Thus agencies usually decide what level of risk is acceptable and then use extrapolation procedures to construct a worst possible case scenario. Exposure limits are then set at a level that would not exceed this risk, which frequently turns out to be at a level of not more than one additional cancer for every million people exposed to a substance throughout their lifetimes.

SUGGESTED READING

AYER, ALFRED J. *Language, Truth and Logic,* 2d ed. New York: Dover Publications, 1936.

BRANDT, RICHARD B. *Ethical Theory.* Englewood Cliffs, N.J.: Prentice-Hall, 1959.

EWING, ALFRED C. *The Definition of the Good.* New York: Macmillan Co., 1947.

FOOT, PHILIPPA, ED. *Theories of Ethics.* Oxford: Oxford University Press, 1967.

HARE, RICHARD M. *The Language of Morals.* Oxford: Oxford University Press, 1952.

HARNOCK, ROGER N. *Twentieth-Century Ethics.* New York: Columbia University Press, 1974.

HARRISON, JONATHAN. *Our Knowledge of Right and Wrong.* New York: Humanities Press, 1971.

HARTLAND-SWANN, JOHN. *An Analysis of Morals.* London: George Allen & Unwin, 1960.

HUDSON, W. D., ED. *The Is/Ought Question: A Collection of Papers on the Central Problem in Moral Philosophy.* New York: St. Martin's Press, 1970.

HUME, DAVID. *A Treatise of Human Nature.* Oxford: Oxford University Press, 1978.

LADD, JOHN, ED. *Ethical Relativism.* Belmont, Calif.: Wadsworth Publishing Co., 1973.

MOORE, GEORGE EDWARD. *Principia Ethica.* Cambridge: Cambridge University Press, 1903.

MONRO, DAVID H. *Empiricism and Ethics.* Cambridge: Cambridge University Press, 1967.

NAGEL, THOMAS. *Moral Questions.* Cambridge: Cambridge University Press, 1979.

ROSS, WILLIAM DAVID. *The Right and the Good.* Oxford: Oxford University Press, 1930.

STEVENSON, CHARLES L. *Facts and Values: Studies in Ethical Analysis.* New Haven: Yale University Press, 1963.

WARNOCK, GEOFFREY J. *Contemporary Moral Philosophy.* New York: St. Martin's Press, 1967.

WESTERMARCK, EDWARD. *Ethical Relativity.* Paterson, N.J.: Littlefield, Adams & Co., 1960.

7

Isn't It All a Matter of Self-Interest?

The problem that egoism or self-interest poses for business ethics is an important one that has to be discussed. Even if ethical statements can and should be taken seriously, egoism still threatens to make ethics an unimportant and irrelevant endeavor for business managers. Perhaps it would not be overstating the case to say that if this problem can't be resolved satisfactorily, ethics either has no meaning as far as practical application to business is concerned and thus business is an amoral undertaking, or the business system has no ethical foundations and is an immoral system that doesn't deserve our allegiance. This problem, then, is more than a philosophical debate that can be safely ignored; it goes to the heart of business and the attempt to relate normative ethical theories and principles to business organizations.

The reason egoism poses this kind of problem is simply that self-interest is elevated in the free-enterprise system as a universal moral or motivating principle that is a key component along with private ownership of capital and limited government intervention in our understanding of how the system is supposed to function. People are encouraged to operate in their own self-interest in the sense of seeking the highest return on their investment they can obtain, seeking the highest wages or salaries they can receive in return for their labor, seeking the maximum satisfaction from their purchases on the marketplace, and in general seeking the maximum advantage for themselves in all their marketplace transactions.

The pursuit of self-interest is held to be kind of a categorical imperative in order for the system to function. If people were truly altruistic and pursued the interests of others to the detriment of their own, the system wouldn't function properly because of the lack of incentives. It is believed that people will be more highly motivated to work hard, take risks, innovate, and all those other virtuous activities necessary to the operation of a capitalistic system if they are encouraged to pursue their own self-interest rather than the interest of the state or the general welfare. The libertarian principles that are a part of an ideal capitalistic system emphasize the freedom and liberty of people to use their abilities and property to pursue their own interests, and the state should interfere with this right only to the extent it may be necessary to protect the right of others to pursue their interests.

This pursuit of self-interest is given a moral justification based on a utilitarian argument. Such a justification was first provided by Adam Smith in his now famous quote dealing with the end result of a system founded on self-interest. The general welfare is more likely to be promoted, Smith argued, as a side effect of self-interest than if people were to give self-conscious thought about promoting the general welfare of the society. People will work harder and contribute more to society in the pursuit of their own interests than if they are made to contribute to the society in a direct fashion.

> As every individual, therefore, endeavors as much as he can both to employ his capital in the support of domestic industry, and so to direct that industry that its produce may be of the greatest value; every individual necessarily labours to render the annual revenue of society as great as he can. He generally, indeed, neither intends to promote the public interest, nor knows how much he is promoting it. By preferring the support of domestic to that of foreign industry, he intends only his own security; and by directing that industry in such a manner as its produce may be of the greatest value, he intends only his own gain, and he is in this, as in many other cases, led by an invisible hand to promote an end which was no part of his intention. Nor is it always the worse for the society that it was no part of it. By pursuing his own interest he frequently promotes that of the society more effectually than when he really intends to promote it.[1]

This argument still provides a powerful justification for the pursuit of self-interest. Better consequences for society will be the result if all individuals pursue their own interests than if they sacrifice their interests for the sake of the general welfare. Smith is in a sense arguing that people have a moral duty to pursue their self-interest rather than the interests of others and are duty bound to let their own interests take priority over the interests of others as far as economic behavior is concerned. The entire society will enjoy a larger pie and experience greater economic growth if this moral principle is followed.

A completely unregulated system based on self-interest can run amok if one or more interests begin to dominate and threaten the ability of all individuals to pursue their interests as defined by themselves. Competition is, of course, the great regulating mechanism that is supposed to keep this from happening. The competition of different interests in the marketplace will prevent anyone from attaining a monopoly position where he or she could begin to ride roughshod over other people's interests and threaten the operation of the system. In a free society, new forms of competition

---

[1] Adam Smith, *The Wealth of Nations* (New York: Modern Library, 1937), p. 423.

will always evolve that will provide a balance and keep the system in harmony. Competition is like a governor on an internal combustion engine in keeping the engine from going too fast and self-destructing.

Whether we like it or not, those of us who teach in business schools are teaching our students to pursue their self-interest in their business careers. Most of the courses in the business school curriculum are geared to teaching students how to make more money, encouraging them to climb the corporate hierarchy as far as they are able, giving them tools and techniques to gain competitive advantages—we are not teaching them to be concerned about helping others or about contributing to the general welfare. By exalting competition, we treat others as a threat to the pursuit of our own interests rather than as valued human beings and thus try to gain tactical and strategic advantages in the pursuit of our own interests.

It has been suggested that indeed business organizations should not be subject to the ethics of organized society, that a business is a game of strategy subject to its own set of specialized ethics. Albert Z. Carr, for example, in a controversial *Harvard Business Review* article, compared business with a game of poker.[2] The game of poker is characterized by bluffing, misstatement, concealment, exaggeration; poker calls for distrust, cunning deception, and concealment of one's strengths and intentions, behavior that would not necessarily be acceptable in ordinary civilized relationships. The game of poker ignores the claims of friendship and does not involve kindness and openheartedness. Yet we do not think less of the poker player for exemplifying this kind of behavior because such behavior is accepted as part of the game. Poker has its own set of special ethics. There are certain things, like marked cards, that are unacceptable in poker, and thus it is not entirely without rules and standards of behavior. But these rules are different from those operative in the society at large.

Business, Carr argued, also has the impersonal characteristics of a game—a game that demands both a special strategy and an understanding of its special ethics. Business operates according to a special set of ethical principles that are different from the ethics of society in general. Business executives are compelled to practice some form of deception. This deception could take the form of conscious misstatements, concealment of pertinent facts, or exaggeration—behaviors that Carr believes are all forms of bluffing. The need to bluff is a central fact of life for business executives, according to Carr. If they feel obligated to tell the truth in all situations, they will be ignoring many business opportunities and putting themselves at a heavy disadvantage in many business dealings.

Business is the main area of competition in our society, and it has been ritualized into a game of strategy. The basic rules of this game are set by the government, which attempts to detect and punish outright fraudulent behavior. But as long as a company does not transgress the rules of the game set by law, it has the right to shape its strategy without reference to anything but its profits, and this strategy will sometimes run counter to the ethical ideals of society at large.

[2]Albert Z. Carr, "Is Business Bluffing Ethical?" *Harvard Business Review* 46, no. 1 (January–February 1968), 143–53.

Carr's article, when it first appeared, received a good deal of comment. Some agreed with his basic thrust. One executive, after citing several examples that supported Carr's view of business as being realistic, stated, "What is universal about these examples is that these managers, each functioning on a different corporate level, are concerned with one thing—getting the job done. Most companies give numerous awards for achievement and accomplishment, for sales, for growth, for longevity, and loyalty, but there are no medals in the business world for honesty, compassion or truthfulness."[3]

Others disagreed with the thrust of the article, however, and argued that the comparison of business to poker was unfair and inaccurate, that business is too important an area of human endeavor to be regarded as a game. Other readers complained that the article condoned unethical business practices, that a business executive cannot separate the ethics of his or her business life from the ethics of his or her home life, and that the article is one-sided and extreme in its description of what goes on in business.[4]

Is business ethics, then, a special kind of ethics, where self-interest is acceptable as a universal ethical and motivating principle and is actually a moral duty that leads to the best consequences for society as a whole? If the answer is yes, the whole ethical enterprise is threatened because ethics assumes that people are able or should be encouraged to set aside their interests for the sake of the general good or that they should perform their moral duty regardless of the consequences for themselves. If managers can't do that or if they can't set aside their own interests and be successful business executives within the free-enterprise system, then what relevance does ethics have to managerial behavior? The pursuit of self-interest is not one of the virtues that have been mentioned by virtue theorists. Does this mean that business is an immoral activity?

TYPES OF EGOISM

In general, an egoist contends that all human choices do involve or should involve self-interest as their sole objective. A person's moral duty is to pursue self-interest, and he or she owes no sacrifices and obligations to others or to the general welfare. Egoism involves rational self-love as a principle of morality or as a substitute for morality. This theory has never been well accepted by moral philosophers, who have judged it to be unprovable, false, inconsistent, or totally irrelevant to morality and moral discourse.[5] As stated previously, it is generally believed that morality involves the ability to set aside one's immediate interests on certain occasions in order to promote the general welfare or fulfill one's moral obligations.

---

[3]Timothy B. Blodgett, "Showdown on Business Bluffing," *Harvard Business Review* 46, no. 3 (May–June 1968), 163.

[4]Ibid., pp. 163–66.

[5]Tom L. Beauchamp, *Philosophical Ethics: An Introduction to Moral Philosophy* (New York: McGraw-Hill Book Co., 1982), p. 57.

The first type of egoism, called psychological egoism, holds that people cannot act voluntarily against what they believe to be in their own interest. People always do what pleases them or what they perceive to be in their own interest. Everything people do is in some sense an act of self-promotion or tinged with self-interest. To act in the interests of someone else or in the interests of the general welfare would be contrary to human nature. Self-interest cannot be set aside in the interests of morality or anything else. We cannot avoid the pursuit of self-interest in order to do what may be hypothetically the right thing.[6]

Psychological egoism is thus really a theory of human motivation and is a psychological theory rather than an ethical theory. It provides an explanation of human behavior rather than a justification of human conduct. People by nature always act in their self-interest and cannot choose to do otherwise. Thus, self-interest is not only a universal principle of human behavior, it is a universal explanation of the way humans do in fact behave in all of their endeavors.

This view of human nature poses a serious challenge to moral philosophy and the effort to promote moral behavior. The task of normative ethics is to develop moral principles and prescribe ways in which people ought to behave whether or not such behavior promotes one's own interests. It assumes that people can choose to be moral and pursue moral goals and objectives even when these conflict with self-interest. But if people, because of their psychological makeup, always have to act in their self-interest, it would be pointless to ask them to do otherwise. It would be a useless exercise to try to determine what is a moral duty or perform a benefit-cost analysis to determine which alternative would contribute most to the general welfare. People are going to do that which promotes their own interests and cannot do otherwise.[7]

Critics of psychological egoism will point to acts of heroism or self-sacrifice as examples where people have obviously set aside their self-interest in the interests of saving other people or promoting the welfare of others. The story told in chapter 4 of the man in the Air Florida accident who passed the rope to others shows an example of such heroism.

How could anyone not believe that this man placed the safety of others ahead of his own and sacrificed his own life so that others might live? How could anyone argue that the man had acted in his own self-interest? A staunch defender of psychological egoism, however, may not be impressed by this example. People do not always have to behave in an outwardly selfish manner and can appear to perform acts that on the surface, at least, appear to be totally self-sacrificing and disinterested. But if one digs deeply enough under the surface, one can find self-interested motives.

The man who passed the rope along to others so they could be rescued may have been brought up to act in this manner. His sense of integrity or sense of self was structured around acts of self-sacrifice under crisis circumstances. For him to have done other than he did would have been impossible because it would have led

---

[6]Ibid.
[7]Ibid., pp. 57–58.

to destruction of his self-image and integrity. If the man had allowed himself to be rescued and someone else had drowned, he may not have been able to live with himself, face his family and friends, and continue a normal life. Thus he had no choice, so it could be argued, but to act as he did to preserve his sense of self-worth and the image that had been carefully constructed over the years. In a sense, the man was in a no-win situation. He could either allow himself to be rescued before the others, in which case he would be psychologically destroyed, or do as he did, in which case he was physically destroyed.

The man may also have unconsciously assumed that he would be around later, perhaps in some kind of afterlife, to receive the praise of his friends and colleagues and receive fame and fortune for having been such an unselfish person. He may also have imagined that he would get a reward from his superego, an imaginary parent who would be pleased with his action and might unconsciously exaggerate how bad he would have felt if he had not been a hero in this situation. Thus, the egoist can always escape into the unconscious and make assumptions that are hard to refute.[8]

Or to take another example, we all may have known people who were very generous with the monetary resources they had available. They contributed generously to charitable causes and were always ready to help out people who were legitimately in need at certain times of their lives. These people may have lived very modestly themselves or at least did not lead the kind of lives their means could have afforded. Aren't these kinds of people genuinely altruistic, and don't they think of others' needs before they think of their own? How can they be acting in their own interests when on the surface they appear to be acting otherwise?

The egoist could argue that not all people are out to acquire more material goods or money and follow more and more affluent lifestyles. Some people's interests are tied up with doing things for other people rather than accumulating more wealth, power, or fame. They derive great personal satisfaction from being charitable and generous and doing things for other people, far more satisfaction than they would get from spending their money on themselves. But they are still acting on the basis of self-interest in doing the things that give them the greatest pleasure and satisfaction in life. They are not acting out of a sense of duty or acting as utilitarians because they hope to produce good consequences as a result of their generous actions.[9]

Thus, the egoist can find egoist explanations for any example of heroism or self-sacrifical behavior that's used as a counterexample to the theory. If a case of benevolent behavior is presented, the egoist can argue that the person really acted for self-interested reasons and then invent some self-interested motives, as in the cases above. If an example of heroic behavior is presented, the egoist can invent other motives that have to do with self-interest, as in the case of the Air Florida crash. The egoist can always assert that some unconscious wishes or desires were

[8]Gilbert Harman, *The Nature of Morality: An Introduction to Ethics* (New York: Oxford University Press, 1977), p. 142.

[9]Beauchamp, *Philosophical Ethics,* p. 60.

driving the person to do what he or she did, and these are not readily apparent by examining only surface behavior.

Anyone who has had any kind of psychological counseling that helped to uncover unconscious motives would have a hard time refuting this argument. However, it is just this kind of retreat into the unconscious that makes psychological egoism vulnerable to criticism, for in the final analysis, psychological egoism is simply an assumption about human nature that cannot be proven or disproven by an appeal to any kind of observable behavior. It is a theory that is self-evident to those who believe it but cannot be proven to those who hold other views. It is simply an assumption that can be readily dismissed by those who hold to other assumptions about human nature.

> Here the unargued and unarguable character of the egoist's strategy clearly comes into focus. No longer with any evidence and in the teeth of counterevidence, the egoist asserts an a priori thesis about an empirical question. The egoist is driven to cite unconscious motives because no plausible conscious motive remains. It may of course be true that all human behavior is unconsciously motivated, and that we have yet to discover its deepest causes. The point nonetheless remains that egoism has no proof of this thesis and defends it only in order to salvage what started out as an empirical account of human motivation. The salvaging operation winds up with an ad hoc, a priori, and quite unempirical defense.[10]

Perhaps a more realistic assumption about human nature is to argue that self-interest is not the whole story about human behavior, that every act we do is obviously done to satisfy some kind of personal goal or to fulfill some desire. But we have many interests in mind when we perform acts, not only our own self-interest. We can be self-interested and interested in the welfare of others at the same time. It seems both absurd and offensive to argue that the person in the air crash acted solely to preserve his own integrity and did not legitimately have the interests of those who were saved in mind when he passed the rope along to the other people.

People may also derive satisfaction from doing things for other people, but it is not necessarily true that they perform acts for the sole purpose of self-satisfaction. It is not necessarily true that such acts disregard the interests of others for reasons of self-promotion. Thus, people can be charitable and derive a great deal of personal satisfaction out of their charitable acts, but they may also have a genuine concern for the welfare of others and their economic condition. People can care about others for their own sake and have an intrinsic desire for other people's happiness. And this genuine concern for others is related to one's own happiness and sense of well-being.

> There are also self-interested reasons of a different sort for one to develop intrinsic concerns for others. The life of someone who is concerned with other people is likely to be a much happier life than the life of someone who is mainly self-interested. If you care about others, then your life will be more interesting, more varied, more exciting.

[10]Ibid., p. 62.

> Their happiness will lead to your happiness. You will not be subjected to the destructive agonies of competition. In competing with others, if you and they are self-interested, one person wins, the others lose. Most are therefore made unhappy. If instead you and the others are concerned not only with yourselves but with each other as well, then there is no real competition. If any of you gains, you all gain, because you will all be happy about that person's success.[11]

In the final analysis, psychological egoism is probably not an adequate theory of human motivation and does not square with everyday observations we make regarding human behavior. People do seem genuinely capable of motivation that is not totally self-interested. We do things every day that are not strictly in our own interests. Children grow up to acquire many non-self-interested concerns with little conscious calculation of the consequences for themselves. Thus psychological egoism can easily be rejected as a legitimate theory of human motivation in favor of a more adequate explanation.

But what of the second type of egoistic theory called ethical egoism, which holds that one ought always to act so as to promote or maximize one's own personal good in any given circumstance. This theory assumes people have a choice, that they are not psychologically bound to always act in their self-interest but rather are morally obligated to promote their own well-being above the welfare of others. Always look out for number one, says ethical egoism. To sacrifice one's own interests for the interests of others is contrary to reason. Therefore ethical egoism is a valid moral principle that ought to be followed.[12]

It should be noted that ethical egoism is an ethical theory and does not refer to a pattern of action of a set of character traits. An ethical egoist need not be an egoist or selfish person as we ordinarily use those terms. A person may act consistently with what the theory requires but may not do things that we ordinarily call egoistic or selfish. An ethical egoist may think that modesty and concern for others are the best policy to follow in promoting one's own interests. Ethical egoists may be enlightened egoists who think about long-run advantages to themselves. They need not be narrowminded and openly selfish in all their actions.[13]

There are different kinds of ethical egoism. One kind is individualistic and holds that a person ought to promote himself or herself above others at all times. This assertion is not held to apply beyond oneself and thus would be a self-defeating theory if advocated universally. To instruct others to follow this principle might convince them to adopt it for themselves, which would undermine the promotion of one's own interests above theirs. Thus, an individualistic theory cannot be universalized and work in practice. It is more in the nature of a personal creed that one hopes no one else adopts so that there are no competing interests to worry about.[14]

A second form of ethical egoism holds that everyone else ought to promote one person's interests above the interests of all others. This form is not generally

---

[11]Harman, *The Nature of Morality*, p. 149.

[12]Beauchamp, *Philosophical Ethics*, p. 57.

[13]William K. Frankena, *Ethics*, 2d ed. (Englewood Cliffs, N.J.: Prentice-Hall, 1973), p. 18.

[14]Beauchamp, *Philosophical Ethics*, p. 62.

believed to be a valid moral theory because others would never act voluntarily to promote the interests of a specific individual for all times and places. They may do so in some circumstances and in some time periods because they are coerced or perceive some long-run benefit for themselves, but they would never do so for any long period of time under usual circumstances. Thus, this form of the theory also has serious problems.[15]

The third form of ethical egoism is most plausible and can be stated as "everyone ought to promote himself or herself above all others at all times."[16] This theory, however, has the same problem as the individualistic theory if it is universally advocated. There is an inherent contradiction that makes the theory implausible. People in any society are going to have different interests, and many of these interests are going to be in direct conflict. It is highly unlikely that what is to one person's advantage coincides with what is to everyone else's advantage, that there is a sort of preestablished harmony in the universe. Yet in holding to the pursuit of self-interest as a universal principle, egoists are, in practice, going to limit their ability to attain their interests because they are going to confront competing interests.[17] Thus, to be consistent, it is not in the self-interest of an egoist to advocate the pursuit of self-interest for everyone. Yet an individualistic egoism is also untenable, as seen earlier. So the theory has some serious contradictions that render it questionable as an acceptable moral theory that can be rationally defended.

For example, in strategy classes we teach students how to gain competitive advantages. But we teach these concepts and techniques to all our students. We do not just teach one student and then instruct all the others that they are to help the one student to gain competitive advantages. We teach them all to seek competitive advantages, meaning we are in some sense limiting the ability of any one of them to gain a competitive advantage, because somewhere along the line they will most likely come into competition with each other. Thus, the pursuit of competitive advantage is contradictory if we universalize it, and we must be advocating such behavior on other moral grounds.

This brings us back to Adam Smith because we most likely support competition in a free-enterprise context on utilitarian grounds and believe that we will have more economic growth and innovation if people compete with each other for market share, profits, and other economic objectives. But then we aren't justifying self-interest on the basis of egoistic theory but because of its utilitarian advantages for the society as a whole. So egoism doesn't turn out to be a theory at all but collapses into utilitarian theory, and the pursuit of self-interest has to be justified on utilitarian grounds, which is then a valid moral theory that can be debated.

Questions, then, have to be asked as to whether self-interest does indeed promote the general good more than would some other arrangement, such as cooperation. Would cooperation in a world of limited resources make more sense and produce even greater growth? And on deontological grounds, would cooperation as

[15]Ibid., pp. 62–63.
[16]Ibid., p. 63.
[17]Frankena, *Ethics*, p. 19.

a way of relating to other people treat people as ends and respect their autonomy more than a system where competition is not only encouraged but exalted as a universal motivating principle. These are valid moral questions that then come to the surface for debate and discussion. Thus, ethical egoism has to be justified on other grounds and is not a valid moral theory in and of itself.

A final objection to ethical egoism can be made on other grounds by attacking it as an evil moral doctrine, which because of this evil tendency is really not a valid moral theory that deserves serious consideration. It is believed to be evil because it advocates the pursuit of selfish goals even when the pursuit of these goals imposes enormous suffering on other people.[18] The rich are encouraged to attain more and more wealth and ignore the needs of poor people. Politicians are encouraged to lie to their constituents if lying will help them to get elected. Such a doctrine encourages defense contractors to defraud the government if they think they can get away with it in order to earn more profits. Ethical egoism encourages us to ignore the welfare of others and pursue our own narrow interests, a form of behavior that is believed not only to be intrinsically evil but also to lead ultimately to the complete breakdown of civilized society.

The pursuit of self-love, when it is made the primary basis of action and judgment, is usually regarded as the essence of immorality. Even if there are some situations where it is prudent to consider our own welfare, there is hardly sufficient basis for an acceptable moral theory. The moral point of view is a disinterested one, not one of self-love or self-interest, even if enlightened in some sense.[19] Use of the word *moral* itself implies respect for other participants in the universe and some concern for their interests. Valid moral reasons are generally held to be based on a concern for others and not solely on the basis of one's own interests.[20] Thus, ethical egoism may not be a moral theory at all but simply a disguised appeal for people to act immorally.

IMPLICATIONS

What are the implications of this discussion for the questions raised at the beginning of the chapter? If psychological egoism is not an adequate explanation of human behavior, and ethical egoism can be discredited as a valid moral theory, where does that leave us? Because the fact of the matter is that we will always advocate self-interest as an essential component of business and managerial behavior as long as we have something resembling a free-enterprise system. Does this mean the system is inherently immoral and ought to be rejected on moral grounds? Does it mean, as Carr suggests, that business is analogous to a poker game and has its own set of special ethics that are different from the ethics operative in society at large? Or does it mean that business is an amoral activity, and ethics and moral considerations

---

[18]Beauchamp, *Philosophical Ethics,* p. 63.

[19]Frankena, *Ethics,* pp. 19–20.

[20]Harman, *The Nature of Morality,* p. 151.

simply don't apply? Business is an economic activity and as such follows economic laws and principles that are scientific in nature.

To try to answer these questions, it must first be restated that business and management are profoundly moral activities because management creates values that ideally enhance human welfare. Thus, moral categories apply, and business and management can be morally evaluated as to whether they are contributing to human welfare or whether they are using resources to the detriment of society. The market system does this evaluating—it makes a moral evaluation of management's ability to economize in the use of resources. The government does this evaluating—it evaluates management's impact on social and ethical values that are important in society. And society as a whole makes this evaluation every time people buy a product or support a particular candidate or piece of legislation that affects business.

The second thing that must be said is that self-interest is very much a part of every ethical theory and concept that we have thus far discussed. People are asked to consider the consequences of their actions because these consequences have moral significance, not only for the general good but for the good of the individual making the decision. People are encouraged to fulfill their moral duties not just for the sake of duty itself but because it will make them moral persons. Rawls argues that people would adopt or should adopt his two principles of justice behind the veil of ignorance because they might find themselves in a disadvantageous position once they step into society. Thus, they ought to agree to rules that would work to their advantage should they end up in this position. Anyone who promotes rights is certainly not only interested in promoting the rights of others but most likely motivated by promoting rights for themselves.

Thus, self-interest can't be ignored, but it is simply not the whole story about human behavior and can't be made into a comprehensive and acceptable moral theory. Furthermore, and this is most critical, self-interest is an empty set—it is an abstraction. It has no meaning until it is seen in relation to a particular goal or objective. Self-interest is never pursued for its own sake but for the sake of obtaining some object of interest. Thus, the question of which objects are worth pursuing and which are not is of great moral interest. Is money worth pursuing? Fame? Power? All these are legitimate objects of self-interest and must be morally evaluated in terms of their contribution to human welfare and the creation of a life worth living.

To return to the points developed in the first chapter, the pursuit of profit, while important to the business organization, may not be enough to capture the moral imagination of executives and provide them with the total satisfaction they desire as human beings. There are other objects worth pursuing that are within their power and ability to pursue. They can make more contributions to the welfare of society than simply economizing in the use of society's resources. The goal of business ethics, then, is to link the self-interest of managers and employees who are concerned about being ethical to the broader interests of society.

The Dalkon Shield case in the second section of the book illustrates the pursuit of self-interest and its consequences for the company and for consumers. In reading news stories and books about this situation, one gets the distinct impression that throughout this controversy A. H. Robins failed to have the consumer's interests in mind because the company never issued a formal recall of the product and never admitted it was causing serious health problems. Its strategy has been one of trying to delay and frustrate the efforts of those who would like to resolve the issue and see the victims justly compensated for their damages. The end result is that the company will likely be taken over by another company or else run by a court-appointed trustee. Thus, the sole pursuit of self-interest without taking the interests of others into account has not, at least in this case, worked to the advantage of even Robin's management.

SUGGESTED READING

BAIER, KURT. *The Moral Point of View*. Ithaca, N.Y.: Cornell University Press, 1958.

BRANDT, RICHARD B. *Ethical Theory*. Englewood Cliffs, N.J.: Prentice-Hall, 1959.

FREUD, SIGMUND. *Beyond the Pleasure Principle*. New York: W. W. Norton & Co., 1961.

GAUTHIER, DAVID P., ED. *Morality and Rational Self-Interest*. Englewood Cliffs, N.J.: Prentice-Hall. 1970.

MILO, RONALD D., ED. *Egoism and Altruism*. Belmont, Calif.: Wadsworth Publishing Co., 1973.

NAGEL, THOMAS. *The Possibility of Altruism*. Oxford: Clarendon Press, 1970.

OLSON, ROBERT G. *The Morality of Self-Interest*. New York: Harcourt Brace Jovanovich, 1965.

PETERS, RICHARD S. *The Concept of Motivation*. London: Routledge & Kegan Paul, 1958.

RAND, AYN. *The Virtue of Selfishness*. New York: Signet Books, New American Library, 1964.

SCRIVEN, MICHAEL. *Primary Philosophy*. New York: McGraw-Hill Book Co., 1966.

8

Is the Corporation a Moral Agent?

Thus far we have for the most part been discussing ethics and morals in relation to individual human beings and looking at theories and principles as they apply to human behavior. The question we must now deal with is the question of institutional behavior in relation to these same ethical theories and principles. Since institutions are such an important part of modern society, and most of us earn our livelihood in some kind of an institution, this is not idle question. In the philosophical literature, this question about the relationship of ethics and morals to institutions has been called the question of moral agency.

The question of moral agency has to do with moral responsibility and moral accountability. Is the corporation a moral agent in some sense so that it can be held morally accountable for its actions? Or is the corporation no more than the people who are a part of the organization so that moral responsibility and accountability make sense only when applied to these individuals? Can the corporation be considered as something distinct from its individual members and thus be held morally responsible as an organizational entity? Or in holding a corporation morally accountable, are we simply holding individuals in the corporation accountable?

This question has implications for the manner in which corporations are controlled and their behavior directed toward ethically acceptable goals and objectives. If the corporation in and of itself is nothing more than an impersonal but complicated machine without moral responsibility, then control must be accomplished through some external mechanism that is powerful enough to change corporate behavior. This external-control mechanism for nonmarket concerns will most likely be government. If corporations are no more than the people who work for them, then the behavior of these people must be directly controlled, and they must be held morally accountable for the harms done to society. Responsibility for corporate actions must be parceled out somehow to these people based on their individual contributions to the action.

Corporations are considered as persons under the law and have some of the same rights as persons. They can sue and be sued; they own property, conduct business, conclude contracts and enter into agreements; they have freedom of the press and are protected from unreasonable searches and seizures the same as individuals. Corporations are considered citizens of the state in which they are chartered. They can be fined and taken to court by governments for violation of laws or regulations. Since the law treats corporations the same as individuals in many respects, does this mean that corporations are also moral agents with moral responsibilities?

Corporations can be seen as voluntary associations of people who come together to conduct business and pursue a profit in the course of producing goods and services for society. Incorporation is less a privilege granted by the state than it is a right to be protected by the state. The act of incorporation does not create a corporation but merely is an act of legal recognition that it exists and has a right to exist. Corporations produce goods and services for the use of society, provide work and income for the members of a community, pay taxes for the support of the government, and provide for future economic growth and development. Do these responsibilities make them analogous to a person in the sense that they are morally responsible for these activities?

Usually a moral act is considered to be an act that is done knowingly and intentionally, that a choice was involved, and the person making the choice knew what he or she was doing. The action was not forced but was done freely and deliberately. It would be folly to hold someone morally responsible for an act that was coerced or where little or no choice was involved. We also excuse people from moral responsibility if they are not in control of their mental faculties or have a temporary condition that renders them incapable of making a conscious choice.[1]

Moral responsibility generally involves a causal connection to an action, that the action in question was actually caused by a moral agent who acted knowingly and freely. If there are no excusing conditions, the act can be morally evaluated. Excusing conditions include (1) conditions that preclude the possibility of action, for instance, a particular action might be impossible for a person to perform; (2) conditions that preclude or diminish knowledge that is required to perform the action as when a reasonable person cannot be expected to know the consequences of an action; and (3) conditions where freedom to perform or not perform an act is precluded or diminished, for instance, where there is external coercion or internal compulsion.[2]

Given this definition, it may seem obvious on the surface, at least, that the corporation cannot be held morally accountable for its actions. The corporation as such does not make choices; the people in the corporation make choices. People act

[1]Richard T. DeGeorge, *Business Ethics,* 2d ed. (New York: Macmillan Co., 1986), p. 83.
[2]Ibid., pp. 83–87.

intentionally and deliberately. The corporation cannot act intentionally, at least in the way we usually use and understand that concept. The corporation is not a moral person. It has no conscience and no feelings of moral compulsion or obligation. The corporation cannot act on its own volition. It can act only through the people who make up its work force. What sense does it make, then, to say that the corporation is morally responsible for its actions?

While the corporation may not be a moral person, it may, however, be a moral agent in the sense that the corporation was created for specific functions in society and thus is responsible to society for the fulfillment of those functions. Corporations do act through a hierarchical decision-making procedure, and those actions have impacts on people. When a decision is made to close a plant, that decision affects stockholders, employees, the community in which the plant is located, and other people. This decision has moral consequences and involves moral duties that should be taken into account by management.

The corporation could thus be seen as an agent created by society for special purposes and accountable to society for its decisions. It has been created to fulfill certain roles in society and is allowed to function as long as these roles are adequately fulfilled. The primary role of a corporation is, of course, economic, but its social and political roles are of increasing importance. If the corporation does not fulfill its economic responsibilities, the marketplace may force it to declare bankruptcy. If its social role is not fulfilled adequately, the government may regulate the corporation in the public interest. The corporation has a responsibility connected with its agency and the roles it is expected to play in society.

Because the corporation has these characteristics of agency, it may be appropriate to ascribe moral responsibility to the corporation as an entity rather than simply talk about the responsibility of the individuals who work for the corporation. The corporation can be held morally responsible and accountable for its actions even though it is not a moral person. There are certain practical advantages to this ascription of responsibility that stem from the complexity of a corporate organization and the difficulty of identifying the appropriate individuals and affixing responsibility for the decisions made by the corporation.

The fact that the corporation may be a moral agent, however, does not mean that it possesses other properties that are associated with human agents, such as intentions, feelings, pleasures, and human rights and responsibilities. The corporation as such has no right to vote in a democratic society, nor is it required to obtain a driver's license. There is a difference between corporate moral agency and personal or human moral agency. This difference is important to keep in mind because the moral agency of a corporation is of a special kind and deserves special consideration.[3]

This question of moral agency is important when it comes to questions of controlling or directing corporate behavior. The marketplace is a control mechanism directing corporations to produce goods and services people want at prices they can afford. External regulatory mechanisms exist to direct corporate behavior toward

[3]Ibid., p. 30.

noneconomic goals and objectives such as pollution control. If the corporation is not in some sense a moral agent, these external control mechanisms have to be relied upon to direct corporate behavior toward moral or social objectives. These external controls are directed at the corporation as such with individuals then having to conform their behavior and abide by rules and regulations developed by some external source. If the corporation is a moral agent, however, it would seem that internal control mechanisms could be relied upon to a greater extent to change the behavior of individuals within the corporation to conform to the moral standards and expectations of society.

THE PHILOSOPHICAL DEBATE

The question of corporate moral agency and responsibility has been debated extensively in the philosophical literature. People like John R. Danley, for example, argue that collective entities are not the kinds of things that are capable of having intentions. When we speak of corporations as being responsible, we are speaking elliptically of certain individuals in the corporation who are responsible. Only individuals within the corporation can be held responsible and punished for their actions.[4]

Danley compares the corporation to a machine and argues that if a complicated machine got out of hand and ravaged a community, there would be something perverse about directing moral outrage and indignation at the machine. Such moral fervor should be addressed to the operators and designers of the machine. They and not the machines are morally responsible.[5] In the Bhopal tragedy, for example it would make no sense to direct our moral outrage at the technology in which MIC was stored and controlled. Such outrage is appropriately directed toward the operators of the plant, the designers of the facility, and the management of the company.

Michael Keeley agrees that it is difficult to talk intelligently about the corporation as a single collective entity. It does not make sense to talk about corporate intentions and responsibilities in contrast to the intentions and responsibilities of individual persons in the corporation. While a corporation can act in the sense of producing an effect, this does not mean that it acts in the sense of intending an effect. When we talk about intentions it does not seem possible to speak of organizational intentions without resorting to the intentions of participating individuals. What we commonly call organizational goals are those potential consequences of organizational behavior that are goals for at least some participating individuals.[6]

---

[4]John R. Danley, "Corporate Moral Agency: The Case for Anthropological Bigotry," *Business Ethics: Readings and Cases in Corporate Morality,* W. Michael Hoffman and Jennifer Mills Moore, eds. (New York: McGraw-Hill Book Co., 1984), p. 173.

[5]Ibid., p. 178.

[6]Michael Keeley, "Organizations as Non-Persons," in *Ethical Issues in Business: A Philosophical Approach,* 2d ed., Thomas Donaldson and Patricia H. Werhane, eds. (Englewood Cliffs, N.J.: Prentice-Hall, 1983), pp. 120–25.

John Ladd asserts that corporations should not be expected to display the same moral attributes we expect of persons. Formal organizations or their representatives acting in their official capacities cannot and must not be expected to be honest, courageous, considerate, or sympathetic, or have any kind of moral integrity. Because of its structure a corporation is bound to pursue its goals single-mindedly and cannot, by definition, take morality seriously. Decisions are made for the organization with a view to its objectives and not on the basis of the personal interests or convictions of the individuals who make decisions. The decisions made by management must take as their ethical premises the objectives that have been set for the organization. They cannot take their ethical premises from the principles of morality. It is improper to expect organizational conduct to conform to ordinary principles of morality. Corporate decisions are subject to the standard of rational efficiency, whereas the actions of individuals as such are subject to ordinary standards of morality. There exists a double standard, then, one for individuals when they are working for the company and another when they are at home among friends and neighbors.[7]

Kenneth Goodpaster and John Matthews in an article entitled "Can A Corporation Have a Conscience?" attempt to attack this notion of the double standard.[8] They argue that a corporation can and should have a conscience—that organizational agents such as corporations should be no more and no less morally responsible than ordinary persons. In supporting these assertions, they define and apply two key concepts of corporate behavior. One of these is rationality. Taking a moral point of view includes features usually attributable to rational decision making, such as lack of impulsiveness, care in mapping out alternatives and consequences, clarity about goals and purposes, and attention to details. The other key concept is respect, defined as awareness and concern for the effect of one's decisions and policies on others. Respect means that other people are not seen merely as instrumental to accomplishing one's purposes. It means taking their needs and interests seriously.

The principle of moral projection is then advocated as a means of projecting rationality and respect to organizations. It is not sufficient to draw a sharp line between an individual's private ideas and efforts and a corporation's institutional efforts. The latter can and should be built upon the former. The principle of moral projection helps to conceptualize the kinds of moral demands we might make of corporations and other organizations and offers the prospect of harmonizing those demands with the demands we make of ourselves. In this way the double standard between individual and corporate moral responsibility can be overcome.[9]

Peter French argues that corporations can be full-fledged moral persons and have whatever privileges, rights, and duties as are, in the normal course of affairs, accorded to moral persons. Moral responsibilities are created through promises,

[7]John Ladd, "Morality and the Ideal of Rationality in Formal Organizations," in *Ethical Issues in Business,* Donaldson and Werhane, eds., pp. 125–36.

[8]Kenneth E. Goodpaster and John B. Matthews, Sr., "Can a Corporation Have a Conscience?" in *Business Ethics: Readings and Cases in Corporate Morality,* Hoffman and Moore, eds., pp. 150–62.

[9]Ibid.

contracts, compacts, hiring, assignments, and appointments. French relies on a corporation's internal decision-making structure (CID) as the basis for corporate morality, that the CID structure is the requisite device that licenses the predication of corporate intentionality. Corporations have policies, rules, and decision-making procedures, all of which when considered together qualifies them for the status of a moral agent. A functional CID structure incorporates the acts of biological persons who can then be praised or blamed for decisions, and their decision-making capacity entails that they are intentional beings and have essentially the same responsibilities and rights as ordinary persons. When a corporate act is consistent with the implementation of established corporate policy, then it is proper to describe it as having been done for corporate reasons and as having been caused by a corporate desire coupled with a corporate belief, in other words, as corporate intentional.[10]

Finally, Tom Donaldson argues that in order for a corporation to be raised above the level of a mere machine, the corporation must have reasons for what it does, not just causes; and some of these reasons must be moral ones in order for the corporation to be considered a moral agent. A second condition for moral agency, according to Donaldson, is that corporations must be able to control the structure of policies and rules; in other words, they must have the freedom to develop policies and rules of operation free from internal compulsion or external coercion.[11]

MORAL AGENCY

What are the implications of this debate for the question of corporate moral agency and responsibility? The argument by Peter French mentions corporate policies as a possible focus of moral responsibility. Policies can be defined as courses of action taken with respect to a particular problem or issue. These policies reflect the best thinking of the corporation and in a sense represent the collective wisdom of the organization. In modern complex organizations these policies are not the responsibility of one person but are a true collective product, the result of inputs from many different people. They have, however, moral dimensions and impacts and can be evaluated from a moral point of view.

It seems reasonable to assume that corporations do have moral reasons for what they do, either implicit or explicit, and certain degrees of freedom in the development of policies and rules of operation. It can be assumed that corporations act rationally according to a rational decision-making structure. These decisions affect the welfare of people and hence can be morally evaluated. Thus, corporations can be held morally accountable for the moral dimensions of policies and the actions that result from these policies.

Corporate policies toward AIDS victims, for example, have moral implications. Do these policies respect the rights of individuals to privacy, the right to a

---

[10]Peter A. French, "Corporate Moral Agency," in *Business Ethics: Readings and Cases in Corporate Morality*, Hoffman and Moore, eds., pp. 163–71.

[11]Thomas Donaldson, *Corporations and Morality* (Englewood Cliffs, N.J.: Prentice-Hall, 1982), p. 30.

job, and the right to equal opportunity? These are moral questions. Other policies regarding the disposal of toxic wastes have moral implications. Are these wastes being disposed of properly so as to protect drinking water and human health and thus promote human welfare and fulfillment? Policies with respect to customer complaints entail moral considerations. Do these policies respect persons as ends with valid concerns that the company has an obligation to treat in a responsible fashion?

These are all legitimate moral questions that apply to the policies of the organization. The organization accomplishes much of its work through the implementation of these kinds of policies. Yet it does not seem realistic, let alone ethical, to assign moral responsibility for the effects of these policies to an individual or even to specific individuals in the organization. The organization is a collective entity, and many people at all levels of the organization are involved in policy making and implementation with regard to various issues and problems. The question of assigning or affixing responsibility in this kind of context is difficult under the best of conditions. The following methods or models have been suggested as ways to assign responsibility:

1. Each member of the collective is assigned and/or assumes full responsibility for the action.
2. Assign only partial responsibility to all the members of a firm or, as a variant, to those involved in any decision or action taken by the firm.
3. The firm is fully responsible, with responsibility assigned to individuals as in the first model.
4. The firm is fully responsible, with responsibility assigned to individuals as in the second model.
5. Assign responsibility to the firm as such, not to any of its members individually.[12]

Because of the size and complexity of modern corporate organizations, it is difficult if not impossible to identify the individuals within the corporation to whom responsibility should be assigned. Who is responsible for the Bhopal disaster, for example, when so many people were involved? How much responsibility should be assigned to the workers who panicked and ran away when they realized that the tank containing MIC might explode? How much blame should be assigned to the designers of the facility, who made a decision to store the chemical in large tanks rather than in smaller ones where the risks might have been lessened? How shall responsibility be allocated between the management of the Indian facility and top management of the company located in the United States? What responsibilities should be assigned to the board of directors of the parent company?

These difficulties are compounded when one recognizes that many of these decisions were probably made in a committee structure where no single individual could be held responsible for what was essentially a group decision. The modern corporation is a complex bureaucracy where it is seemingly impossible to parcel out individual responsibility for policies and decisions. How does one sort through the

---

[12]DeGeorge, *Business Ethics*, p. 12.

maze of bureaucracy and accountability in a disaster like Three Mile Island, where corporate employees from top to bottom were involved, where government agencies played a crucial role, and where design considerations were of critical importance?

All too often such responsibility can be avoided in a large, complex organization. Those who are at or near the end of the line as far as implementation of policies are concerned believe that they have little or no choice in the matter. They have received their orders, and the choices open to them are limited. They did not initiate the action or practice but are just following corporate policy or the orders of their superiors. Those at the top echelons of the company who are responsible for major policies can claim that they do not see the specific results of the policies they initiated and are far removed from their concrete implementation. They may claim that they did not intend to cause the specific harms that people at the receiving end of policy may have suffered. Thus, at both ends of the chain of command people can escape moral responsibility for corporate policies and actions.

There are more than practical reasons, however, as to why all of the actions of a corporation cannot be reduceable to individual actions. There are philosophical reasons as well, having to do with the nature of a corporation as a collective entity. There is something called collective corporate action even though the actors are individuals who make individual contributions to the collective action. But one individual action in itself is not sufficient to produce a collective action. In a collective action, each individual action is mixed with others and transformed into an action or policy of the organization. Because of this process of transformation the collective action of the corporation is quite different from the primary inputs of any of the individual contributors. In principle, at least, it is possible for an immoral collective action to be the result of a mixture of moral primary actions, thus making the moral evaluation of corporate actions and policies different from the moral evaluation of individuals within the corporation who played a role in the action.[13]

Policies are truly acts of the corporation, and the corporation as such can be held responsible for their effects. This does not mean that the corporation is a moral person but only that it is a moral agent in acting as an agent of society to accomplish specific purposes. The corporation can be held responsible for corporate policies that result in actions that have moral impacts. The corporation as such has obligations; it enters into contracts; it makes agreements and commitments. Thus, it belongs in some sense to a moral community and can be ascribed moral responsibility for its actions. While it may not have a conscience, it does have purpose and intentionality of a sort, and the people who collectively make decisions within the corporate structure and formulate and implement policies for the organization are acting on behalf of the corporation and not strictly for themselves. While individuals make corporate policy decisions, these decisions are not personal but are choices made for and in the name of the organization.[14]

---

[13]Patricia H. Werhane, *Persons, Rights, and Corporations* (Englewood Cliffs, N.J.: Prentice-Hall, 1985), p. 56.

[14]Kenneth E. Goodpaster, "The Concept of Corporate Responsibility," in *Just Business: New Introductory Essays in Business Ethics,* Tom Regan, ed. (New York: Random House, 1984), p. 295.

The social-contract model provides a justification for the existence of a corporation and describes its relationships with society as a whole. Achieving a complete picture of a corporation's moral responsibilities involves a consideration not only of its capacity to create wealth but of the full range of its impacts on society and on individuals. There is sort of an implicit contract between a corporate organization and society in that the corporation's right to exist derives from society, whose members buy its products and take jobs with the organization. This contract idea expresses the conviction that corporations exist to serve more than themselves. The goal of a productive organization such as a corporation can be defined as the enhancement of the welfare of society through a satisfaction of society's needs and desires. But these needs and desires change over time as society changes. Thus, the corporation must adapt its behavior to meet the changing expectations of society. It is accountable to society for the use of resources and for the social impacts its activities have on people and communities.

As mentioned previously, this argument about the moral status of a corporation has serious implications when it comes to controlling corporate behavior. If the corporation is viewed as essentially an amoral entity and in no sense a moral agent, then guidance as far as moral purposes are concerned must be external. The law and the political process are then seen as the appropriate sources for this guidance. Government regulation is then the major mechanism for the implementation of moral concerns rather than self-regulation. The corporation is a machine where people perform economic roles and should not take the morality of their actions into account. If the corporation is not a moral agent, it is meaningless to ask what behavior society should expect from the individual persons that make up the organization. Thus, the corporation should be subject to external regulation as far as moral purposes are concerned. If corporations are similar to large machines that have capacity to harm society, then they must be externally controlled. If they are only profit-generating machines, then they must be regulated to perform their activities in a morally acceptable manner.

If the corporation is viewed in some sense as a moral agent, however, and its policies and actions have moral impacts, then a different view of implementation results. Moral pressure can then be brought to bear within the organization so that each of those individuals involved in policy and decision making as agents of the corporation might consider the actions and policies of the corporation and their own participation in decision making from a moral point of view and examine their moral responsibilities. They could, as Goodpaster and Matthews suggest, project rationality and respect into corporate actions and policies. Thus, some form of self-regulation, at least under certain conditions, might be a possibility.

Individual responsibility is therefore still important even if the corporation is considered to be a moral agent, but it must be considered in a collective context. If the corporation is considered to be a moral agent, an inquiry can be made into the nature of a corporation's rights and responsibilities. But a focus on moral agency should not allow us to ignore individual responsibility. While moral responsibility may be ascribed to corporations as collective entities, this responsibility must be assumed by the individuals within the corporation in order for it to mean anything and for change to take place if it is necessary. Moral responsibility can be refused, in which case no action will be taken to correct whatever moral deficiencies are alleged to exist.

The law treats corporations and individuals in a way that perhaps has application to the question of moral agency. Most laws, such as those in the antitrust area, hold both the corporation and individuals guilty of violations and subject to separate penalties. Both the corporation and the individuals who are determined to be responsible for the illegal action are fined some amount of money. In some cases the fine is the same, in other cases the corporation as such is subject to a greater fine. Jail sentences, of course, can be assigned only to individuals, but even here it has been alleged that corporations pick individuals whose job it is to serve the sentences on behalf of the corporation.

To develop a moral corporation, all persons in the company must hold themselves morally responsible for the job they were hired to do, and they must hold others morally responsible for doing their jobs. In this way, a culture of moral responsibility can be created where moral conduct is institutionalized throughout the organization. Where this takes place, there is more likely to be a consistency between moral actions on the part of individuals and moral actions that are the result of collective action on the part of the organization. Such a firm would have a moral integrity that is more than the sum of the integrity of the individuals who make up the organization. The organization itself could be said to be moral in that it has accepted its responsibility and recognizes the moral dimensions of its policies and actions.

SUGGESTED READING

BOWIE, NORMAN. *Business Ethics.* Englewood Cliffs, N.J.: Prentice-Hall, 1982.

DONALDSON, THOMAS. *Corporations and Morality.* Englewood Cliffs, N.J.: Prentice-Hall, 1982.

DEGEORGE, RICHARD T. *Business Ethics,* 2d ed. New York: Macmillan Co., 1986.

HEYNE, PAUL T. *Private Keepers of the Public Interest.* New York: McGraw-Hill Book Co., 1968.

REGAN, TOM, ED. *Just Business: New Introductory Essays in Business Ethics.* New York: Random House, 1984.

WERHANE, PATRICIA H. *Persons, Rights, and Corporations.* Englewood Cliffs, N.J.: Prentice-Hall, 1985.

9

Can a Corporation Be Made Moral?

Assuming that it can be determined what a corporation ought to do in a given circumstance and that the corporation can in some sense be treated as a moral agent with moral responsibilities, the question remains as to how society can be assured that corporations will act as they ought. How can morality be implemented in a corporate organization? How can organizational behavior be controlled so as to contribute toward the attainment of social and moral goals society deems important? How can the corporation be directed to produce values other than economic when there is no market mechanism to guide managerial behavior?

The problem has been stated in terms of a weakness of will—that oftentimes we know what is morally right but yield to the temptation to do what is morally wrong.[1] This is a common characteristic of human behavior, and it is no less true of organizational behavior. The problem is more complex, however, as in an organizational context the problem involves organizational structure, authority relationships, organizational culture, and similar organizational characteristics. Managers may know what ought to be done and have the will to do the ought but may also be legitimately confused as to how to institutionalize ethical concerns throughout the organization and be assured that all the employees involved in implementing policies and making decisions are adhering to ethical standards.

There are two strategies for dealing with these problems of implementation and assuring that corporations adhere to the moral standards of society. The first strategy consists of external constraints on business that impose certain obligations to meet the expectations of society with regard to the creation of noneconomic

[1]Norman Bowie, *Business Ethics* (Englewood Cliffs, N.J.: Prentice-Hall, 1982), p. 89.

115

values. The major form of external constraint is government regulation, but social pressure irrespective of formal government action is also a factor with respect to certain issues, such as corporate involvement in the South African situation. The second strategy consists of internal mechanisms of self-control, such as codes of ethics and the social audit, which can be used to direct and control employee behavior in the corporation toward the attainment of ethical and social goals that are not dictated by the marketplace.

GOVERNMENT REGULATION

Despite the emphasis on social responsibility in many corporations, government regulation of business became a growth industry in the 1960s and 1970s. Society came to rely more and more on external constraints to direct corporate behavior with respect to certain social goals, such as cleaning up the environment and providing safer workplaces. There was a strong consensus in society that business had a serious problem with weakness of will and faced organizational constraints with respect to responding to the changing social values and expectations of society. Thus, regulation was relied on to change corporate behavior and make the corporation moral by forcing it, for example, to clean up its pollution and in this way make another kind of contribution to social welfare. Regulation forces business to internalize the social costs of production and take social impacts that it might otherwise ignore into account in the production and pricing of products.

Regulation of business by the federal government eventually became so pervasive and comperehensive in American society that it was the subject of a national debate. One of the main components of the Reagan economic program in the early 1980s was a reduction in the regulatory burden on business, to reduce inflation and increase productivity in the American economy. Thus, regulation became a national issue in and of itself, as this role of government had expanded more during the 1960s and 1970s than any other role of government, and eventually, it was difficult to find an area of business that was untouched by government regulation.

> No business, large or small, can operate without obeying a myriad of government rules and restrictions. Costs and profits can be affected as much by a directive written by a government official as by a management decision in the front office or a customer's decision at the checkout counter. Fundamental entrepreneurial decisions—such as what lines of business to go into, what products and services to produce, which investments to finance, how and where to make goods, and how to market them, and what prices to charge—are increasingly subject to government control.[2]

Government regulations came to affect every department or functional area in the corporation. Exhibit 9.1 shows in detail the impact of regulation on specific decisions in each functional area and the government agencies involved in regulat-

---

[2]Murray L. Weidenbaum, "Government Power and Business Performance," in *The United States in the 1980s,* Peter Dunignan and Alvin Robushka, eds. (Palo Alto, Calif.: Stanford University, Hoover Institution, 1980), p. 200.

ing business. Regulations also came to affect every level of management in the organization. Top management in particular often found itself spending a great deal of time involved in matters that were regulatory in nature. They also faced varying and rising penalties under federal statutes, as many of the new laws that were passed dealing with social issues carried with them some kind of penalties for noncompliance.

EXHIBIT 9.1 Operational Decisions and Regulatory Constraints

BUSINESS FUNCTION	DECISIONAL AREA	GOVERNMENT BODY OR LEGISLATION
Production	Material Selection	OSHA, EPA, and CPSC
	Plant Layout	OSHA
	Plant Location	EPA and Corps of Engineers
	Quality Control	CPSC
	Energy Utilization	DOE
	Production Tasks	OSHA and EPA
	Waste Materials	EPA
Marketing	Price	FTC and Department of Justice
	Promotion (Labeling and Advertising)	FTC
	Place (Distribution and Packaging)	FTC and CPSC
	Product (Recall and Liability)	FTC, CPSC, EPA, and NHTSA
Research and Development	Process Design	OSHA, EPA, DOE
	Production Design	CPSC, FTC, DOE, and EPA
Finance	Investment, Financing, and Dividend	SEC
	Public Disclosure	SEC
Accounting	Financial Standards	SEC
	Cost Standards	Cost Accounting Standards Board (Government Contracts)
Personnel	Selection and Retention	EEOC, OFCC, and NLRB
	Employee Development	EEOC, OFCC, and NLRB
	Rewards	EEOC, NLRB, and ERISA
	Health and Safety	OSHA

CPSC—Consumer Product Safety Commission
DOE—Department of Energy
ERISA—Employee Retirement Income Security Act
EPA—Environmental Protection Agency
EEOC—Equal Employment Opportunity Commission
FTC—Federal Trade Commission
NHTSA—National Highway Traffic Safety Administration
NLRB—National Labor Relations Board
OSHA—Occupational Safety and Health Administration
OFCC—Office of Federal Contract Compliance
SEC—Securities and Exchange Commission

Source: Henry A. Tombari, *Business and Society: Strategies for the Environment and Public Policy* (New York: Dryden Press, 1984), p. 439.

Over the past two decades, then, a vast regulatory system has been created to constrain business activities and make the corporation respond to ethical and social values that are not a part of marketplace transactions. The volume of regulations that affect business is now so large that no corporation in the country can possibly comply with all the laws and regulations to which it is subject. Small companies in particular may not even be aware of all the regulations affecting them. Large corporations have created staff functions in many of these areas to keep abreast of regulations and assure that the corporation is in compliance with those regulations that affect its behavior.

Types of Regulation

Government regulation aims at the adjustment of commercial conduct to serve, through the political process, certain objectives that are deemed desirable by society.[3] To attain these objectives, government can use the threat of force, including penalties and possible jail sentences that go with criminal law violations. Government thus regulates by making legally enforceable rules and decisions with respect to certain kinds of corporate behavior. Some have called the regulatory system that has evolved in this country a command-and-control system where government commands certain kinds of corporate responses and can control corporate behavior by the use of coercive measures.

Regulatory activities of government are not all the same. In fact, they vary a good deal, depending on the area being regulated. Different types of regulation have different objectives, use different methods to accomplish these objectives, affect different segments of business, and involve different costs to society. The major types of government regulation are regulation of competitive behavior, industry regulation, social regulation, and regulation of labor-management relations. The list of agencies in exhibit 9.2 is by no means exhaustive, but it is representative of these different types of regulation.

Regulation of Competitive Behavior.   Since the Sherman Antitrust Act of 1890, the government has been regulating competitive behavior by investigating such illegal practices as price fixing and price discrimination and the structure of industries when they become highly concentrated. The agencies of the federal government involved in regulating competitive behavior are the Antitrust Division of the Justice Department and the Bureau of Competition in the Federal Trade Commission. This type of regulation is designed to maintain what has been called a workable competition by making it illegal to engage in certain kinds of anticompetitive behavior and by allowing the government to pursue what it regards as highly concentrated areas of the economy where monopoly or near-monopoly conditions are believed to exist. Regulation of competitive behavior is supposed to keep the competitive system operating and prevent unethical behavior that would destroy the system.

---

[3]Tibor R. Machan, "Should Business Be Regulated?," *Just Business: New Introductory Essays in Business Ethics*, Tom Regan, ed. (New York: Random House, 1984), p. 209.

EXHIBIT 9.2 Types of Government Regulation

  I. Competitive Behavior
     A. Justice Department
     B. Federal Trade Commission
 II. Industry Regulation
     A. Utilities—FERC
     B. Communications—FCC
     C. Surface transportation—ICC
     D. Finance and securities—SEC
III. Social Regulation
     A. Occupational safety and health—OSHA
     B. Equal employment opportunity   EEOC
     C. Advertising and deceptive practices—FTC
     D. Product safety—CPSC
     E. Physical environment—EPA
     F. Food and drugs—FDA
     G. Auto safety and economy—NHTSA
 IV. Labor-Management Relations
     A. National Labor Relations Board
     B. Labor-Management Services Administration

Industry Regulation. This type of regulation is the oldest, beginning with the Interstate Commerce Commission of 1887, which was established to provide continuous surveillance of private railroad activity across the country. While some states had practiced such regulation before the federal government, the inability of the states to regulate railroads effectively led to the passage of this act, which set the pattern for additional regulatory commissions of this type. It was followed by the Federal Power Commission, the Civil Aeronautics Board, and the Federal Communications Commission, all examples of industry regulation.

One reason for this type of regulation is the belief that certain natural monopolies exist where economies of scale in an industry are so great that the largest firm would have the lowest costs and thus drive its competitors out of the market. Since competition cannot act as a regulator in this situation, the government must perform the function to regulate these industries in the public interest.

Another reason for industry regulation is that an agency may be needed to allocate limited space, as in the case of the airlines and broadcasters. The threat of predatory practices or destructive competition is another rationale for regulation that is often used to justify regulation of the transportation industry. Regulation may be needed, it is often argued, to provide service to areas that would be ignored by the market. An example is the provision of railroad and airline service to small towns and cities. Finally, some argue that regulation is needed to prevent fraud and deception in the sale of securities.

Industry regulation focuses on a specific industry and is concerned about its economic well-being. While the original impetus for regulation may have come from consumers who believed they needed protection, the so-called capture theory suggests that these agencies eventually become a captive of the industry they are supposed to regulate. This happens because of the unique expertise possessed by members of the industry or because of job enticements for regulators who leave government employment. The public, or consumer, interest is often viewed as subordinate as the agency comes to focus on the needs and concerns of the industry it is regulating, and the industry becomes something of a government-maintained cartel. These beliefs about industry regulation became dominant in the late 1970s, when a deregulatory trend began in the airline industry and spilled over into other areas, such as railroads, trucking, communications, and banking. Vast changes took place in these industries, where more and more competition was introduced.

Social Regulation.   A new wave of regulation appeared in the 1960s and 1970s in response to the change in the social values and concerns of society. This type of regulation is a radical departure from the industry type of regulation. Health and safety regulation, for example, affects virtually all of business, not just a particular industry, and thus is far broader in scope. The effects of the Interstate Commerce Commission, for example, are limited to surface-transportation companies, while safety and health regulations apply to every employer engaged in a business affecting commerce. Thus, social regulation is issue oriented rather than industry oriented.

Furthermore, this new style of regulation affects the conditions under which goods and services are produced and the physical characteristics of products that are manufactured rather than focusing on markets, rates, and the obligation to serve. The Environmental Protection Agency (EPA), for example, sets constraints on the amount of pollution a manufacturer may emit in the course of its operations. The Consumer Product Safety Commission (CPSC) sets minimum safety standards for certain kinds of products.

These agencies are concerned with noneconomic matters and sometimes pay little or no attention to an industry's basic mission of providing goods and services to the public. Their impetus comes from social considerations related to improving the quality of life or the general welfare of society, and they often ignore the effects of their regulations on such economic matters as productivity, growth, employment, and inflation. Social regulation also means that the government becomes involved with very detailed facets of the production process, interfering with the traditional prerogatives of business management. For example, the Occupational Safety and Health Administration (OSHA) sometimes specifies precise engineering controls that must be adopted. The CPSC mandates specific product characteristics that it believes will protect consumers from injury. These activities involve the government in many more details of business management than industry regulation does.

The pressures for this new type of regulation primarily come from a variety of interest groups concerned with the social aspects of our national life—environmentalists, consumer groups, labor unions, and civil rights organizations. The traditional capture theory does not apply to this type of regulation. Industry, by and large, has shown no enthusiasm for social regulation because it interferes with the basic economic mission of business. If anyone comes to dominate these new functionally oriented agencies, it will be the special interest concerned with the agency's specific task of regulation.[4]

One reason for this type of regulation is related to the nature of today's workplace and marketplace. It is often argued that when goods and technology are complex and their effects largely unknown, consumers are incapable of making intelligent judgments of their own, and workers may not know the risks they face on various jobs or may not be able to get the necessary information. Expert judgment is needed in these areas to protect consumers and workers from unnecessary risks that they cannot assess for themselves.[5]

Another reason for this type of regulation is the existence of externalities where the actions of a firm have a harmful effect on third parties. The cost of external diseconomies, such as air and water pollution, cannot be voluntarily assumed by firms unless a government agency exists to enforce standards equally across all firms in an industry. Voluntary assumption by some firms would place them at a competitive disadvantage. Regulation is needed to make all companies meet the same standard, leaving them in the same competitive position.

Labor-Management Relations.   This area of regulation grew out of the depression years, when the Wagner Act established the right of employees to form unions and collectively bargain with management over wages and working conditions and other aspects of labor-management relations. Before this act was passed, labor unions had a difficult time becoming established because of the power management had to take action against them. Government, then, took upon itself the role of passing and enforcing rules related to the creation and operation of labor unions and thus made collective bargaining a matter of national or public policy. The two principal agencies involved in this aspect of regulation are the National Labor Relations Board (NLRB), which was created by the Wagner Act to administer the laws related to collective bargaining between companies and labor unions, and the Labor-Management Service Administration, which regulates certain aspects of union activity and shares, with the Internal Revenue Service, the administration of legislation pertaining to benefit plans of corporations.

The Nature of Regulation

An administrative agency, such as those mentioned in exhibit 9.2, has been defined as "a governmental body other than a court or legislature which takes action that affects the rights of private parties."[6] These agencies may be called

[4]Murray L. Weidenbaum, "The Changing Nature of Government Regulation of Business" (Paper presented at the AACSB Conferences on Business Environment/Public Policy, Summer 1979), p. 14.

[5]Robert E. Healy, ed., *Federal Regulatory Directory 1979–80* (Washington, D.C.: Congressional Quarterly, 1979), p. 5.

[6]John D. Blackburn, Elliot I. Klayman, and Martin H. Malin, *The Legal Environment of Business: Public Law and Regulation* (Homewood, Ill.: Richard D. Irwin, 1982), p. 65.

boards, agencies, administrative departments, and so forth, but in the regulatory area they are most often called commissions. They have specialized functions to implement governmental policy in specifically defined fields. Congress cannot immerse itself in all the details of each activity regulated or pass legislation that mandates specific forms of business behavior. Thus, it passes laws that are broad in scope and sets general goals to be accomplished that promote the general welfare. The task of implementing these laws is given to the regulatory agencies. Congress, for example, gives the Occupational Safety and Health Administration (OSHA) the power to set standards to improve safety and health conditions in the workplace, but Congress does not specify what kinds of standards should be established or for what conditions. It is up to OSHA to determine these standards based on its expertise.

Regulatory activities may be pursued in a number of ways: rate making, licensing, granting of permits, establishing routes, establishing standards, requiring disclosure of information, or pursuing formal litigation against violators of federal standards. In general, however, the traditional industry-oriented agencies have used adjudication procedures more than rule-making procedures to carry out their responsibilities. Rates and routes for trucking companies, for example, are set in trial-like circumstances, where interested parties present their oral arguments and are cross-examined. After a lengthy process of review, the agency eventually reaches a decision, which may be appealed in the courts. The agency thus proceeds on a case-by-case basis, making law and policy much the same as a regular court. This procedure gives the agency considerable flexibility in developing precedent over a period of time.

The rule-making procedure is generally preferred by the newer social regulatory agencies. Rule making is the process of promulgating rules, resulting in regulations of greater certainty and consistency and allowing for broader input from the public. A rule is defined in the Administrative Procedures Act as "an agency statement of general or particular applicability and future effect designed to complement, interpret, or prescribe law or policy."[7] Thus rule-making is the enactment of regulations that will generally be applicable at some future time period.

Under the rule-making process, an agency must first publish a proposed regulation in the *Federal Register*. The *Federal Register* is a legal newspaper in which the executive branch of the United States government publishes regulations, orders, and other documents of government agencies. It was created by Congress for the express purpose of providing a means for the government to communicate with the public about the administration's activities on a daily basis.

This procedure provides an opportunity for public comment. Any interested individual or organization concerned with a pending regulation may comment on it directly in writing or orally at a hearing within a certain comment period. The *Federal Register* gives detailed instructions on how, when, and where a viewpoint can be expressed. After the agency receives and considers the comments, it may publish a final version of the regulation in the *Federal Register* or discontinue the rule-making process. If a final regulation is published, the agency must also include a summary and discussion of the major comments it received during the comment

[7]Ibid., p. 77.

period. The final regulation may take effect no sooner than thirty days following its publication.

On February 17, 1981, President Reagan issued an executive order that required agencies in the executive branch to prepare a regulatory impact analysis for each major rule being considered. The purpose of this analysis was to permit an assessment of the potential benefits and costs of each major regulatory procedure. The executive order also required that agencies choose regulatory goals and set priorities to maximize the benefits to society and choose the most cost-efficient means among legally available options for achieving the goals. This regulatory impact analysis must be submitted to the Office of Information and Regulatory Affairs (OIRA), which has the power to delay issuance of the regulation in either its proposed or final form.

Government agencies are very important in the regulatory process. They combine the functions of the legislative branch in making administrative law, the executive branch by enforcing agency actions, and the judicial branch in adjudicating disputes. This administrative process has grown because of the need for specialized application of the laws Congress passes. Congress did not wish to increase executive power by giving these functions to the president and created administrative agencies as an alternative. These agencies are subject to control by the other branches of government through congressional oversight, the presidential power of appointment and issuance of executive orders, and judicial review of agency actions. But they have also shown a great deal of autonomy in formulating public policy and have been called a fourth branch of government.

The Growth of Regulation

There is little doubt that regulation was a growth industry during the 1970s, with the leading product being the newer areas of social regulation. While many of the more traditional industry regulatory agencies were created during the New Deal era, the 1970s saw a surge in federal regulation with the creation of many new agencies dealing with social regulation. Figure 9.1 shows the growth in the number of agencies from before 1900 to 1979, the end of the last period of rapid agency growth.

During the decades of the 1960s and 1970s Congress enacted over a hundred laws regulating business activity. In addition, existing or new federal agencies issued thousands of rules and procedural requirements. The number of pages in the *Federal Register* grew from 20,036 in 1970 to 42,422 in 1974. In March 1979 the Office of the Federal Register reported that 61,000 pages of government regulations had been issued, a 305 percent increase in eight years.[8]

The Reagan administration came into office promising to cut back or at least slow the growth of this regulatory onslaught. Immediately upon taking office, the administration froze dozens of regulations that were promulgated during the final days and hours of the Carter administration. It also ordered a halt to the issuing of any new rules for at least sixty days. Soon thereafter, the president established a

[8]Healy, *Federal Regulatory Directory,* p. 10.

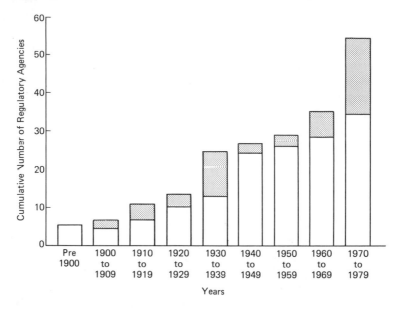

FIGURE 9.1   **A Historical Perspective to Agency Growth**   From Kenneth Chilton, *A Decade of Rapid Growth in Federal Regulation* (St. Louis, Mo.: Washington University, Center for the Study of American Business, 1979), p. 5. Reprinted with permission.

Presidential Task Force on Regulatory Relief chaired by the vice-president. The major purposes of the task force were to review new proposals by regulatory agencies in the executive branch, assess regulations already in effect, and oversee the development of legislative proposals as appropriate.

The president also staffed major regulatory agencies, such as the EPA, OSHA, FTC, and NHTSA, with indviduals who shared his commitment to reduce the regulatory burden on business. Budgets were cut in some of the agencies, there was a slowdown in enforcement activities, and staffing was reduced. The Reagan administration thus adopted a strategy of working through the bureaucracy itself to effect change. This strategy has been called the purse-strings approach to regulatory reform.

The net effect of these measures has been to at least level off the growth of the regulatory bureaucracy. (See figure 9.2.) But this trend has led some to conclude that an appraisal of the purse-strings approach to regulatory reform reveals more continuity than change. The rapid growth that occurred in the 1970s is no longer evident, but this is a familiar pattern for growth industries. Regulation may now have become a mature industry—one that may not be expanding rapidly but one that is not likely to wither away either.[9] Political pressures, lawsuits, and bureau-

---

[9]Kenneth W. Chilton and Ronald J. Penoyer, *The Hazards of "Purse Strings" Regulatory Reform: Regulatory Spending and Staffing under the Reagan Administration, 1981–85* (St. Louis: Washington University Center for the Study of American Business, 1984), p. 8.

cratic resistance have caught up with administrative efforts to slow down and cut back the regulatory apparatus.

Thus, an extensive regulatory system is still in place as society continues to rely on external constraints to shape business behavior and make it respond to nonmarket concerns. The basic statutory framework supporting this regulatory system has not been changed, and the purse-strings approach to reform has only leveled off the growth of regulation and not cut it back in any significant manner. The regulatory thrust, particularly with regard to social regulation, has matured and is likely to continue to be relied on as an external control mechanism for the foreseeable future.

Problems With Regulation

There are many problems with regulation, not the least of which is the cost to business and society. These costs are largely hidden from public view, as the only visible costs of regulation are the costs of running the agencies themselves that are contained in the federal budget. But these administrative costs are only the tip of the iceberg. The bulk of the costs of regulation are compliance costs—the costs of developing and implementing affirmative-action programs, the costs of installing pollution-control equipment, the cost of installing safety devices, and other com-

FIGURE 9.2 Trends in Federal Regulatory Spending Source: Kenneth W. Chilton, *The Effects of Gramm-Rudman-Hollings on Federal Regulatory Agencies* (St. Louis: Washington University Center for the Study of American Business, 1986), p. 7. Reprinted with permission.

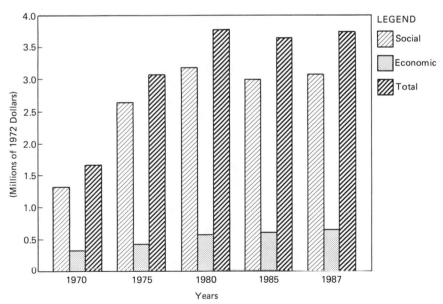

pliance measures. While the benefits of regulation may be shared by society at large, or at least by significant segments of a society, which may include business itself, the costs of regulation are largely borne by business organizations.

The total costs of regulation, including administrative and compliance costs, were estimated to be in the neighborhood of $100 billion, based on a study released by the Center for the Study of American Business (CSAB), a research center directed by Murray Weidenbaum, former chairman of the Council of Economic Advisors in the Reagan administration.[10] The Business Roundtable subsequently completed a study of the compliance costs imposed on part of its membership by six regulatory agencies or programs.[11] This study, released in March 1979, covered forty-eight companies in more than twenty industries. The total compliance cost for these forty-eight companies with respect to regulations issued by the six agencies and programs for 1977 was $2.6 billion. Besides these comprehensive studies covering the entire economy or a select number of companies, some corporations have estimated regulatory costs for themselves. There have thus been a few efforts to measure the direct costs of complying with government regulations, and these costs are not insignificant.

Besides these direct, or first-order, costs of regulation, the cost to the firm of directly complying with government regulations, there are also what Murray Weidenbaum calls the indirect, or second-order, effects of regulation.[12] The most serious of these costs, according to Weidenbaum, is losses in productivity. Edward Denison of the Brookings Institution, for example, estimated that business productivity in 1975 was 1.4 percent lower than it would have been if business had operated under the regulatory conditions existing in 1967. Of that amount, 1 percent was due to pollution-abatement requirements and 0.4 percent to employee safety and health programs. That productivity loss, according to Denison, amounted to a reduction of about $20 billion in the level of gross national product for that year.[13]

Besides this indirect effect on productivity, regulation can also affect employment. Older, marginal facilities may have to be closed down because they cannot meet regulatory standards and remain profitable. The minimum wage law also affects employment by pricing teenagers out of the market. Other plants that were proposed have been cancelled because of the difficulty of obtaining all the regulatory permits from federal, state, and local agencies.[14]

A final category of regulatory costs is the induced, or third-order, effects. These are the actions that the firm takes to respond to the direct and indirect effects

[10]Murray L. Weidenbaum and Robert De Fina, *The Rising Cost of Government Regulation* (St. Louis: Washington University Center for the Study of American Business, 1977).

[11]Arthur Andersen & Co., *Cost of Government Regulation Study* (New York: Business Roundtable, 1979).

[12]Murray L. Weidenbaum, *The Future of Business Regulation* (New York: AMACOM, 1979), pp. 16–23.

[13]Ibid., p. 20.

[14]Dow Chemical Company canceled plans in January 1977 for building a $300 million petrochemical complex in California. After two years and a $4 million expenditure, Dow had obtained only four of the sixty-five permits that were needed from federal, state, local, and regional regulatory agencies in order to build the facility. Weidenbaum, *The Future of Business Regulation*, pp. 18–20.

of regulation. Weidenbaum believes that these "difficult to measure impacts may, in the long run, far outweigh the more measurable costs resulting from the imposition of government influence on private sector decision making."[15]

One of these third-order effects is on capital formation. This situation arises from the closing down of plants that cannot remain economically viable and meet government standards. The other side of the coin is the difficulty in obtaining all the necessary permits and clearances necessary to construct new facilities. The effect of many of these regulations is to halt or limit new capital formation and hence economic growth.

Government regulation also has an effect on innovation in some industries. In the drug industry, for example, the volume of new drug products and new chemical entities has declined since the 1962 amendments to the Pure Food and Drug Act. These amendments required extensive premarket testing of new drugs. This drop in innovation has been accompanied by increases in the cost, duration, and risk of new-product development. The results have been a sharp reduction in the rate of return on R&D investment in the drug industry and an erosion of American technological leadership in new-drug development.[16]

Finally, regulation diverts management attention from its basic function of running the enterprise. Management sometimes has to devote a significant portion of its time to dealing with the impacts of regulation on the economy. The net result of these third-order effects, Weidenbaum says, "can be seen in the factories that do not get built, the jobs that do not get created, the goods and services that do not get produced, and the incomes that are not generated."[17]

The use of external constraints to make corporations moral or socially responsible is thus not a free good. Business organizations have to internalize the costs of public-policy objectives related to a safe workplace, equal opportunity, product safety, clean air and water, and other public goods. These costs are reflected in the cost of products, in the wages and salaries paid to employees, and in dividends paid to shareholders. Business organizations cannot simply absorb these costs, they must pass them on to the rest of society. While the costs of public policy at first glance appear to be concentrated on business organizations, they are in reality diffused throughout society.

These costs constitute the most obvious problem with regulation and the regulatory process. Many regard these costs as excessive, that the economy is overregulated in the sense that the costs exceed the benefits to society. But there are other problems with regulation. Many regulations are unclear and vague, requiring a good deal of effort in interpretation and clarification. Regulations are often adopted on the basis of inadequate information not only about the costs but also about the status of affected groups. Another problem is the haphazard enforcement of government regulations. John T. Dunlop, former U.S. secretary of labor, pro-

[15]Ibid., p. 23.

[16]Jerome E. Schnee, "Regulation and Innovation: U.S. Pharmaceutical Industry," *California Management Review* 22, no. 1 (Fall 1979), 23–32.

[17]Weidenbaum, *Future of Business Regulation,* p. 30.

vides a useful list of regulatory problems in an article entitled "The Limits of Legal Compulsion."

1. Simplistic thinking about complicated issues is encouraged. Agencies oftentimes do not do enough research into the actual causes of social problems the regulations are supposed to address. Thus some regulations are counterproductive.

2. Designing and administering a regulatory program is an incredibly complicated task. To do the job right requires more money than is usually allocated to the agencies. Thus they have to cut corners in both research and enforcement activities.

3. Often policies that appear straightforward will have unintended consequences which can create problems as severe as those with which the regulations were intended to deal.

4. The rule-making and adjudicatory procedures of regulatory agencies tend to be very slow, creating conflicts among the different groups involved, and leading to weak and ineffective remedies for the people the programs aim to help.

5. The rule-making and adjudicatory procedures do not include a mechanism for the development of mutual accommodation among the conflicting interests. They more or less force the interested parties to take adversarial positions and do not encourage compromise and negotiation.

6. Regulatory efforts are rarely abandoned even after their purpose has been served. It is far easier to pass regulations than to remove them after they have been in effect. Political considerations come into play and make a rational approach to the removal of regulations difficult.

7. Legal game-playing occurs between the regulatees and the regulators. This may enable the lawyers involved to earn high salaries, but society pays and does not necessarily receive any benefits in return.

8. As the rule-making and compliance activities of regulatory agencies become routine, it grows increasingly difficult for the president and the agency to attract highly qualified and effective administrators to leadership positions.

9. Uniform national regulations are inherently unworkable in many situations because the society is not uniform. Yet leaving regulations up to the states faces business with the impossible task of having to adapt their activities to fifty possible variations of the same basic regulations, creating unnecessary expense and headaches.

10. Regulatory overlap, where a number of different regulatory agencies share some of the same responsibilities causes problems. There have been many instances of agencies that have required two diametrically opposed actions on the part of business. This would seem to be inevitable when two or more agencies have responsibility for the same area and no effective coordinating mechanism exists. Some effort has been made to deal with this problem with the formation of interagency committees when jurisdictional responsibilities overlap among two or more agencies.[18]

Kangun and Moyer point out that the regulatory agencies are dominated by lawyers, which means there is a lack of quantitative skills for analysis, inattention to priorities regarding the cost and benefits of actions, and an overemphasis on the adversary system in making economic decisions. External review of the agencies is also hampered by industry dominance and bias, underfunding of the agencies deal-

[18]John T. Dunlop, "The Limits of Legal Compulsion," in *A Managerial Odyssey: Problems in Business and its Environment,* Arthur Elkins and Dennis W. Callaghan, eds. (Reading, Mass.: Addison-Wesley, 1978), pp. 369–73.

ing in industry regulation, thereby forcing the agencies to place a heavy reliance on industry-generated data, and the tendency of regulatory bodies to make less than socially optimal decisions in order to avoid strong challenges to their mandates.[19]

Because so much sensitive information has to be reported to regulatory agencies, there is also the danger that trade secrets will be disclosed to competitors. Agencies are required by law to keep such trade secrets confidential, but mistakes inevitably happen. The Freedom of Information Act can cause problems as it has in several situations, including the disclosure of Monsanto Corporation's formula for Roundup, one of the largest selling herbicides in the world, to a competitor.[20] Such blunders can cause irreparable harm and damage to companies.

Finally, it is impossible to keep politics out of regulation. The nondegradation and new-source performance standards built into the Clean Air Act have their most severe impact on the high-growth southern and western regions of the country, where more new plants are being built. Some research suggests that such policies were designed not so much to control pollution as to hold down growth in these regions. One study found that congressional support for strong environmental measures came principally from representatives of high-income, low-growth states in northern sections of the country. These votes are not correlated with local air or water quality.[21]

Another study found that votes for the nondegradation policy in particular came from the urban, industrialized congressional districts of the North, not from the clean air districts in other parts of the country.[22] The conclusion drawn from these studies is that members of Congress from the Frost Belt are the strongest supporters of a set of environmental policies that deliberately discourage the construction of new plants elsewhere. The Sun Belt states end up paying "far more than their wealthier midwestern counterparts in control costs per dollar of polluting economic activity."[23]

SELF-REGULATION

Relying on internal mechanisms of self-control or self-regulation involves institutionalizing ethics and moral concerns into the corporation itself. Moral concerns must be integrated into daily business operations, making ethics a normal and regular part of doing business. This would seem to involve integrating ethics into

---

[19]Norman Kangun and R. Charles Moyer, "The Failings of Regulation," *MSU Business Topics* 24, no. 2, (Spring 1976), p. 13.

[20]Pete Earley, "EPA Blunder Discloses Trade Secret," *Dallas Times Herald*, September 9, 1982, P. A3.

[21]Robert W. Crandall, "Clean Air and Regional Protectionism," *Brookings Review* 2, no. 1 (Fall 1983), 18.

[22]See B. Peter Pashigan, *The Political Economy of the Clean Air Act: Regional Self-interest in Environmental Legislation* (St. Louis: Washington University Center for the Study of American Business, 1982).

[23]Crandall, "Clean Air," p. 20.

policy making at all levels of the organization and into the decision-making and work practices of all employees. There are various internal control mechanisms that can be useful in this regard.

Company Codes of Ethics.   These codes can be developed for the company as a whole, prescribing general ethical practices for all employees, or they can be developed for specific functions such as purchasing and deal with ethical problems that are unique to that activity. Ethical codes are generally developed by a committee and communicated to the rest of the organization through training programs or other means designed to impress upon employees the importance of adhering to the code's precepts. For a code to be effective, there have to be some disciplinary measures instituted to punish offenders and positive rewards of some kind for ethical actions that correspond to the code's directives. Codes are not unlike government regulations in some respects, but of course, they are developed and implemented internally and thus constitute a form of self-regulation.

Corporate Ethics Committee.   Such a committee can provide the board and top-level management with a group of advisors who are well versed in ethical issues that should be of concern to the company. Typical functions of such a committee could include (1) raising ethical issues at board meetings or at high-level management meetings, (2) communicating a code of ethics to all corporate managers and employees, (3) enforcing the code through the development of sanctions, (4) reviewing and revising the code based on annual corporate reviews by management and on changing business conditions, and (5) reporting to the board of directors on all committee actions. Such a committee might also function as a judiciary board in investigating possible violations of the code and deciding where violations have occurred and then disciplining violators by imposing sanctions. These functions are sometimes located in a separate committee.[24]

Management-Training Programs.   The inclusion of an ethics module or ethical issues in management-training programs is another possibility that might be useful to implement ethical concerns into company operations. Such programs could aid middle and lower levels of management by reviewing the ethical content of decisions they must make every day and assist them in discovering new and better ways to deal with these decisions. This emphasis might also assist the corporate ethics committee by pointing out areas in the code that need review or revision and could further institutionalize ethics into the corporate decision-making structure.[25]

The Social Audit.   The social audit is an attempt to measure the social and ethical performance of the corporation and report on this performance in a systemat-

---

[24]James Weber, "Institutionalizing Ethics into the Corporation," *Ethical Theory and Business,* 2d ed. Tom L. Beauchamp and Norman E. Bowie, eds. (Englewood Cliffs, N.J.: Prentice-Hall, 1983), p. 536.

[25]Ibid., pp. 537–38.

ic manner. The social audit can be used as an internal management tool to determine if codes of ethics are being followed and if resources are being used effectively to deal with social problems and also as a reporting device to the stockholders and general public as to how well the corporation is fulfilling its obligations to society that go beyond financial performance. The social-audit concept stems from the idea of a changing social contract and changing public expectations.

> Society in America and elsewhere grants the corporation the right to exist. By issuing a corporate charter, it endows the corporation with certain privileges . . . and many unspecified but valuable rights. . . . In return for these and other legal privileges and rights society expects certain standards of behavior. . . . In the intervening years society has vastly increased its expectations. . . . It follows from this that the corporation will be called upon, formally or by the subtle pressures of public opinion, to make known how it is measuring up to its responsibilities. Thus the social audit flows logically from the social contract and from the expectations rooted in this contract.[26]

During the 1970s there was a great deal of interest in the social audit on the part of companies and academics. The accounting profession itself became extensively involved in developing the concept. There were numerous proposals as to what a social audit ought to look like, and various kinds of social audits were actually implemented by many companies. Many books and articles were written about the social audit. The head of the Commerce Department even proposed the development of a corporate social index that would be used to measure the social performance of corporations in a consistent manner. Since that time, however, interest in the social audit has declined dramatically. While many companies still use some form of the social audit for internal purposes, not much is written about it anymore, and discussion about the idea is not very extensive.

Institutionalization of Ethical Concerns

The Center for Ethics at Bentley College conducted a survey to determine how extensively these mechanisms for internal control were being implemented by corporations. Of the 279 companies that responded to the survey, almost 80 percent indicated that they were taking steps to incorporate ethical concerns into their daily operations. Being a socially responsible corporation was the goal most often mentioned by these corporations as their primary reason for an interest in ethics rather than simply the need to comply with state and federal regulations.[27]

The survey examined seven specific mechanisms through which ethical concerns could be institutionalized. These included (1) codes of ethics, (2) ethics committees, (3) judiciary boards, (4) ethical ombudsmen, (5) ethics training, (6) social audits, and (7) changes in corporate structure. As shown in table 9.1, a code of ethics is the most frequently used mechanism, with 93 percent of the companies that had implemented ethical concerns in some fashion using such codes. Almost all

[26]John J. Corson and George A. Steiner (CED), *Measuring Business's Social Performance: The Corporate Social Audit* (New York: Committee for Economic Development, 1974), pp. 43–44.

[27]Center for Business at Bentley College, "Are Corporations Institutionalizing Ethics?" *Journal of Business Ethics*, 5 (1986), p. 85.

TABLE 9.1   Incorporation of Ethical Values into the Corporate Environment

	YES		NO		TOTAL #
	#	%	#	%	RESPONSES
Code of conduct	208	93.3%	15	6.7%	223	100%
Ethics committee	40	17.9%	183	82.1%	223	100%
Judiciary board	3	1.3%	220	98.7%	223	100%
Ombudsman	17	7.6%	206	92.4%	223	100%
Employee training in ethics	99	44.4%	124	55.6%	223	100%
Social auditing and reporting	98	43.9%	125	56.1%	223	100%
Changes in corporate structure	46	20.6%	177	79.4%	223	100%
None of the above	2	0.9%	221	99.1%	223	100%

Source: Center for Business Ethics at Bentley College, "Are Corporations Institutionalizing Ethics?" *Journal of Business Ethics* 5 no. 2 (April 1986), 87. Copyright © 1986 by D. Reidel Publishing Company. Reprinted by permission.

of the companies that had codes informed their employees about the code through printed materials, and over 80 percent of these companies used dismissal as a sanction for enforcement. A significant number of these companies also used formal reprimands and demotion as enforcement mechanisms.[28]

Ethics training, which was the second most frequently used means to institutionalize ethical concerns, was primarily addressed to managers, but a large percentage of these programs also included executive officers, management trainees, and administrative staff. Hourly workers were not included in most of the training programs. Companies generally listed the following two reasons for establishing such training programs: (1) developing employee awareness of ethics in business and (2) drawing attention to ethical issues to which an employee may be exposed.[29]

The most surprising finding of the survey was that almost 44 percent of the companies engaged in some form of social auditing and reporting. This figure is surprising because the social audit seemed to have declined as an area of interest in both academia and corporations. However, the information obtained in such an audit is disclosed mostly through internal memoranda and circulated only at the highest levels within the company. Only 22 percent of the companies disclosed the social audit to the general public, and only 21 percent did so to their shareholders. This may indicate that the social audit is being used as a management tool to determine how well the company is in compliance with federal and state regulations pertaining to social areas, such as health and safety and pollution control.[30]

Few companies have ethics committees or ombudsmen, and the profile of those that do suggests that their thrust is very much upper management directed.

[28]Ibid., p. 86.
[29]Ibid., p. 88.
[30]Ibid.

They are generally designed without much input or representation from lower-level employees or from people outside the company.[31] Few of these ethics committees handle violations of the code of ethics or employee complaints. Finally, almost 80 percent of the companies have made no changes in corporate structure to accommodate ethical concerns, and of those that have made structural changes, only 24 percent have adopted worker participation in decision making, and only 7 percent have an employee bill of rights.[32]

Ethical Codes

As the Bentley College survey shows, one of the most popular ways for companies to deal with ethical problems within the corporation is to develop a code of ethics. An article in the *New York Times* stated: "Over the last decade, nearly every major company has put together some form of written code of ethics, ranging from the Exxon Corporation's one-page 'Policy Statement on Business Ethics,' to Citicorp's 62-page booklet on 'Ethical Standards and Conflict of Interest Policy.'"[33]

Many companies have had such codes for years, but other codes were developed in response to the Watergate crisis and the foreign-payments controversy. An extensive study of codes by Donald R. Cressey and Charles A. Moore examined the codes of 119 corporations. Almost two-thirds of these codes were written or revised between 1975 and 1977, with 43 percent of them drafted or revised in 1976 alone. Cressey and Moore believe the codes of these 119 companies are fairly representative of the ethical thinking of America's top business executives during the years when discussion of internal codes of ethics reached its highest intensity.[34]

Table 9.2 shows the policy areas covered by these codes. Three different tabulations were made in these areas: (1) the number of codes in which a policy is mentioned, (2) the number of codes in which a policy is discussed in detail, and (3) the number of codes in which a policy area is emphasized. A detailed discussion was defined as a measure of the amount of attention given to a policy area, while emphasis was defined as measuring the relative importance of policy areas within a given code.[35]

The authors make two observations with regard to these findings. First, they conclude that there appears to be little in the way of consensus among business executives as to the proper subject matter of a code of ethics. The diversity evident in the codes may reflect an attempt by corporate officials to tailor the codes to a firm's individual concerns in a highly complex national and international economy. The second observation concerns the fact that policies regarding conflict of interest

[31]Ibid., p. 87.

[32]Ibid., p. 90.

[33]Tamar Lewin, "Business Ethics' New Appeal," *New York Times*, December 11, 1983, p. 4F.

[34] Donald R. Cressey and Charles A. Moore, "Managerial Values and Corporate Codes of Ethics," *California Management Review* 25, no. 4 (Summer 1983), pp. 53–77.

[35]Ibid., p. 55.

TABLE 9.2 Policy Areas[1]

POLICY AREA	DISCUSSED %	DISCUSSED N	DISCUSSED IN DETAIL %	DISCUSSED IN DETAIL N	EMPHASIZED %	EMPHASIZED N
Conduct on behalf of the firm	76.7	(89)	5.2	(6)	6.0	(7)
Relations with U.S. governments[2]	75.0	(87)	13.8	(16)	16.4	(19)
Relations with customers/suppliers	52.6	(61)	10.4	(12)	5.2	(6)
Employee relations	50.0	(58)	12.1	(14)	12.1	(14)
Relations with competitors	42.2	(49)	2.6	(3)	6.0	(7)
Relations with foreign governments	41.4	(48)	5.2	(6)	7.8	(9)
Relations with investing public	34.5	(40)	0.9	(1)	1.7	(2)
Civic and community affairs	26.7	(31)	3.5	(4)	3.5	(4)
Third-party commercial transactions[3]	19.8	(23)	0.9	(1)	0.9	(1)
Environmental affairs	12.1	(14)	4.3	(5)	6.0	(7)
Host country commercial relations Other	2.6	(3)	—		—	
Conduct against the firm	69.0	(80)	36.2	(42)	31.0	(36)
Conflict of interest	16.4	(19)	1.7	(2)	0.9	(1)
Other white-collar crimes[4]	9.5	(11)	1.7	(2)	0.9	(1)
Personal character matters Other	1.7	(2)	0.9	(1)	—	
Integrity of books and records[5]	49.1	(57)	6.9	(8)	13.8	(16)

[1]Percentages are based on the 116 codes containing discussions of specific policy areas. Percentages do not toal 100 percent because most codes discuss more than one policy area.
[2]Includes participation in public life (such as office holding).
[3]Includes transactions with agents, consultants, and distributors.
[4]Acts other than those relating to conflict of interest (such as embezzlement).
[5]Includes discussions of off-book accounts, false or misleading records and supporting documents, and candor with internal and independent auditors.

Source: Donald R. Cressey and Charles A. Moore, "Manager Values and Codes of Ethics," *California Management Review* 25, no. 4 (Summer 1983), 56. Copyrighted © 1983 by the Regents of the University of California. Reprinted by permission of the Regents.

received significantly more attention than other policy areas. When both detail and emphasis are considered, the codes seem more concerned about conflict of interest than with actions that affect the public at large. The authors state that this observation may in part be explained by the fact that conflict-of-interest behavior is of long-standing concern to public officials, while matters pertaining to the public interest have only recently come to be perceived to be of ethical as well as economic significance to corporations.[36]

With regard to compliance procedures, i.e., methods of enforcing, sanctioning, or otherwise ensuring compliance with a code's provisions, table 9.3 shows that the majority of the codes relied on internal controls rather than external—control through company oversight or control based on the personal integrity of corporate personnel rather than control effected by outside agents or agencies. This

[36]Ibid., pp. 57–58.

reliance on internal control is, of course, consistent with the use of codes as a method of self-regulation to make public or external regulation unnecessary.

The authors, however, are not very optimistic that codes of ethics can accomplish this result. They conclude that any improvements taking place in business ethics in the last decade are not a consequence of business leaders' calls for ethics or of the codes themselves. They believe, instead, that any changes in business ethics have stemmed from conditions imposed by outsiders. Such codes have not been effective in stemming the tide of government regulation or in increasing public confidence that business leadership is concerned about protecting and promoting the public interest.

> The codes we have examined thus reflect a misplaced confidence that behavioral change will follow from mere ethical preaching and ethical modeling. Organizational steps to eliminate the organizational "place" that unethical behavior has had in corporations is all but ignored. Corporation personnel have been told in sincere publications that they should be ethical, but these codes have done very little to relieve the organizational pressure to be unethical.[37]

TABLE 9.3 Compliance Procedures[1]

TYPE OF COMPLIANCE PROCEDURE	DISCUSSED %	DISCUSSED N	EMPHASIZED %	EMPHASIZED N
Internal, oversight			72.2	(65)
Supervisor surveillance	53.3	(48)		
Inernal audits	35.6	(32)		
Read and understand affidavits[2]	23.3	(21)		
Routine financial-budgetary review	14.4	(13)		
Legal department review	13.3	(12)		
Other oversight procedures	5.5	(5)		
Internal, personal integrity			35.6	(32)
Reporting misconduct of self/others[3]	52.2	(47)		
Compliance affidavits	38.9	(35)		
Employee integrity	33.3	(30)		
Senior management role models	4.4	(4)		
External			1.1	(1)
Independent auditors	20.0	(18)		
Government agencies/law enforcement[4]	5.6	(5)		
Reporting of misconduct by outsiders	1.1	(1)		

[1]Percentages are based on the 90 codes mentioning compliance procedures. Percentages do not total 100 because some codes give equal emphasis to two or more compliance categories.
[2]Affidavits affirming that the individual has read and understood the firm's code.
[3]Excludes conflict of interest disclosure forms. These are included under the category, "compliance affidavits."
[4]Includes all forms of law enforcement and all types of government regulatory agencies.

Source: Donald R. Cressey and Charles A. Moore, "Managerial Values and Codes of Ethics," *California Management Review* 25, no. 4 (Summer 1983), 65. Copyrighted © 1983 by the Regents of the University of California. Reprinted by permission of the Regents.

[37]Ibid., pp. 73–74.

The ethical dilemmas people in business experience and the factors that have the greatest impact on business suggest that ethical codes alone will not substantially improve business conduct. Some of the major problems with such codes include the difficulty of determining who in the corporation should have the power and authority for enforcement, the difficulty of getting information about violations, and the problem of uniform and impartial enforcement.

> Codes of ethics by themselves are not sufficient devices to provide the climate for a desirable record on business ethics. Codes of ethics must be buttressed by internal mechanisms within the corporation if they are to be effective. They must be interpreted adequately and enforced effectively by ethical persons. Ethics is not simply a matter of good laws. Nor is ethics simply a matter of having good people. If the ethical perspective is to be effective in human behavior, both good laws and good people are necessary.[38]

Clearly, a written policy cannot be drawn up to cover every ethical difficulty faced by corporate employees. Yet, in general, written policies can help employees handle the usual ethical problems they confront in a consistent manner that helps achieve the goals of the organization. And the vast majority of ethical problems have probably happened before and are thus more routine than unusual. Among the advantages that codes can bring to an organization and employees are the following:

1. They provide more stable guides to right and wrong than do human personalities. When individuals have to decide on a case-by-case basis whether certain actions are ethical or unethical, their judgments are likely to be variable and dependent on many different kinds of pressures and circumstances. Ethical codes focus management and employee attention on key problems to provide sounder and more logical solutions that can be applied consistently.

2. Ethical codes communicate the importance of the policy to those affected by it as the collective standard of the organization. If it's in writing, it's got to be important. Thus, they can help foster the development of a culture that is ethically aware and committed to high standards of behavior.

3. Codes provide guidance in ethically ambiguous situations where a clear understanding of right and wrong is not readily apparent. Thus they set limits on the behavior of individuals who might be tempted to go astray and provide justification for a person to act in the way he or she wants to act anyway.

4. Ethical codes can help to control the power of employers and supervisors who may ask their subordinates to do something not only unethical but also illegal. Codes can provide a degree of legal protection for the organization as well as employees.[39]

Ethical codes also have several disadvantages including the following: (1) they can require substantial amounts of time and money to develop and communicate to employees; (2) they are often too broad and emorphous to operationalize and relate to specific problems; (3) if they are too concrete, however, they can suggest,

---

[38]Bowie, *Business Ethics,* p. 102. Reproduced by permission of Prentice-Hall, Inc. Englewood Cliffs, New Jersey.

[39]Ibid., pp. 91–93. Adapted by permission of Prentice-Hall, Inc., Englewood Cliffs, New Jersey.

by implication, that everything not explicitly covered by the code is acceptable practice; and (4) they compel management action to penalize offenders for violations.[40]

Management must weigh the benefits and costs of written policies dealing with ethical problems. When policies become too detailed, they run the dual dangers of being increasingly inflexible and of going unread. Perhaps the most realistic statement about ethical codes is the following quote from a study of business ethics. After analyzing data concerning the ethical dilemmas employees encountered on the job, the practices respondents would most like to eliminate, and the factors causing shifts in standards, the authors then asked where ethical codes could have an impact on employee and organizational behavior.

> In general the responses suggest that codes can be most helpful in those areas where there is general agreement that certain unethical practices are widespread and undesirable. Ethical codes do not, however, offer executives much hope for either controlling outside influences on business ethics or resolving fundamental ethical dilemmas. This is not to minimize the potential for codes to have an impact in narrow areas of concern. It is to emphasize that regardless of form they are no panacea for unethical business conduct.[41]

Can a corporation be made moral? The answer has to be affirmative. Government regulation has made the corporation respond to the changing social values of society and spend money on pollution control, provide more equal opportunities for minorities and women, respect employee rights to know what toxic substances they are exposed to in the workplace that may have adverse effects on their health, and deal with other, similar problems. Ethics codes have helped employees to know what to do in ambiguous situations and have helped to create a corporate culture where ethics is an important consideration. There seems to be little doubt on a practical level that a corporation can be made to respond to ethical values by both external constraints and internal mechanisms of control.

Surely a more significant question for corporate management, however, is whether internal control mechanisms can ever completely replace external constraints, particularly government regulation. The answer to this question has to be answered in the negative. There are too many personal and institutional barriers to a system of complete self-regulation that would be acceptable in our society. The weight of opinion and common-sense observation of business behavior suggests that a system of self-regulation that would replace government regulation is a pie-in-the-sky type of thinking.[42]

[40]William Rudelius and Rogene A. Buchholz, "What Industrial Purchasers See as Key Ethical Dilemmas," *Journal of Purchasing and Materials Management* 15, no. 4 (Winter 1979), 2–10.

[41]Steven N. Brenner and Earl A. Molander. "Is the Ethics of Business Changing?" *Harvard Business Review* 55, no. 1 (January–February 1977), 68. Copyright © 1977 by the President and Fellows of Harvard College; all rights reserved.

[42]In a study financed by the Justice Department and conducted by Marshall B. Clinard, some 57 percent of retired middle-management executives agreed that government regulation is needed to correct corporate misdeeds and that industry can't police itself. See "Retired Corporate Aides Say Regulation Needed to Prevent Misdeeds, Poll Finds," *Wall Street Journal*, November 2, 1983, p. 29.

Nonetheless, there are certain situations where companies have demonstrated that self-regulation can be effective. Johnson & Johnson is generally given high marks because of the way it responded to the Tylenol poisonings. The company did not debate whether or not it had a moral responsibility in this situation and did not postpone action and hope the crisis would go away without any action on the company's part. The company responded quickly and effectively by taking the product off the market to protect consumers' interests and preserve its goodwill. When Tylenol was then reintroduced in tamper-resistant packaging, it quickly regained its market share. And during the second phase of the tragedy, the company responded again by quickly abandoning the capsule form of the painkiller entirely. The company credo was given some credit for having instilled a certain philosophy throughout the company that consumers' interests must be given top priority in this kind of a situation. Thus, the case presents a situation where self-regulation did work effectively.

SUGGESTED READING

BACKMAN, JULES, ED. *Regulation and Deregulation*. Indianapolis: Bobbs-Merrill, 1981.

BARAM, MICHAEL S. *Alternatives to Regulation*. Lexington, Mass.: Lexington Books, 1982.

BARDACH, EUGENE, AND ROBERT A. KAGAN, EDS. *Social Regulation: Strategies for Reform*. San Francisco: Institute for Contemporary Studies, 1982.

BOWIE, NORMAN. *Business Ethics*. Englewood Cliffs, N.J.: Prentice-Hall, 1982.

DONALDSON, THOMAS. *Corporations and Morality*. Englewood Cliffs, N.J.: Prentice-Hall, 1982.

GRAMLICH, EDWARD M. *Benefit-Cost Analysis of Government Programs*. Englewood Cliffs, N.J.: Prentice-Hall, 1981.

HEYNE, PAUL T. *Private Keepers of the Public Interest*. New York: McGraw-Hill Book Co., 1968.

LAVE, LESTER B. *The Strategy of Social Regulation*. Washington, D.C.: Brookings Institution, 1981.

MACHAN, TIBOR R., AND M. BRUCE JOHNSON, EDS. *Rights and Regulation: Ethical, Political, and Economic Issues*. Cambridge, Mass.: Ballinger Publishing Co., 1983.

MELNICK, SHEP R. *Regulation and the Courts: The Case of the Clean Air Act*. Washington, D.C.: Brookings Institution, 1983.

MITNICK, BARRY M. *The Political Economy of Regulation*. New York: Columbia University Press, 1980.

MORRISON, ALAN B., AND ROGER G. NOLL. "Government and the Regulation of Corporate and Individual Decisions in the Eighties." In *A Panel Report of the President's Commission for a National Agenda for the Eighties*. Englewood Cliffs, N.J.: Prentice-Hall, 1980.

REGULATING BUSINESS: *The Search for an Optimum*. San Francisco: Institute for Contemporary Studies, 1978.

SCHULTZE, CHARLES L. *The Public Use of the Private Interest*. Washington, D.C.: Brookings Institution, 1977.

SHEPARD, WILLIAM G., AND THOMAS G. GIES, EDS. *Regulation in Further Perspective*. Cambridge, Mass.: Ballinger Publishing Co., 1974.

STRICKLAND, ALLYN DOUGLAS. *Government Regulation and Business*. Boston: Houghton Mifflin Co., 1980.

WEIDENBAUM, MURRAY L. *Business. Government and the Public,* 3d ed. Englewood Cliffs, N.J.: Prentice-Hall, 1986.

_____. *The Costs of Government Regulation of Business.* Subcommittee on Economic Growth and Stabilization of the Joint Economic Committee, Congress of the United States. Washington, D.C.: U.S. Government Printing Office, 1978.

_____. *The Future of Business Regulation,* New York: AMACOM, 1979.

WHITE, LAWRENCE J. *Reforming Regulation: Processes and Problems.* Englewood Cliffs, N.J.: Prentice-Hall, 1981.

10

Does Business Ethics Have a Future?

As stated in the first chapter, there has been an increasing interest in business ethics over the past several years. More schools of business and management have developed business ethics courses, more chairs in the subject have been established, and more centers promoting research in the area of business ethics have been started. Companies have been increasingly concerned to have some kind of ethical considerations built into their management-training programs and have developed codes of ethics related to employee behavior throughout the company or to specific functions, such as purchasing or accounting. Is all this activity just a passing fad that started because of certain scandals in the corporate world, or is it indicative of something more significant taking place in the way business is conducted and in the values held by society?

Recalling the points made in the first chapter, there has been a change over the past several decades in the way the market system is perceived that has made ethical concerns of greater importance. As long as there was a consensus that the marketplace was a mechanism that could be relied upon to coordinate the efforts of thousands of economic actors and direct these efforts toward the enhancement of human welfare, there was no need to deal with ethical concerns in an explicit manner. Those ethical concerns that were expressed were largely limited to such matters of human conduct as honesty and fair dealing in marketplace transactions. But no serious questions were raised regarding the responsibilities of business to the larger society. These responsibilities were considered to have been fulfilled if business performed its economic mission successfully.

The market was also relied upon to resolve value questions that the society had to make. Questions about what goods and services should be produced were resolved through the supply-and-demand conditions that existed with respect to specific goods and services. People made individual value choices about buying products, working at specific jobs, and investing in particular companies, and these choices were aggregated by the market mechanism into the supply-and-demand conditions faced by individual companies. These individual choices determined what resources were available, what prices could be charged, what technologies could be employed in the production process, what wages and salaries had to be paid, and other economic factors. There was no need for explicit ethical considerations on the part of society as a whole because the important value questions were answered by the individual value choices people made in the marketplace.

This situation began to change, as was described in the first chapter, with the advent of the social-responsibility discussion. In that discussion, it was advocated that while business organizations were enhancing economic welfare, they were creating many adverse side effects, such as pollution, that did not enhance human welfare and in many cases threatened the health of significant numbers of people, if not the continued survival of the human race. The market mechanism did not take these so-called social costs into account and internalize them so that they would be reflected in the costs of raw materials and in the final prices for goods and services. The market mechanism ignored these social costs and left them for someone else to consider.

That someone else turned out to be the government, as new legislation and regulations were passed to control business behavior and force it to internalize these social costs in its routine operations. The result was a dramatic change in the way business functions in society in that the marketplace no longer determines by itself the prices business can charge for its products, the technologies that can be employed, the wages and salaries that can be paid, who can be hired, and other such decisions. These decisions are now affected by government in a direct manner through enforcement of pollution standards, application of equal opportunity legislation, implementation of job safety and health standards, and hundreds of other such activities related to the regulatory apparatus that has been created in the past several decades. Business is now controlled by both the market mechanism and a command-and-control system consisting of government regulation.

The social-responsibility concept lacked solid ethical foundations and was difficult to implement in a market society; thus, a regulatory mechanism developed to see that social concerns were taken into account by business. Value questions relative to these social concerns, what could be called the production of public goods and services, had to be resolved through the political process. The money and effort spent to clean up waste dumps, to protect workers' health, to promote equal opportunity, to provide safe cars, and to handle other such concerns reflect in some crude manner the values society holds relative to these social or public goods and services. These values are expressed in voting patterns, interest-group activity, and other political endeavors. The outcome of these activities shows the concern society has in enhancing human welfare through successful dealing with these social dimensions of human existence.

Public policy has thus come to complement the market mechanism as a means to control corporate behavior and direct it toward the enhancement of human welfare and fulfillment. But there are serious problems with regulation, as became apparent several years ago before and during the 1980 election campaign. Regulation costs a great deal of money; it is inefficient in many situations; it takes a great deal of time and effort on the part of both the private and public sectors; regulations often conflict with each other—the list of criticisms could be extended almost endlessly. Perhaps a most severe criticism is that ethical issues are not necessarily considered in the determination of public policy to any more of an extent than they are in market decisions. Whatever ethical concerns are present in decisions about product safety, mileage standards for automobiles, or health standards for workers, they are often lost in the political battle that takes place in Congress, in the executive branch where the agencies implement the laws passed by Congress, or in the courts that decide whether regulations should be allowed to stand.

Political criteria are thus largely responsible for the outcome of the debate about these social problems, and ethical considerations are either not debated at all or become tools of politicians who try to advance their particular causes. Perhaps some will think this to be too harsh a judgment, but it is difficult to draw any other conclusion after watching the political battles that have recently taken place over reauthorization of the Superfund, revision of the Clean Water Act, continuation of affirmative-action programs, and other such areas of social concern. Political power and influence determine the outcome of these debates, not ethical considerations. Whatever ethics may mean in any of these considerations is determined in a political context where ethical issues are not necessarily explicitly debated. This may be inevitable given the political nature of human existence, but at least one could hope for more of an explicit ethical debate on some of these matters.

In any event, these changes provide evidence that something fundamental has happened in American society over the past several decades and that ethical considerations have become more important to corporations and schools of business and management because of these changes. There is something going on regarding conceptions of human welfare and how best to attain the kind of society where human fulfillment can be attained. Old myths and ideologies are no longer accepted and functional, and yet there is no consensus that has yet developed to replace the old ones that served us in the past. We are groping our way toward some new understanding of society and its goals and objectives, and the outcome of this search will have significant implications for business organizations.

> Executives today are living ''between the times''—that is, they are caught between the time when there was a strong social consensus that the market mechanism was the best way to control business activity, and some possible future time when society has a clear consensus about just how business institutions ought to advance human welfare. We are now searching for a new consensus: economic language, which has in the past often provided the sole rationale for corporate decisions, no longer, in itself, strikes a note of legitimacy for the American public. While corporate critics speak in ethical language employing terms such as fairness, justice, rights, and so on, corporate leadership often responds solely in economic language of profit and loss. Such discussion generates much heat but little light, and the disputing parties pass like ships in the night.[1]

[1]Oliver F. Williams and John W. Houck, eds., *The Judeo-Christian Vision and the Modern Corporation* (Notre Dame, Ind.: University of Notre Dame Press, 1982), pp. 2–3.

If these observations have any truth to them, it would seem that ethics does indeed have a future, as ethical considerations are of prime importance in the creation of some new consensus. It would thus seem important to managers and future managers in schools of business and management to learn something about ethical concepts and ethical language. Again, the problem is not necessarily that vast numbers of people are unethical or not concerned about ethics but simply that they are ethically ignorant. Most people have not received formal education in ethics and probably base whatever ethical notions they have on religious training they may have been exposed to in their youth or on some rather vague humanistic notions of human fulfillment. While these sources of morality are important, they are most likely woefully inadequate to cope with the modern complex world in which we live today. Managers are thus encouraged to take ethics seriously and devote some time to learning about ethical concepts and dealing explicitly with the ethical issues that are important to their function.

ETHICAL CONSIDERATIONS
IN MANAGEMENT

Managers are constantly making ethical decisions whether consciously or unknowingly. They are creating the future not only for their organizations but for the people who work for them, for consumers who use their products, for stockholders who may have invested their life savings in the company, and for the society as a whole. Managerial decisions affect human well-being and social welfare and have ethical impacts that are significant for those affected by the decisions. Managers are constantly helping direct people toward or away from human fulfillment by offering persons better working opportunities or assigning them to uselessness, by making products that enhance people's lives or give them serious illnesses, and by contributing to community life or exploiting physical and human resources that devastate the community.

As we expand our knowledge of the world and develop technology to control the world, we have more and more choices to make concerning the kind of world in which we want to live. These choices cannot be avoided and are based on some kind of ethical notions that are often not consciously examined and debated. The future is thus created by default and is not the result of an explicit dialogue between those who make decisions and those who have to live with the results. The application of technology is most often under the the the control of managers of business organizations. This is an awesome responsibility and one that calls for ethical reflection of the highest nature. The decisions managers make create or destroy important values and affect the lives of hundreds and thousands of people, sometimes scattered around the entire planet.

There was a time when the church tried to legislate morality for all the situations in which members might find themselves. Perhaps many of us still rely on some vague notions about the Ten Commandments and the Golden Rule as our basis for moral judgments. Such unsophisticated approaches to morality are no longer good enough in today's world. In business, as in many other areas of life, only the experts who work in a specialized area understand the factors that are involved and the implications of various courses of action that can be taken with respect to a particular problem. These experts have to take responsibility for the ethical dimensions of the decisions they make. Society should be able to trust their judgments. This means that each manager has to become his or her own moral philosopher and apply moral thinking and principles to the decisions they make and the actions they take in their daily lives as managers. This responsibility cannot be dumped on theologians or moral philosophers but is the responsibility of managers themselves.

The vision managers have about the kind of world in which they want to live is all important, but such a vision must be realistic and consistent with human welfare. There is no perfect man or woman or no perfect society that can ever be reached. Reality is dynamic and always changing. Human beings have neither an end nor a nature in the sense of some fixed, invariable, uniform condition in which they reach a static state. The nature of society and humankind is open and is created by the kind of decisions we make in the present. The future is not the result of some deterministic process whether guided by an all-knowing deity or by some fatalistic belief process. The future is largely under our control and depends on the vision we have and the will to implement that vision and move toward it in decision and action. Perfection must be understood in dynamic terms as creating a better world than the one we know at present and laying hold of the possibilities for the future that are offered in the present.

> Perhaps the simplest answer to the question about man's end is to say: "Man's end is to be!" He attains his end when he is, in the fullest manner that is open to him. In this sense, his end need not be regarded as coming at the end, but can be present in the midst of his life. . . . man really is when he ventures forward in hope, as one on his way and not bound to an unchanged and unchangeable order; when he accepts his life in this world and lays hold on the rich possibilities that it offers; when he acknowledges his being-with-others and joins with them in building a community of concern and love; when he enlarges his freedom of actions; when he exercises his power in responsibility.[2]

Managers are thus encouraged to think more broadly and highly of their task. They are encouraged to recognize business as a multiple-purpose institution that has many impacts besides economic ones. Managers create or destroy many different kinds of values that are of importance in society; social, ethical, and human value in addition to economic value. Managers have rich and exciting opportunities to create a future that is better for people in many aspects, not just in terms of their material existence. Making a profit is not enough to justify a manager's existence nor is it enough of a challenge for a creative and ambitious manager who wants to contribute the best that he or she has to society. There is more to be done, and there are more possibilities for managers of business organizations.

Managers must think of their jobs as primarily ethical in nature and of the organizations they manage as ethical organizations. They cannot rely on the market

---

[2]John Macquarrie, *Three Issues in Ethics* (New York: Harper & Row, Publishers, 1970), p. 79.

ot the invisible hand to take care of moral and ethical concerns. The idea that human welfare is best served when each agent and corporation pursues its competitive advantage should be assigned to the scrap heap of human ideas. It has outlived its usefulness. The working of a free and competitive marketplace will not ensure moral behavior on the part of the organizations and managers in the system. Moral responsibility resides in the hands of the managers of business organizations, not in the invisible hand of the free-market system.

Nor should the laws and regulations of government be relied upon to promote moral behavior of corporations and management. If managers think of themselves as no more than rational economic actors with only economic responsibilities, the law and the political process will continue to be used to turn these objectives to the common good. Moral direction will be provided by political managers, who will be seen as custodians of the public purpose. Corporations are not, however, amoral entities, and an emphasis on government regulation as the key to business ethics underestimates the capacities for moral responsibility in the private sector and overestimates the capacities of government for moral guidance. Neither the market system nor the public-policy process can be relied upon to carry the moral freight of society. Managers must make an explicit effort to introduce ethics into their day-to-day decision making.[3]

This does not mean that the marketplace or government is going to be replaced by managerial discretion. The competitive marketplace is always going to be the major factor in guiding managerial behavior with respect to economizing in the use of resources and directing managerial efforts toward producing something people are willing to buy at prices they can afford. And government may always be the major factor in guiding managerial behavior where substantial matters affecting the public interest are concerned. But management cannot abandon its ethical responsibilities to these two systems and claim that all of its moral concerns are either exhausted by marketplace performance or by adherence to government regulations.

Managers have considerable discretion in the marketplace, particularly managers of large organizations, and have a great deal of leeway to bring products to market and stimulate a demand for them. They are not managing machines that automatically respond to consumer demand in a mechanical fashion. Management has a good deal of discretion in gaining competitive advantages through marketing and distribution of products and through planning for sources of supply. Management is an active, not a passive, task and involves the creation of new products and services that fulfill needs that consumers didn't know they had. Thus they must be stimulated to buy those goods and services.

By the same token, managers are not passive when it comes to government regulation. They have become increasingly sophisticated over the last several years in influencing government and the rules by which they are going to have to live. Through political involvement, managers have been able to influence public policy and have in some cases prevented legislation from being passed that would adverse-

---

[3]Kenneth E. Goodpaster, "The Concept of Corporate Responsibility," in *Just Business: New Introductory Essays in Business Ethics,* Tom Regan, ed. (New York: Random House, 1984), p. 316.

ly affect their interests. Thus, the public-policy dimension of the managerial task has come to be of increasing importance as the impact of government has become more significant.

In both of these areas, then, management has considerable discretion, and the ethical dimension of their task has relevance. They might even be able to increase their discretion if they could win the trust of the public and adhere to ethical standards in all their activities. As long as the public does not trust management to take their interests into account, regulation will continue to be relied upon to promote social and ethical values of concern to the public. The pursuit of self-interest is not enough. Managers must self-consciously pursue human fulfillment and the social good in all their activities. Economic self-interest must be subsumed under a broader and more comprehensive notion of the common good or social welfare.

This broader notion is a possibility if managers take ethics seriously. The institutionalization of business ethics should not just be seen as another control mechanism for management to extend its power over employees or various aspects of society. Business ethics must be seen as a management responsibility. The questions raised in this book must be dealt with in order to develop a philosophy of management that is ethically sound. Every manager has a philosophy, but most likely it has not been very well articulated. Management and business school students are encouraged to develop a philosophy that can serve them well throughout their careers.

The development of such a philosophy, one that incorporates ethical concerns, requires commitment. External justifications can go only so far, and eventually one may reach a level beyond which such attempts no longer make sense. At that point, a choice is involved, a choice to live a moral life, a nonmoral life, or perhaps something in between. Individual managers must accept responsibility for whatever choice they make and abandon the hope for some higher level of justification. Their own fulfillment as human beings is at stake in the choice they make because human beings in the final analysis are moral beings. They live in a web of moral relationships, institutional and personal, and how these relationships are responded to determine the quality of a person's life.

It is hoped that managers will recognize the web of moral relationships in which they and the organizations they direct function. This recognition is the first step toward realizing that a choice is involved, a choice to promote human fulfillment and welfare in the decisions they make or to pursue some more narrow goal, such as the pursuit of profit or market share, and ignore the moral implications of their decisions. In this case, these moral dimensions will be pursued by others, who will take action to shape managerial and business behavior to match their conceptions of the good life and the life they believe is worth living. To abandon this moral debate to others, however, would seem to be an irresponsible act of management and an abdication of their responsibilities to shareholders, let alone all the other stakeholders who have an interest in corporate activities.

Managers want freedom to make decisions, and business organizations want to be free to pursue their own interests. External control mechanisms of whatever kind are always seen as burdensome and an undue interference with management prerogatives. Freedom, however, is a moral concept and is granted only to moral agents. Thus, if business wants freedom to conduct its affairs with a minimum of outside interference, it must see itself as a moral agent accountable to the society as to how this freedom is used to the benefit of society. It makes sense to ascribe moral freedom to corporations only under conditions of moral accountability. Only when corporations acknowledge moral responsibility will they be able to carry out their obligations with relative independence from external control mechanisms.[4]

Managers may be prone, because of their training and background, to think in terms of utilitarian morality, to make decisions intended to bring about the greatest possible balance of good consequences for the parties affected. It may very well be, however, that this way of thinking about morality is dependent on an even more basic principle, namely, that one ought to do good and to prevent or avoid doing harm. If this more basic obligation did not exist, there would be no basis on which to suppose that good is better than evil.[5] Perhaps this principle is the one that calls for commitment, the basic decision that being human obligates one to think about the good that can be done and the possible harms that can result from decisions and actions. If this commitment is there, then seeking to find some way of analyzing good and harm and determining what decisions are best in this regard would seem to follow.

> The point is that corporate moral responsibility, like its analogue in the individual, requires management; management of people and resources, but most importantly what we might call self-management. The modern challenge for the professional manager lies not with the growing number of tasks associated with the growing complexity of the role. Though formidable, the quantitative dimensions of the challenge can be met by more sophisticated approaches to control, production, and organizational structure. The most dramatic challenge lies in the qualitative domain—the domain in which management must exercise judgment and self-understanding. The competitive and strategic rationality that has for so long been the hallmark of managerial competence must be joined to a more "disinterested," community-centered rationality. Gamesmanship must be supplemented with moral leadership.[6]

Such moral leadership means recognizing the corporation as basically an ethical system that affects various kinds of values that are important to human welfare. The challenge to management is to incorporate these other kinds of value into routine decision making and develop methods of analysis that are appropriate to determining trade-offs between objectives. The holistic perspective is captured in the notion of human welfare, and the decisions of management affect human welfare by affecting economic, social, ethical, and human values. All of these dimensions are important to consider in making a decision. Economic values must not always be assumed to be dominant but in most instances must be balanced against

[4]Patricia H. Werhane, *Persons, Rights, and Corporations* (Englewood Cliffs, N.J.: Prentice-Hall, 1985), p. 76.

[5]William K. Frankena, *Ethics* (Englewood Cliffs, N.J.: Prentice-Hall, 1973), p. 45.

[6]Goodpaster, "Concept of Corporate Responsibility," p. 319.

other values in determining the best actions to take that will contribute most to human welfare.

AN AGENDA FOR ACTION

The implementation of such a moral vision requires action on several fronts. Building ethical concerns into the corporation and business education is not an easy task, but there are several avenues that can be followed in order to begin the process of integrating ethical concerns into the organization and the curriculum where future managers are being developed. The following areas constitute what could be called an ethical or moral agenda for the society in relation to business institutions:[7]

1. In the educational realm, such an agenda would seem to call for a thorough integration of moral and ethical concerns into the functional courses like marketing, production, finance, control, and human resources management. While separate courses in ethics should be continued in order to deal with basic issues and concepts related to ethical discussion, integration of ethical concerns into the functional courses is essential to make ethics more directly related to management decision making and help students see the relevance of ethics to the role of management.[8]

2. Management-development programs of corporations need to develop parallel efforts to continue the effort begun in the academic setting. Education is a lifelong process, and questions about the ethical and moral aspects of management decision making must continue as graduates take jobs in business institutions and begin their management careers. Such a concern would convey the importance of ethics to those who may move into higher management ranks within the corporation.

3. Boards of directors must demonstrate a concern about ethics by raising ethical questions where appropriate. The moral implications of decisions and actions must be evaluated by the board along with traditional business concerns. The board can help legitimize ethical discussion throughout the corporation by raising these questions in relation to strategic planning and corporate practices. Corporations might think of establishing ethics committees to accomplish this task or at least making ethical concerns part of the public-policy committee's task. But ethical concerns again should be integrated throughout all the board's deliberations.

4. Management at all levels, but particularly top management, must recognize the most important role they play in institutionalizing ethical responsibility throughout the organization. Managers have many avenues available to them to shape the corporate culture including the setting of objectives for individuals and subunits in the corporation, developing and implementing the reward structure for other individuals in the organization, modifying organizational structures for the accomplishment of ethical goals, and developing measures of ethical performance. Managers not only have responsibility for efficient and effective use of the material and human resources the corporation has available but must also be concerned to create a responsible institution that cares about the ethical and moral impact of its actions and will take corrective action when ethical issues arise that need to be considered.

5. Business-government relations need attention from an ethical standpoint. Public-pol-

[7]See ibid., pp. 320–21.

[8]Thomas W. Dunfee et al., *Ethics and the MBA Curriculum: A Proposal for Integration of Ethics into the MBA Core Curriculum* (Philadelphia: Wharton School, 1986).

icy questions are fraught with ethical questions, and these must be more explicitly debated. But business has a role to play in this debate by helping design the rules of the game it is going to follow. Business must recognize its responsibility to work with government in a partnership arrangement in designing these rules and do more than just engage in political manipulation. But government must also recognize the important contributions business has to make in formulating regulations and must not seek to replace corporate decision making with more and more government regulations. Business must be given freedom to respond to ethical issues out of its own sense of responsibility, and rules and regulations should be implemented only where necessary because of the inherent limitations of a competitive system.

6. More research must be encouraged by academia, business, and government into the ethical aspects of management decision making. One of the themes of this book is that many of us in this society are ethically ignorant, not really having a good understanding of ethical issues and how they can be analyzed and debated. Research into ethical and moral issues can help to overcome this ignorance. Management scholars need to bring their expertise in empirical research to bear on ethical questions and combine this with the work of the philosophers in conceptual and theoretical developments. Business can help by opening its doors to researchers, and government can provide financial support by encouraging more proposals for research in ethics and morals.

This is an ambitious agenda but one that seems to cover most of the important areas that need attention if ethics is to be implemented and integrated into the business system. The future of business may indeed depend on how well this task is accomplished. Business managers cannot assume that because they run institutions that produce material goods without which life cannot exist, society cannot do without them and therefore their place in society is secure. Business organizations can be controlled in many different ways and business behavior shaped to satisfy the wishes of society. While the ideology that pervades thinking in our country will probably not allow outright ownership of the means of production to any significant degree, it has certainly allowed government to control more and more aspects of business behavior through the regulatory mechanism.

This development reminds us once again of the thesis advocated some years ago in a classic book, *The Modern Corporation and Private Property,* by Adolf A. Berle and Gardiner C. Means, the thesis about the separation of ownership and control in the modern corporation. While Berle and Means applied this thesis to the relationship between shareholders and professional management in private corporations, the thesis applies no less to the relationship between business and government. The government doesn't have to own the means of production in order to control the behavior of private business organizations and have a significant impact on the way these organizations can allocate their resources. The important factor in this thesis is control, and government can extend its control over private organizations if it finds sufficient moral and political support to justify and implement its public-policy agenda.

Regarding the educational enterprise, ethics can serve to integrate the various functional fields of management that have developed over the past several decades. These functional fields of accounting, marketing, finance, and production have become more and more specialized with their own bodies of knowledge that are not very well integrated with each other. Thus finance, for example, has developed its own theories and principles, and people who teach and research in the finance area have difficulty in communicating with people in the other areas of management. Each functional area has dug its own tunnel of specialization deeper and deeper and, in the process, become more and more isolated from the other areas.

Supposedly, all of these functional areas have something to do with management, but the integration of all these specialized areas into a meaningful whole is a problem for students and faculty alike. At one time, most schools of business and management had a capstone policy course, an integrating course that provided an opportunity for students to use their functional knowledge to solve case problems. In the last few years, however, policy has been linked more closely with strategic management or strategic planning, which has developed its own literature and body of knowledge. Thus, strategy has become a field in its own right and has further fragmented knowledge in schools of business and management. This leaves no integrating device in the curriculum that can fit all of the functional areas into some holistic framework where the student's knowledge and experience can be related to a meaningful whole.

Perhaps ethics can serve this integrating function. If the management task is fundamentally ethical in nature, as has been argued throughout the previous chapters, then ethics could be the glue that holds all the functional areas together. These functional specialties have to do with the creation of values, values that should enhance human welfare and lead to the development of a better life for everyone. Most of the functional areas have to do with the creation of economic value and contribute to economizing in the use of resources. Courses in business and society or public policy could be said to deal primarily with the creation of social value; courses in human and organizational behavior, the creation of human value.

All of these courses are meant to contribute to the development of a manager who can guide the fortunes of modern complex business organizations. But every manager has some kind of a philosophy of management, either explicit or implicit, that has been learned in the various courses and through experience in organizations. One would hope that this philosophy is based on some broader ideas about human welfare and contributions to society than are apparent in the notion of self-interest and profit making. Ethics has a primary contribution to make in the development of this philosophy and can serve as an integrating force to make sense out of all the functional areas and fit them into some kind of an ethical framework.

In any event, thinking along these lines needs to be done and is important to the educational task. Courses in business ethics are not necessarily going to make better managers or good people who have ethical sensibilities. But they can contribute to the more limited task of helping students develop an understanding of management that can then serve them throughout their careers. They need to understand that management is more than just some loose integration of the functional areas and is more than just making money or gaining an ever larger market share. The task of management is fundamentally ethical, having to do with the creation of values that enhance human welfare and contribute to the development of human civilization. There is no task that can be more important nor more challenging.

SUGGESTED READING

CHAMBERLAIN, NEIL W. *Social Strategy and Corporate Structure.* New York: Macmillan Co., 1982.

The Changing Expectations of Society in the Next Thirty Years. Washington, D.C.: AACSB/EFMD, 1979.

Commission on Population Growth and the American Future. *Population and the American Future.* Washington, D.C.: U.S. Government Printing Office, 1972.

EWALD, WILLIAM R., JR., ED. *Environment and Change: The Next Fifty Years.* Bloomington: Indiana University Press, 1968.

KAHN, HERMAN. *The Future of the Corporation.* New York: Mason & Lipscomb, 1974.

KAHN, HERMAN, AND B. BRUCE-BRIGGS. *Things to Come: Thinking about the Seventies and Eighties.* New York: Macmillan Co., 1972.

_____, AND A. WIENER. *The Year 2000.* New York: Macmillan Co., 1967.

LIPSET, SEYMOUR MARTIN AND WILLIAM SCHNEIDER. *The Confidence Gap: Business, Labor, and Government in the Public Mind.* New York: Free Press, 1983.

Management in the XXI Century. Washington, D.C.: AACSB/EFMD, 1979.

MORRIS, DUBOIS, S., JR., ED. *Perspective for the 70's and 80's: Tomorrow's Problems Confronting Today's Management.* New York: National Industrial Conference Board, 1970.

PERLOFF, HARVEY S., ED. *The Future of the U.S. Government: Toward the Year 2000.* Englewood Cliffs, N.J.: Prentice-Hall, 1971.

THEOBALD, ROBERT. *An Alternative Future for America Two: Essays and Speeches.* Chicago: Swallow, 1968.

_____. *Futures Conditional.* New York: Bobbs-Merrill, 1971.

MANVILLE CORPORATION: JUSTICE
AND RIGHTS

INTRODUCTION

On Thursday morning, August 26, 1982, a team of lawyers for the Denver-based Manville Corporation arrived at the United States district court building in New York City and filed for the company's reorganization under chapter 11 of the Federal Bankruptcy Act. Public reaction to the filing ranged from sympathetic understanding to outright rage. Manville was the largest industrial company in corporate history to ever file under the act, and the action promised to open a Pandora's box of legal, political, moral, and environmental questions. The request for reorganization was made to protect the company from the overwhelming number of product-liability lawsuits relating to the manufacture and use of asbestos. "Manville . . . decided to seek protection under chapter 11 after a study by Epidemiology Resources, Inc., of Brookline, Massachusetts, indicated that Manville faced a potential total of 52,000 suits at a possible cost of $2 billion—nearly twice the company's net worth. Officials said this was the 'low projection'; the 'high projection' was for 120,000 suits at a liability of more than $5 billion."[1] Manville president, John A. McKinney, said, "Our businesses are in good shape . . . [but] we are completely overwhelmed by the cost of the asbestos health lawsuits filed against us."[2]

Manville's action stunned the financial community, outraged those who had filed asbestos suits against it, put stockholders in a panic, and raised a complex tangle of issues that may have far-reaching implications for the millions of Americans who have routinely worked with asbestos or other toxic chemicals like benzene, vinyl-chloride, and formaldehyde. By filing for bankruptcy, Manville won at least a temporary respite from its legal woes. Chapter 11 does not divest any court of jurisdiction over litigation in which Manville was a party at the time of its filing, but it does suspend all such future claims requiring such claimants to look to the bankruptcy court for relief, taking their place in line behind secured creditors.

THE MANVILLE CORPORATION

The Manville Corporation is a diversified manufacturing, mining, and forest-products company. Its principal manufacturing businesses consist of production of fiberboard, glass, forest products, nonfiberglass insulation, pipe products and systems,

---

[1]"Company Besieged by Claims, Files Bankruptcy," *Monthly Labor Review*, 105, no. 11 (November 1982), 48.

[2]William Marbach and others, "An Asbestos Bankruptcy," *Newsweek*, September 6, 1982, p. 54.

roofing products, and industrial and specialty products. Its principal mining businesses are the mining and processing of asbestos, diatomite, and pearlite.[3]

In 1858 Henry Ward Johns was awarded a patent for an asbestos product described as an "improved compound for roofing and other purposes." He founded the H. W. Johns Manufacturing Company, which along with the Manville Covering Company, incorporated in 1901 to become the Johns-Manville Corporation. The company was renamed Manville Corporation in 1981 with twenty-two principal subsidiaries and various affiliates located throughout the world. Over the years the company has grown considerably through a number of competitive mergers and by developing revolutionary products and designing innovative processes that use technology to help solve some of our most pressing environmental problems. Some examples of these are Spillguard, an effective container of oil spills; HEAF, an industrial exhaust filter; and M.B.F., a continuous, moving bed filter for municipal sewage treatment. Johns-Manville's product development and technological advances have been considered state of the art.

Manville also believed itself to be at the forefront of developing standards that protected asbestos workers. According to Manville's 1973 *Annual Report,* for as long as it has been known that asbestos could be harmful to those handling the fiber, the company has been spending millions of dollars for equipment and technology to prevent inhalation of dust by workers in its mines, mills, and plants. Manville also contributed to the U.S. Department of Labor studies that led to the occupational health standards in 1972 for all U.S. manufacturing operations using asbestos. Manville established an environmental affairs department in 1973 to distribute technical information to help customers meet health standards and ensure safe handling practices in asbestos-manufacturing operations.[4]

With the cooperation of experts from five of the nation's leading medical institutions and the joint support of the International Association of Heat and Frost Insulators and Asbestos Workers, AFL/CIO, Manville established a nationwide program to provide early detection of carcinogenic substances taken into the body. The company also helped establish an environmental cancer therapy research center at the City University of New York's Mount Sinai School of Medicine, which concentrated on research into preclinical diagnosis and treatment of mesothelioma, a cancer that affects the lining of the chest or abdomen, to which asbestos has been related.[5]

ASBESTOS

Asbestos gained importance as a product because it is resistant to fire, rot, rust, and decay. The word comes from the Greek and means "unquenched" or "incombusti-

---

[3]"Manville Corporation," *Standard Corporate Descriptions,* Standard and Poor's Corporation, May 1982, p. 4959.

[4]Johns-Manville, *Annual Report,* 1973.

[5]Johns-Manville, *Annual Report,* 1976.

ble.'' Asbestos is the generic name given to a group of hydrated silicate minerals, which have one common attribute: the ability to be separated into light, silky, but strong fibers, which have many industrial and commercial uses.[6] The fibers can be woven into noncombustible fabrics, or they can be added to other materials to produce floor and ceiling tile, roofing shingles, siding, asbestos cement, and various types of commercial insulation materials. Rocks containing asbestos fiber have even been used for road construction.

As the world became industrialized, the demand for asbestos fiber increased, and a worldwide asbestos mining and processing industry came into being. For many applications, asbestos has no acceptable substitute owing to its unique qualities. Thus, like many important products—ethical drugs, for example—it carries the risk of serious side effects. Asbestos is categorized as ''unavoidable, unsafe'' under product-liability law, but through the years it has saved countless lives and billions of dollars in property damage by preventing or checking the spread of fire.[7]

The first clue that asbestos may be a health hazard was observed ''as early as the first century by the Greek geographer, Strabo, and by the Roman naturalist, Pliny the Elder, both of whom mentioned in passing a sickness of the lungs in slaves whose occupation was to weave asbestos into cloth.''[8] Modern evidence, however, dates from 1900 when a physician from London's Charing Cross Hospital performed a postmortem examination on a thirty-year-old who had worked in an asbestos-textile factory for fourteen years. The physician found ''spicules of asbestos in the lung tissues . . . [and] was able to establish a . . . connection between the man's occupation and the disease that killed him.''[9] By now, it is well known that inhaled asbestos dust can cause several serious illnesses: asbestosis, a chronic disease of the lungs causing shortness of breath similar to emphysema; mesothelioma, a fatal cancer of the chest or abdominal lining; and lung cancer.

Dr. Irving Selikoff, a leading medical authority on asbestos exposure, conducted research on 632 members of the International Association of Heat and Frost Insulators and Asbestos Workers. Starting with 1942, he traced their individual medical history over a twenty-year period. At the conclusion of his study, he observed that 421 deaths occurred among asbestos workers, although according to mortality tables, only 280 deaths should have occurred. These excess deaths were attributed to higher-than-usual incidences of (1) asbestosis, (2) mesothelioma, and (3) other diseases including cancer of the esophagus, stomach, colon, and rectum, which were believed to have been caused by some form of ingested asbestos.[10]

---

[6]*Asbestos Exposure—A Desk Reference for Communicators,* U.S. Department of Health, Education and Welfare, NIH 79-162, May 1979, pp. 3–5.

[7]Steven Solomon, ''The Asbestos Fallout at Johns-Manville,'' *Fortune,* May 7, 1979, p. 202.

[8]Paul Brodeur, *Asbestos and Enzymes* (New York: Ballantine Books, 1972), p. 9.

[9]Ibid., p. 11.

[10]A. Karim Ahmed, Donald F. MacLeod, and James Carmody, ''Control for Asbestos,'' *Environment,* 14, no. 10 (December 1972), 17–18.

CONTROLLING POLLUTION

Public policy to control pollution was brought about by the passage of the National Environmental Policy Act of 1969, with the general purpose to (1) declare a national policy that would encourage productive and enjoyable harmony between people and their environment, (2) promote efforts that would prevent or eliminate damage to the environment and biosphere and stimulate people's health and welfare, and (3) enrich the understanding of the ecological system and natural resources important to the nation.[11] The act created the Council of Environmental Quality, which has the responsibility to evaluate federal programs to determine if they are consistent with national policy on the environment, to advise the president in environmental matters, and to develop national policies in the environmental area.[12]

The Environmental Protection Agency (EPA) came into being on July 9, 1970. It is involved in protection and enhancement of the physical environment. Responsibility for pollution control has been established in the following environmental areas: air, water, pesticides, toxic substances, radiation, and noise. In general, its responsibilities cover (1) establishing and enforcing standards, (2) monitoring pollution in the environment, (3) conducting research into environmental problems, and (4) assisting state and local governments in their efforts to control pollution. The major focus of the EPA is to control the industrial sources of pollution. (Air pollution existed before the advent of modern industrial society, but natural causes of pollution cannot be controlled). Industrial processes that produce sulphur oxide, particulate matter, carbon monoxide, ozone, nitrous oxides, hydrocarbons, and lead get most of the attention.[13]

While all pollutants in the environment are considered harmful, only particulates in the air are of concern in the asbestos case. Particulates include solid particles like dust, soot, and smoke, which may be irritating but are usually not poisonous, and bits of solid or liquid substances that may be highly toxic. Particulates are measured together by filtering all the particles from a known amount of air and weighing them. The EPA standard for particulates is only a rough indication of the health hazards since it does not separate toxic particles from those that are merely annoying. Research is under way to find quick, economical methods of measuring various kinds of particles and their sizes. The smaller the particles, the more likely they are to reach the innermost part of the lungs and work their damage.

The harm may be physical: clogging the lung sacs, as in anthracosis, or coal miners' "black lung," caused by inhaling coal dust; asbestosis or silicosis in people exposed to asbestos fibers or dust from silicate rock; and byssinosis, or textile workers' "brown lung," from inhaling cotton fibers.[14]

[11]National Environmental Policy Act, 1969, PL 91-190, sect. 4321.

[12]Ibid., PL 91-191, sect. 4344.

[13]Rogene A. Buchholz, *Business Environment and Public Policy,* (Englewood Cliffs, N.J.: Prentice-Hall, 1982), pp. 382–83.

[14]*Air Pollution and Your Health,* Environmental Protection Agency, Washington, D.C., March 1979, pp. 7–8.

The public-policy approach to pollution control is many faceted. To control ambient air quality, the EPA set primary and secondary standards for the most harmful pollutants. The primary standards prescribe the minimum level of air quality necessary to keep people from becoming ill and are aimed at protecting human lives. The secondary standards are concerned with the protection and prevention of damage to animals, plants, and property. Substances like asbestos, beryllium, mercury, and vinyl-chloride are strictly limited in the amounts that can be emitted into the atmosphere because they are known to be dangerous.[15]

THE VICTIMS

The health hazards have long been recognized for workers who are heavily exposed to asbestos, such as in shipbuilding and asbestos mining. The carpenter who saws wallboard containing asbestos, and the garage mechanic who air hoses out a brake housing are subject to the fibers that are spread throughout their workplaces. Since the early 1940s as many as eleven million American workers may have been exposed to harmful concentrations of asbestos, including some 4.5 million in the shipbuilding yards during World War II.[16] Recent studies of shipyard workers, including those with only a month or two of exposure, indicate the presence of asbestos-related diseases. Some workers who did not work directly with asbestos but whose jobs were located near contaminated areas have developed diseases associated with asbestos. There is also some evidence that members of the families of exposed workers face an increased risk of developing asbestos-related diseases as a result of the dust brought into the home on workers' shoes and clothing.

In recent years concern has been expressed for the general public as well as for workers and their families because of evidence that suggests even relatively light exposure to asbestos fibers can lead to the development of several different types of cancer. Among those whose health may be endangered are children, teachers, and others in schools where asbestos insulation and fireproofing materials have been used.

Between 1940 and 1973 hundreds of thousands of tons of asbestos was sprayed or applied on ceilings and other parts of schools and other buildings for fireproofing, sound deadening, insulation, or decoration. Some of this asbestos material is deteriorating and releasing harmful fibers into the air. The danger may be particularly grave for children because they are exposed at an early age, and asbestos-induced cancers would have plenty of time to develop. The EPA has launched a program to help school officials identify buildings containing asbestos, inspect these buildings to determine whether asbestos fibers are being released into

[15]Buchholz, *Business Environment*, pp. 387–89.

[16]*Asbestos Exposure: What It Means, What to Do*, U.S. Department of Health, Education and Welfare, NIH 78-1594, 1978, p. 2.

the air, remove or repair the damaged material, and periodically reinspect materials left in the schools.[17]

The major problem for victims has been finding someone to accept responsibility—the manufacturer, the distributor, the contractor, the insurance company, or the government.[18] They cannot sue their employer if that employer is covered by workers' compensation. In many states statutes of limitation prohibit benefit payments for long-latent maladies, which in this case can take up to thirty years to develop. A Labor Department study revealed that only 5 percent of the severely disabled victims received workers' compensation payments.[19]

A lawsuit may seem like a slow and costly remedy, but as things now stand, a victim has little choice. Also, product-liability law is very complex because the laws of fifty states are involved. The asbestos manufacturer is the logical target of these suits, but the present fault system is a lottery—some win and some lose. In long-developing illnesses, it is difficult to prove the cause, and "defendants and insurance companies are conservatively paying out $2.00 in expenses for every $1.00 put into the hands of the victims and that doesn't include the cost to the public in providing judges, juries, and other court expenses."[20] But the victims, many in their sixties, urgently need some kind of help.

THE GOVERNMENT

During World War II asbestos was used extensively in government shipyards or shipyards under government contract. The safety material saved countless lives from fire, smoke, and heat, but it also harmed countless others who worked to put it in the ships. Forty years and many lawsuits later, the federal government denies any tort liability to asbestos victims, contending that they can be compensated through the Federal Employee Compensation Act. Section 8116(c) of the act grants federal employees immediate fixed benefits for workplace injuries on the condition that they give up the right to sue their employer—the federal government. Courts have previously construed the language to mean that defendants sued by federal employees were barred from recovering from the federal government or a civilian contractor even if the government or contractor was liable for the employee's injuries.[21]

---

[17]*Toxic Information Series,* Asbestos Office of Pesticides and Toxic Substances, TS-793, Washington, D.C.

[18]John T. Mascotte, "Technology and the Environment: Who Pays the Piper?" *Vital Speeches of the Day* XLIX, no. 7 (January 15, 1983), 221.

[19]Joann S. Lublin, "Workplace Perils," *Wall Street Journal,* December 20, 1982, p. 1.

[20]Mascotte, "Who Pays the Piper?" p. 221.

[21]Stephan Tarnoff, "Asbestos Defendants Go after Government," *Business Insurance* 17 (March 7, 1983), 26.

On February 23, 1983, the Supreme Court changed the course of the asbestos litigation. Its decision in *Lockheed Aircraft* v. *United States* opened the federal government and its civilian contractors to asbestos lawsuits. Justice Lewis Powell, writing the opinion for the majority, said:

> Section 8166(c) was intended to govern only the rights of employees, their relatives and people claiming through or on behalf of them. These are the only categories of parties who benefit from the quid pro compromise that FECA adopts. Lockheed is not within any of the specified categories.[22]

Since it is estimated that 8000 of the 16,500 plaintiffs suing Manville were exposed to asbestos while working for the federal government, this decision is very important to the company.

Does the solution rest with the federal government? Should the government pass legislation that will provide compensation to the victims—a "white lung"-type legislation—funded by the government and the employers? The asbestos industry lobbied for just such a fund to be administered by a board of experts who would determine which workers were entitled to compensation. The fund was to be paid for by contributions from industry, insurance companies, and the federal government, thereby assessing the federal government for its alleged share of the responsibility. However, the fact that plaintiffs are now receiving punitive damages from asbestos manufacturers somewhat dilutes industry's argument for federal aid. Congress has shown little interest in such a bill, but Manville's bankruptcy filing may have been meant to force Congress into action. "The timetable for legislation is moved up by twelve months, to 1983 instead of 1984," stated William E. Bailey, senior vice-president of Boston's Commercial Union Insurance Co., a longtime supporter of compensation legislation.[23] Fred M. Baron, a Dallas attorney who represented clients suing Manville and others for asbestos damages said, "They are trying to force government's hand. They want a 'bail-out' bill. That's 100% behind their filing."[24]

Representative George Miller (D-Calif.) proposed a bill that would create an asbestos workers' compensation fund. However, his bill put the entire burden on industry. All industries that used some asbestos would contribute. This did not seem to be a feasible solution to the immediate problem, however, owing to the difficulties inherent in obtaining agreement as to the specifics of paying into such a fund in an industry composed of hundreds of firms. Manville contested the bill because of its cost and its failure to deal with the present suits.[25] Another proposal would have reformed the current workers' compensation system and provided government par-

[22]Ibid.

[23]"Manville May Drive Congress to Action," *Business Week,* September 13, 1982, p. 34.

[24]Neal Maxwell, G. Christian Hill, and Raymond A. Joseph, "Radical Tactic," *Wall Street Journal,* August 27, 1982, p. 1.

[25]"Manville," *Business Week,* September 13, 1982, p. 34.

ticipation under a complicated arbitration formula. This idea, however, did not receive much serious consideration or support.[26]

Along with the question of how best to assign compensation payments, the government is also concerned with preventive measures. Educating workers, companies, and the general public on the safe use and handling of asbestos is considered of primary importance. The National Cancer Institute for Occupational Safety and Health is responsible for studying and documenting carcinogenic hazards and operates as an information service to answer workers' questions about hazards. The EPA is charged with monitoring levels of asbestos in air and water, while the FDA is concerned with contamination of foods, drugs, and cosmetics. The Consumer Product Safety Commission has banned the use of asbestos in several products, for instance, asbestos-lined hairdryers. No one knows what risks to health are involved or whether future lawsuits will occur from asbestos use in public buildings, consumer products, or other exposure.

Implicit in the fundamental goal of controlling the human carcinogenic hazard from asbestos is education or increased knowledge about such matters as work processes involving asbestos that lend themselves to dispersion and inhalation or ingestion, diseases that may result from exposure, methods and reasons for environmental monitoring and medical surveillance, and the role of related factors in disease production. One of these factors is smoking. If workers smoke, the risks related to asbestos increase ninety-two times that of the general nonsmoking population.[27]

Because asbestos is considered to be an "unavoidable, unsafe" substance, it must be accompanied by a warning to the ultimate user who can then determine whether or not to risk exposure. The failure to give an adequate warning would make the product "unreasonably dangerous," and liability would attach to any injury. Manufacturers are held to the skill and knowledge of experts and have an affirmative duty to test their products to discover dangers.[28] It was not until 1964, after Dr. Selikoff's study, that Manville began putting a warning on its asbestos products, which read:

> Caution: This product contains asbestos fiber. Inhalation of asbestos in excessive quantities over long periods of time may be harmful. If dust is created when this product is handled, avoid breathing the dust. If adequate ventilation control is not possible, wear respirators approved by the U.S. Bureau of Mines for pneumoconosis-producing dust.[29]

However, the Fifth Circuit Court of Appeals, in *Borel* v. *Fiberboard,* held that this notice was insufficient to warn the worker that exposure might cause

[26]Ibid.

[27]*Asbestos: An Information Resource,* U.S. Department of Health, Education and Welfare, NIH 79-1684, May 1978, p. 31.

[28]"Asbestos Fallout," p. 202.

[29]*Borel* v. *Fiberboard Paper Products Corporation et al.,* 493 F2d 1076 (1973).

asbestosis or cancer. Effective July 1, 1976, OSHA called for the following warning label:

> Caution: Contains asbestos fibers. Avoid creating dust. Breathing asbestos dust may cause serious bodily harm.[30]

MANVILLE'S RESPONSE

As of March 1, 1977, the Johns-Manville Corporation was a defendant or codefendant in 271 suits alleging damage to the health of persons exposed to asbestos and asbestos-containing products manufactured and sold by the company. These suits typically alleged that the company failed in its duty to warn of the hazards of inhalation of asbestos fibers and dust originating from such products. In its defense, Manville maintained that there was no basis for any warning until publication of scientific studies in 1964 that indicated which warnings were appropriate.[31]

The landmark case in asbestos litigation was the case of *Borel* v. *Fiberboard et al.* In October of 1969 Clarence Borel, an asbestos worker for thirty-three years, initiated legal action in the U.S. District Court for the Eastern District of Texas, naming as defendants eleven manufacturers of asbestos insulation, including Manville. Borel sought to hold the defendants liable for negligence, gross negligence, breach of warranty, and strict liability. The alleged negligent acts were failure to (1) take reasonable precautions or to exercise reasonable care to warn Borel of the dangers to which he was exposed as a worker when using the defendants' products, (2) inform Borel as to what would be safe and sufficient wearing apparel and proper protective equipment and appliances or methods of handling and using the various products, (3) test the asbestos products in order to ascertain the dangers involved in their use, and (4) remove the products from the market upon ascertaining that such products would cause asbestosis.

The defendants denied the allegations and used the defenses of contributory negligence and assumption of risk. Borel died of asbestosis before the case came to trial, and his widow was substituted as plaintiff. The jury found that the defendants were negligent but not grossly negligent. As for strict liability, the jury found that all the defendants were liable and awarded $79,436 in total damages. The defendants appealed, but the appellate court upheld the decision of the lower court.[32]

The Borel case and the increased public awareness it brought set the stage for thousands of asbestos-related lawsuits, which have been filed against some 240 manufacturers. Manville and other asbestos producers and users have been asking the federal government to assume a major share of the liability because many of the workers developed cancer or asbestosis from exposure during wartime service in the

---

[30]*Asbestos: Worker Health Alert,* U.S. Department of Labor, Occupational Safety and Health Administration, no. 3069, 1980, p. 5.

[31]"Asbestos Fallout," p. 202.

[32]*Borel* v. *Fiberboard.*

shipyards.[33] Dave Pullman of the Asbestos Compensation Coalition (nine firms that either manufacture asbestos or did in the past) maintains that the government has a degree of responsibility because it, "acted just like the other manufacturer—they bought and sold asbestos fiber, they purchased machinery to give to asbestos manufacturers, they specified the products and controlled the workplace where most of the workers were exposed."[34] In fact, the producers were following government-approved safety standards at the time. After all, it was wartime, and if the manufacturers had not complied, their asbestos operations would have been promptly requisitioned.

Manville believes that since the beginning of 1978, no significant new potential liabilities have been created for the corporation with respect to diseases known to be related to asbestos and arising from asbestos fiber and/or asbestos-containing products manufactured or sold by Manville. It bases this belief on the following facts and assumptions. First, since the mid-seventies Manville has not sold loose-form asbestos in the U.S. Second, by 1973, Johns-Manville had ceased domestic manufacture of thermal insulation products containing asbestos, which are the products principally involved in disease claims made against the company. Third, OSHA established a maximum exposure standard for asbestos fiber of five fibers per cubic centimeter in 1972 and lowered that standard to two fibers per cubic centimeter in 1976. It is assumed that compliance with such standards in the workplace was achieved within a reasonable time following promulgation of the standard.[35]

Since 1968 Manville has been involved in over twenty thousand lawsuits and has paid over $50 million in claims. Manufacturers have been particularly troubled by the prospect of juries assessing punitive damages as well as compensatory awards on the grounds—for which there is some documentary evidence—that the companies in fact knew about the health hazards of asbestos and yet continued to manufacture the product anyway.[36]

THE INSURERS

It takes twenty years or more for some asbestos-related diseases to appear. The question that faces the insurance companies and the court system is whether an insurer's liability starts when workers are first exposed to asbestos or if it begins only when the disease manifests itself many years later. Without a firm answer to this question, the insurers tend to be defensive. With thousands of damage suits filed and the claims so staggering, many insurance companies are going to court when it comes their turn to pay. The issue of exposure or manifestation has prompt-

[33]"Company Beseiged by Claims," *Monthly Labor Review* 105, no. 11 (November 1982), p. 48.

[34]Ibid.

[35]Johns-Manville, *Annual Report,* 1981.

[36]"Manville's Bold Manuever," *Time,* September 6, 1982, pp. 17–18.

ed many court battles. "The U.S. Supreme Court has refused to decide between the conflicting theories of liability. This leaves standing a series of often contradictory state and federal court decisions."[37] Does the insurance company that covered the worker at the time of exposure have the liability or does the insurance company that covered the worker when the disease manifested itself have the liability? Which insurance company has the liability if the worker is no longer working?

A major problem in resolving these questions is that no one has a good handle on what the ultimate liability will be for these claims. At least two major studies have tried to assess the potential impact of asbestos claims on the insurance industry. The first study by Paul W. MacAvoy, a professor of organization and management, at Yale University estimated the indemnity cost at $38.2 billion, compared with a net worth of $11.5 billion for the major insurance companies involved. The second study by insurance industry analysts Conning & Company published in late 1982 estimated the potential liability at a much smaller $4–$10 billion.[38]

What about the workers' compensation systems that were designed by the states to provide protection to workers with job-related injuries, disease, or death? A major university studied one thousand asbestos victims and found that only 30 percent of the survivors of these victims had filed for death benefits under the system. The reason given was that the "worker-compensation awards [don't] match the hefty awards made by juries."[39]

CONCLUSION

Of course, Manville is not the only corporation faced with such insurance claims. The entire asbestos industry has been hit with claims. Companies like Eagle-Pitcher Industries, a former maker of brake linings; Pittsburgh Corning Corporation, which once made insulation; and Combustion Engineering, Inc., also a brake-lining manufacturer, are all faced with litigation.

The problems, of course, go far beyond the environment of the asbestos industry. In the September 10, 1966, edition of Chemical Week, a list of places where asbestos can become airborne was compiled:

Asbestos-lined ducts used in centrally air-conditioned buildings
Asbestos ducts and insulation in home central heating plants
Motor-vehicle brake linings and clutch plates
Auto undercoating
Asbestos ceiling and floor tiles
Asbestos shingles and siding

[37]Daniel Hertzberg, "Policy Fight: Asbestos Lawsuits Spur War among Insurers with Billions at Stake," *Wall Street Journal*, June 14, 1982, p. 1.
[38]Stephen Tarnoff, "The Asbestos Crisis," *Business Insurance* vol. 17 (April 4, 1983), p. 24.
[39]Ibid.

Construction and demolition; fitting, cutting, and removing asbestos-filled wallboards, floorings, piping, and insulation

Incineration of asbestos-filled scrap

Improperly filtered effluent from asbestos-processing plants[40]

A product that has been so useful to our growing economy has also caused considerable harm. How can industry and society guard against such products and substances? It is doubtful that all harmful materials will be or have been identified. Future asbestos exposure can be minimized by physical control of the substance and education of the consumer and the worker. Engineering methods to control airborne asbestos include complete enclosure of the source, local exhaust ventilation, isolation, plant design, treatment of asbestos and/or substitution of alternative materials where possible. In 1955 Johns-Manville Corporation built a twelve-story asbestos-fiber mill in Canada—the largest in the world—which was touted as having the best fiber-aspirating and dust-collecting systems consisting of hoods, ductwork, and cyclones. "The mill was said to be one of the cleanest in the asbestos and mining industry."[41]

Lawsuits arising from asbestos-related disease have the potential of causing considerable financial damage to the manufacturers. Corporations are developing procedures that will help monitor health records of employees so that they can spot problems early and cut their potential liabilities. The courts will expect a tracking of this data as a demonstration of concern and responsibility on the part of the employer. Documentation of work hazards such as noise, radiation, inhalation of fibrous substances and exposure to chemicals will be a necessary act of moral responsibility as well as a legal one. Such acts not only may protect the worker and the consumer from injury but may save the employer from possible financial ruin. To develop this information is complicated and expensive and also raises questions of violating the confidentiality of the doctor-patient relationship. Gathering this information may cause some legal problems.[42]

The right-to-know laws that are pending in state legislatures and that are supported by workers, environmentalists, unions, and other stakeholders must be considered. Such laws might require employers to provide the public with warning and information sheets about hazardous substances.

Until Manville filed for bankruptcy, judges seemed to be convinced that victims must be compensated regardless of fault, and juries concluded that big companies had pockets deep enough to pay for anything.[43] Any relief accorded the industry by either government legislation or judicial ruling may result in the lessening of the victims' opportunity to be provided full compensation for their suffering.

---

[40]"Asbestos Awaiting Trial," *Chemical Week*, September 10, 1966, p. 32. Reprinted by special permission. Copyright © 1966 by McGraw-Hill, Inc., New York, New York.

[41]Goldfield, "Air Handling and Dust Control in Johns-Manville's New Asbestos Mill," *Mining Engineering* 7, no. 11 (November 1955).

[42]"Tracking Chemical Hazards on the Job," *Business Week*, March 21, 1983, p. 142.

[43]"Not Such Deep Pockets," *National Review*, September 17, 1982, p. 1125.

The effects of all these legal maneuvers are difficult to evaluate. What is certain, however, is that some just compromise must be found among the insurers, the manufacturers, the federal government, and the victims.

EPILOGUE

Manville was given many extensions to work out the differences with its creditors and litigants over its proposed reorganization plan. The plan Manville initially filed with the court committed almost all its cash flow to creditors from U.S. operations for as long as it took to pay off its debts. The plan also prevented litigants from seeking a trial by jury to determine their claims but provided fixed benefits to all victims with some flexibility for personal circumstances. In addition, Manville wanted to transfer its operating assets to a new company, which would continue to use its cash flow to pay off the debts of the old company. But the new company would have been immune from any direct claims on its assets by current or future asbestos victims.[44]

The asbestos committee representing litigants believed this plan was designed solely to deprive asbestos victims of reasonable compensation for their claims. This committee filed suit in court to challenge the legitimacy of Manville's Chapter 11 filing. The committee argued that the company used some fictitious figures to make its case. The judge who decided the case ruled in favor of Manville, stating that "the economic reality of Manville's highly precarious financial position due to massive debt sustains its eligibility and candidacy for reorganization."[45] The decision was appealed, and the longer the case continued, the more impatient the creditors became, and the longer asbestos victims remained uncompensated for their suffering.

In the meantime, Manville took itself out of the asbestos business. In September 1983 it sold a mine in Quebec, once the world's largest producer of asbestos, to a Canadian consortium for $117 million. In February of the same year the company sold its Belgian asbestos operation for an undisclosed sum. The company also discontinued land operations in Idaho, taking a $3.6 million write down. Manville's earnings jumped from $10 to $59 million for the first nine months of the year.[46]

In July 1984 the bankruptcy judge set a deadline of January 31, 1985, for the filing of claims on the part of private and public property owners who had removed or may have to remove asbestos from their homes and buildings. Asbestos was widely used in ceiling and pipe insulation until the late 1970s, so owners of buildings ranging from homes to hospitals were potential claimants. As of mid-January

---

[44]Dean Rotbart, "Manville Corp. Faces Increasing Opposition to Bankruptcy Filing," *Wall Street Journal,* January 1, 1984, p. 1.

[45]"Manville Corp. Wins Court Rulings in Fight for Chapter 11 Status," *Wall Street Journal,* January 24, 1984, p. 47.

[46]"Manville's Reorganization Plan Resolves Nothing," *Business Week,* December 5, 1983, pp. 72–73.

1985, only 2,300 claims had been filed, which was believed to be far below the number of potential claimants, many of whom may have been unaware of the deadline. In a last-minute flurry, hundreds of government agencies along with other claimants filed damage claims for more than $1 billion.[47] The eventual amount of all property-damage claims reached $89 billion.

Finally, a reorganization plan began to take shape that eventually became the basis for a settlement. In the summer of 1985 Manville agreed to a flexible scheme to fund the claims against the company that would use some cash left over after normal operations but that could also take as much as 80 percent of the company stock. Under the plan, Manville agreed to a trust fund to deal with asbestos-disease claims. The trust wouldn't be part of the company but would be funded by it with a $1.65 billion bond to be paid in annual installments of $75 million over twenty-two years, $646 million in insurance, and 50 to 80 percent of the company's common stock, depending on the size of the claims that had been filed. Voting rights on the stock would be restricted for four years after Manville emerged from bankruptcy, but after that time the trust could use its stock essentially to take over the company. The trust would be controlled by five people appointed by the bankruptcy court. The company would also pay the trust $200 million in cash and allocate 20 percent of its annual profit indefinitely if the funds were needed. Overall, the company would contribute $2.5 to $3 billion, depending on the value of the stock and future earnings.[48]

The company initially balked at giving up control of the company and the board said it—the board—had to have the final say in who would run the company after it emerged from bankruptcy. Representatives of current and future health claimants insisted that any directors be acceptable to all the creditor groups, and the company finally agreed to let creditors have the final say in board appointments, removing the last major obstacle to gaining approval of the plan.[49] The board also agreed to look for an outsider to run the company after its CEO and chairman, John A. McKinney, retired in September 1986. At this news, the current president of the company, J. T. Hulce, who had been the heir apparent, resigned.[50] The board then named George C. Dillon, an outside director, as chairman and W. Thomas Stephens, the chief financial officer of the company since 1984, as chief executive officer.[51] The company then paid McKinney and Hulce more than $1.8 million in a severance agreement.[52]

---

[47]Jonathan Dahl, "Asbestos Claims against Manville Exceed $1 Billion," *Wall Street Journal,* January 31, 1985, p. 3; Jonathan Dahl, "Many with Potential Asbestos Claims against Manville Won't File in Time," *Wall Street Journal,* January 31, 1985, p. 31.

[48]Jonathan Dahl, "Manville Offers $2.5 Billion Plan to Settle Claims," *Wall Street Journal,* August 5, 1985, p. 3.

[49]Cynthia F. Mitchell, "Manville Is Said to Have Agreed to Let Creditors Decide Board Appointments," *Wall Street Journal,* April 25, 1986, p. 7.

[50]Cynthia F. Mitchell, "Manville President Quits after Dispute with Asbestos Plaintiffs over Top Posts," *Wall Street Journal,* April 30, 1986, p. 34.

[51]"Now Comes the Hard Part for Manville," *Business Week,* July 7, 1986.

[52]Cynthia F. Mitchell, "Manville to Pay Large Severance To 2 Executives," *Wall Street Journal,* June 24, 1986, p. 10.

During the time this reorganization plan was being debated, an estimated 2000 of the 16,500 personal-injury plaintiffs died. The victims or their heirs haven't as yet received a penny for their claims because the bankruptcy filing froze the litigation. The money that will eventually be paid will be little consolation. The chairman and CEO retired and the president resigned. The company, itself, after a four-year reorganization effort, is subject to be taken over by the trust, which could liquidate the company if the money isn't enough to pay claims. The only winners will be the lawyers, who will make about $1 billion in fees from settlements paid by the trust.[53]

Manville thought that bankruptcy would be a quick fix to the endless stream of lawsuits it was facing, and that it could emerge from Chapter 11 in a relatively short period of time after having set aside enough money to cover these claims. It now seems that the company drastically underestimated the complexity of using the bankruptcy code to deal with toxic-torts litigation. This strategy forced Manville to negotiate with more than double the number of creditor groups that are common to such filings. The company had to deal not only with commercial creditors and shareholders but also with about twenty representatives for the plaintiffs, another dozen or so lawyers representing codefendents, and one representative for future claimants. Given this kind of a political context, Manville simply lost control of the situation and lost the store in the process.[54]

QUESTIONS

1. Was the use of bankruptcy laws an effective procedure for Manville to adopt? What was Manville's objective in using this strategy? Was this strategy appropriate? Was it ethical? Should bankruptcy be used to deal with toxic-torts litigation? What approaches to settling these claims might be more effective and appropriate?

2. Identify the parties at fault in this case. How should responsibility be assigned to these parties? Who is legally liable? Who is morally responsible? How should liability and responsibility be divided among the company, the insurance companies, the government, and other responsible parties?

3. Who should decide about the risks involved in using a hazardous substance? Employees? The company? The government? What kind of risk analysis is useful in making these decisions? Who should bear the risk, and how should liability be distributed?

4. Apply the different concepts of justice to this situation. Was the final settlement a just agreement? Why or why not? Was it more egalitarian in nature or more in line with libertarian theory? Are these theories useful in analyzing the situation? Were anyone's rights violated or ignored? Were important rights appropriately respected?

---

[53]Cynthia F. Mitchell, "Negative Verdict: Manville's Bid to Evade Avalanche of Lawsuits Proves Disappointing," *Wall Street Journal*, July 15, 1986, p. 1.

[54]Ibid.

THE FORD MOTOR CAR: ETHICAL THEORIES

Ford Motor Company is the second largest producer of automobiles. With annual sales of over six million cars and trucks worldwide, it has revenues of over $30 billion per year. In 1960 Ford's market position was eroded by competition from domestic and foreign subcompacts, especially Volkswagens. Lee Iacocca, president of Ford, determined to regain Ford's share of the market by having a new subcompact, the Pinto, in production by 1970.

Although the normal preproduction testing and development of an automobile takes about forty-three months, Iacocca managed to bring the Pinto to the production stage in a little over two years. Internal memos showed that Ford crashtested early models of the Pinto before production "at a top-secret site, more than forty times and . . . every test made at over twenty-five mph without special structural alteration of the car . . . resulted in a ruptured fuel tank."[1] Stray sparks could easily ignite any spilling gasoline and engulf the car in flames. Several years later, a spokesman for Ford acknowledged "that early model Pintos did not pass rear-impact tests at twenty mph."[2]

Nonetheless, the company went on with production of the Pinto as designed, since it met all applicable federal safety standards then in effect and was comparable in safety to other cars then being produced. Moreover, a later Ford company study released by J. C. Echold, director of automotive safety for Ford, claimed that an improved design that would have rendered the Pinto and other similar cars less likely to burst into flames on collision would not be cost effective for society. Entitled "Fatalities Associated with Crash-Induced Fuel Leakage and Fires," the Ford study (which was intended to counter the prospect of stiffer government regulations on gasoline tank design) claimed that the costs of the design improvement ($11 per vehicle) far outweighed its social benefits:

The total benefit is shown to be just under $50 million, while the associated cost is $137 million. Thus the cost is almost three times the benefits, even using a number of highly favorable benefit assumptions.

BENEFITS:

Savings	—	180 burn deaths, 180 serious burn injuries, 2100 burned vehicles.
Unit cost	—	$200,000 per death, $67,000 per injury, $700 per vehicle.
Total benefits	—	180 × ($200,000) plus
		180 × ($ 67,000) plus
		2100 × ($ 700) = $49.15 million

SOURCE: Manuel G. Velasquez, *Business Ethics: Concepts and Cases* (Englewood Cliffs, N.J.: Prentice-Hall, 1982), pp. 94–96.

[1]Mark Dowie, "Pinto Madness," *Mother Jones,* September/October 1977, p. 20. See also Joanne Gamdin, "Jury Slaps Massive 'Fine' on Ford in '72 Pinto Crash," *Business Insurance,* February, 20, 1978, p. 76.

[2]"Ford Rebuts Pinto Criticism," *National Underwriter,* September 9, 1977.

Costs:

Sales   — 11 million cars, 1.5 million light trucks
Unit cost   — $11 per car, $11 per truck
Total costs — 11,000,000 × ($11) plus
                1,500,000 × ($11) = $137 million

[From memorandum attached to statement of J. C. Echold][3]

Ford's estimate of the number of deaths, injuries, and vehicles that would be lost as a result of fires from fuel leakage were based on statistical studies. The $200,000 value attributed to the loss of life was based on a study of the National Highway Traffic Safety Administration, which broke down the estimated social costs of a death as follows:[4]

COMPONENT	1971 COSTS
Future productivity losses	
Direct	$132,000
Indirect	41,300
Medical costs	
Hospital	700
Other	425
Property damage	1,500
Insurance administration	4,700
Legal and court	3,000
Employer losses	1,000
Victim's pain and suffering	10,000
Funeral	900
Assets (lost consumption)	5,000
Miscellaneous accident cost	200
TOTAL PER FATALITY:	$200,725

On May 28, 1972, Mrs. Lily Gray was driving a six-month-old Pinto on Interstate 15 near San Bernardino, California. In the car with her was Richard Grimshaw, a thirteen-year-old boy. Mrs. Gray was a unique person. She had adopted two girls, worked forty hours a week, was den mother for all the teenagers in the neighborhood, sold refreshments at the Bobby Sox games, and had maintained a twenty-two-year-long happy marriage.

Mrs. Gray was driving at about 55 mph when the Pinto stalled and was rear-ended by a 1963 Ford convertible. On impact, the Pinto gas tank ruptured and the car burst into flames. Inside the car, Mrs. Gray was burned to death and Richard Grimshaw was severely burned over 90 per cent of his body. It was a hundred-to-one shot, but although badly disfigured, Richard survived the accident and subse-

[3]Ralph Drayton, "One Manufacturer's Approach to Automobile Safety Standards," *CTLA News,* VIII, no. 2., February 1968: 11.
[4]Dowie, "Pinto Madness," p. 28.

quently underwent seventy painful surgical operations. At least fifty-three persons have died in accidents involving Pinto fires, and many more have been severely burnt.[5]

QUESTIONS

1. Using the Ford figures given in the memo, calculate the probability that a vehicle would be involved in a burn death (that is, the number of burn deaths divided by the total number of cars and trucks sold). In your opinion, is there a limit to the amount that Ford should have been willing to invest in order to reduce this figure to zero? If your answer is yes, then determine from your answer what price you place on life and compare your price to the government's. If your answer is no, then discuss whether your answer implies that no matter how much it would take to make such cars, automakers should make cars completely accident proof.

2. In your opinion, was the management of Ford morally responsible for Mrs. Gray's "burn death"? Explain. Was there something wrong with the utilitarian analysis Ford management used? Explain. Would it have made any difference from a moral point of view if Ford management had informed its buyers of the risks of fire? Explain.

3. Suppose that you were on Mr. J. C. Echold's staff and before the Pinto reached the production stage you were assigned the task of writing an analysis of the overall desirability of producing and marketing the Pinto as planned. One part of your report is to be subtitled "ethical and social desirability." What would you write in this part?

A SOUTH AFRICAN INVESTMENT: ETHICAL THEORIES

In April 1977 the Interfaith Center on Corporate Responsibility announced that some of its subscribing members owned stock in Texaco, Inc., and in Standard Oil Co. of California (SoCal), and that these members would introduce shareholders' resolutions at the next annual stockholders' meeting of Texaco and SoCal that would require that these companies and their affiliates terminate their operations in South Africa. The effort to get Texaco and SoCal out of South Africa was primarily directed and coordinated by Tim Smith, project director of the Interfaith Center on Corporate Responsibility. The stockholders' resolution that Tim Smith would have

SOURCE: Manuel G. Velasquez, *Business Ethics: Concepts and Cases* (Englewood Cliffs, N.J.: Prentice-Hall, 1982), pp. 96–100.

[5]"Ford Fights Pinto Case: Jury gives 128 million," *Auto News*, February 13, 1978, pp. 3, 44.

the Interfaith shareholders introduce at the annual meetings of Texaco and SoCal read as follows:

> Whereas in South Africa the black majority is controlled and oppressed by a white minority that comprises 18 percent of the population;
>
> Whereas South Africa's apartheid system legalizes racial discrimination in all aspects of life and deprives the black population of their most basic human rights, such as, Africans cannot vote, cannot collectively bargain, must live in racially segregated areas, are paid grossly discriminatory wages, are assigned 13 percent of the land while 87 percent of the land is reserved for the white population;
>
> Whereas black opposition to apartheid and black demands for full political, legal, and social rights in their country has risen dramatically within the last year;
>
> Whereas widespread killing, arrests, and repression have been the response of the white South African government to nationwide demonstrations for democratic rights;
>
> Whereas Prime Minister Vorster has openly declared his intention to maintain apartheid and deny political rights to South African blacks;
>
> Whereas we believe that U.S. business investments in the Republic of South Africa, including our company's operations, provide significant economic support and moral legitimacy to South Africa's apartheid government;
>
> Therefore be it resolved: that the shareholders request the Board of Directors to establish the following as corporate policy:
>
> > "Texaco [and Standard Oil of California] and any of its subsidiaries or affiliates shall terminate its present operations in the Republic of South Africa as expeditiously as possible unless and until the South African government has committed itself to ending the legally enforced form of racism called apartheid and has taken meaningful steps toward the achievement of full political, legal, and social rights for the majority population (African, Asian, colored)."

The resolution was occasioned by the fact that Texaco and SoCal were the joint owners of Caltex Petroleum Co. (each owns 50 percent of Caltex), an affiliate that operates oil refineries in South Africa and that in 1973 was worth about $100 million. In 1975 Caltex announced that it was planning to expand its refinery plant in Milnerto, South Africa, from a capacity of 58,000 barrels a day to an increased capacity of 108,000 barrels a day. The expansion would cost $135 million and would increase South Africa's *total* refining capacity by 11 percent. Caltex would be obliged by South African law to bring in at least $100 million of these investment funds from outside the country.

The management of Texaco and SoCal were both opposed to the resolution that would have required them to pull out of South Africa and to abandon their Caltex expansion plans, which, by some estimates, promised an annual return of 20 percent on the original investment. They therefore recommended that stockholders vote against the resolution. The managements of both Texaco and SoCal argued that Caltex was committed to improving the economic working conditions of its black employees and that their continued presence in South Africa did not constitute an "endorsement" of South Africa's "policies." The commitment of Caltex to improving the condition of its employees was evidenced, the companies claimed, by its adherence to the 1977 "Sullivan principles."

Early in 1977, Caltex was one of several dozen corporations who had adopted a code of conduct drafted by the Reverend Dr. Leon Sullivan, a civil rights activist who is a minister of Philadelphia's large Zion Baptist Church. The Code was based on these six principles that the corporations affirmed for their plants:[1]

I. Nonsegregation of the races in all eating, comfort, and work facilities.

II. Equal and fair employment practices for all employees.

III. Equal pay for all employees doing equal or comparable work for the same period of time.

IV. Initiation of and development of training programs that will prepare, in substantial numbers, blacks and other nonwhites for supervisory, administrative, clerical, and technical jobs.

V. Increasing the number of blacks and other nonwhites in management and supervisory positions.

VI. Improving the quality of employees' lives outside the work environment in such areas as housing, transportation, schooling, recreation, and health facilities.

> These companies agree to further implement these principles. Where implementation requires a modification of existing South African working conditions, we will seek such modification through appropriate channels.

The code had been approved by the South African government since the principles were to operate within "existing South African working conditions," that is, within South African laws. South African laws requiring separate facilities and South African laws prohibiting blacks from becoming apprentices, for example, would continue to apply where in force.[2] Also, the principle of equal pay for equal work would probably require few changes where blacks and whites did not have equal work.

Caltex, however, was apparently committed to improving the economic position of its workers. It had moved 40 percent of its 742 black workers into refinery jobs formerly held by whites, although most blacks had remained in the lower six job categories (a total of 29 had moved into the top four white-collar and skilled categories).[3] The company had also kept its wages well above the averages determined in studies conducted by the South African University of Port Elizabeth. A basic argument that Texaco and SoCal advanced in favor of remaining in South Africa, then, was that their continued presence in South Africa advanced the economic welfare of blacks.

> Texaco believes that continuation of Caltex's operations in South Africa is in the best interests of Caltex's employees of all races in South Africa. . . . In management's opinion, if Caltex were to withdraw from South Africa in an attempt to achieve political changes in that country, as the proposal directs, . . . such withdrawal would endanger prospects for the future of all Caltex employees in South Africa regardless of race. We are convinced that the resulting dislocation and hardship would fall most

[1]Jack Magarrell, "U.S. Adopts Stand on Apartheid: Backed on Many Campuses," *Chronicle of Higher Education,* March, 12, 1979.

[2]See Herman Nickel, "The Case for Doing Business in South Africa," *Fortune,* June 19, 1968, p. 72.

[3]Investor Responsibility Research Center, *Analysis E Supplement no. 9,* April 7, 1977, p. E 114.

heavily on the nonwhite communities. In this regard, and contrary to the implications of the stockholders' statement, Caltex employment policies include equal pay for equal work and the same level of benefit plans for all employees as well as a continuing and successful program to advance employees to positions of responsibility on the basis of ability, not race. [Statement of Texaco management][4]

It is undeniable that the presence of foreign corporations in South Africa had helped to improve the real earnings of black industrial workers. Between 1970 and 1975, black incomes in Johannesburg rose 118 percent, while between 1975 and 1980 black per capita income was expected to rise 30 percent. In addition, the gap between black and white incomes in South Africa had narrowed. Between 1970 and 1976, the gap in industry narrowed from 1 : 5.8 to 1 : 4.4; in construction from 1 : 6.6 to 1 : 5.2; and in the mining sector from 1 : 19.8 to 1 : 7.7.[5] If the flow of foreign investment came to a halt, however, the South African normal yearly growth rate of 6 percent would drop to about 3 percent and the results would undoubtedly hit blacks the hardest.[6] Unemployment would rise (American companies employ 60,000 blacks), and whatever benefits blacks had gained would be lost.

Tim Smith and the Interfaith stockholders were aware of these facts. The basic issue for them, however, was not whether Caltex adhered to the six Sullivan principles or whether its presence in South Africa improved the economic position of blacks:

> The issue in South Africa at this time is black political power; it is not slightly higher wages or better benefits or training programs, unless these lead to basic social change. As one South African church leader put it, "These [six] principles attempt to polish my chains and make them more comfortable. I want to cut my chains and cast them away." . . . We must look not just at wages but at the transfer of technology, the taxes paid to South Africa, the effect of U.S. foreign policy, and the provision of strategic products to the racist government. If these criteria become part of the "principles" of U.S. investors, it should be clear that on balance many of the corporations strengthen and support white minority rule. This form of support should be challenged, and American economic complicity in apartheid ended. [Statement of Tim Smith][7]

In short, the issue was one of human rights. The white South African government was committed to denying blacks their basic rights, and the continued presence of American companies supported this system of white rule.

> Nonwhites in South Africa are rightless persons in the land of their birth. . . . [The black African] has no rights in "white areas." He cannot vote, cannot own land, and

---

[4]*Texaco Proxy Statement*, 1977, item 3.

[5]Nickel, "Doing Business in South Africa," p. 64.

[6]*Ibid.*, p. 63.

[7]Timothy Smith, "Whitewash for Apartheid from Twelve U.S. Firms," *Business and Society Review*, Summer 1977, pp. 59, 60.

may not have his family with him unless he has government permission. . . . The two major black political parties have been banned and hundreds of persons detained for political offenses . . . strikes by Africans are illegal, and meaningful collective bargaining is outlawed . . . by investing in South Africa, American companies inevitably strengthen the status quo of [this] white supremacy. . . . The leasing of a computer, the establishment of a new plant, the selling of supplies to the military—all have political overtones. . . . And among the country's white community, the overriding goal of politics is maintenance of white control. In the words of Prime Minister John Vorster during the 1970 election campaign: "We are building a nation for whites only. Black people are entitled to political rights but only over their own people—not my people." [Statement of Tim Smith][8]

There was no doubt that the continuing operations of Caltex provided some economic support for the South African government. South African law required oil refineries in South Africa to set aside a percentage of their oil for government purchase. In 1975, about 7 percent of Caltex's oil sales went to the government of South Africa. As a whole, the South African economy relied on oil for 25 percent of its energy needs. Moreover, Caltex represented almost 11 percent of the total U.S. investment in South Africa. If Caltex closed down its operations in South Africa, this would certainly have had great impact on the economy especially if other companies then lost confidence in the South African economy and subsequently also withdrew from South Africa. Finally, Caltex also supported the South African government through corporate taxes.

QUESTIONS

1. In your judgment, are the possible utilitarian benefits of building the Caltex plant more important than the possible violations of moral rights and of justice that may be involved? Justify your answer fully by identifying the possible benefits and the possible violations of rights and justice that you believe may be associated with the building of the plant, and explaining which you think are more important.

2. If you were a stockholder in Texaco or Standard Oil, how do you think you ought to vote on the stockholders' resolution of the Interfaith Center? Justify your answer fully.

3. What kind of response should the managements of Texaco and SoCal make to the Interfaith Center?

4. In your judgment, does the management of a company have any responsibilities (i.e., duties) beyond ensuring a high return for its stockholders? Should the management of a company look primarily to the law and to the rate of return on its investment as the ultimate criteria for deciding what investments it should make? Why or why not?

[8]Timothy Smith, "South Africa: The Churches vs. the Corporations," *Business and Society Review*, 1971, pp. 54, 55, 56.

THE SMOKING CONTROVERSY: FACT VERSUS VALUE

The tobacco industry has been a major employer in the United States since the founding of the country. It has most always been a prosperous industry, but in recent years uncertainty has hit the markets of this once thriving industry. Changing market trends have led to a decline in the sales of tobacco products. Total cigarette sales decreased by about 6 percent in 1983—nearly forty billion smokes—and another 10.2 percent the following year. This trend continued during the first half of 1985 with sales off 8.7 percent.[1]

The factors behind this declining market have to do with changing consumer tastes, health concerns, and demographics. People are learning about the health hazards of smoking and are becoming more aware of the health problems that smoking can cause. The American public today is more health conscious than in previous years, and people are going to greater lengths to improve the general quality of their lives. Increased restrictions on where smokers can practice their habit also contribute to the decline in tobacco sales. The demand for cigarettes might decline still further as the male population ages and employment shifts more toward the service sector.[2]

THE HEALTH ISSUE

The health issue regarding cigarette smoking began to be raised as early as 1953, when findings were presented at the annual meeting of the American Dental Society suggesting a connection between cigarette smoking and lung cancer. In 1954 *Reader's Digest* published an influential article based on medical research that linked smoking with lung disease. In response to these medical reports, which were critical of cigarette smoking and its relationship to lung cancer and other diseases, expenditures for cigarette advertising steadily increased, making cigarettes one of the most heavily advertised products in the late 1950s and early 1960s. Public attitudes toward smoking, however, were changing, with the result that in 1966 Congress passed a law requiring that a health warning be placed on all cigarette packages. Since then, not only has government become more active but so have private citizen

---

[1]John Merwin, "Tobacco," *Forbes,* January 2, 1984, p. 222. See also "U.S. Market for Smoking Tobacco Declines," *Tabak Journal International,* December 1985, p. 463.

[2]In 1986 the General Services Administration announced plans to restrict smoking in 6800 federal office buildings. Smoking would be prohibited in general office space, lobbies, corridors, conference rooms, libraries, and restrooms. Buildings that would be affected house more than half the 2.8 million civilian employees of the federal government. Peter Hecht, "Federal Offices to Limit Smoking," *Dallas Times Herald,* May 5, 1986, p. A1.

groups in support of increased legislation restricting smoking and the tobacco industry.

The annual mortality rate from cigarette smoking in the United States has been estimated to exceed 350,000 lives per year. These deaths are nearly equivalent to the number of American lives lost during World War II and are in excess of the combined losses during World War I, the Korean War, and the Vietnam War. An estimated 30 percent of all annual deaths from coronary heart disease and cancer are attributable to cigarette smoking. This figure does not take into account the estimated 9000 deaths due to oral cancer. Chronic obstructive lung diseases account annually for an additional 62,000 smoking-related deaths.[3] Thus, smoking has been universally condemned by many authoritative medical groups and medical officers who work for the government as a leading cause of death and a major public health problem in developed countries around the world.[4] The surgeon general of the U.S., Dr. Everett Koop, has stated:

> We can say again today, with greater certainty than ever, that cigarettes are the most important individual health risk in this country, responsible for more premature death and disability than any other known agent.[5]

Death rates among smokers are uniformly above those of nonsmokers regardless of sex or age at the time of death. For smokers between the ages of forty-five and fifty-four, the excess mortality rate is proportionately greater than at younger or older ages. A smoker doubles his or her risk of dying before the age of sixty-five.[6] Smokers of low-tar and low-nicotine cigarettes have lower mortality rates than smokers of medium- or high-tar and nicotine cigarettes. However, the death rate among smokers of low-tar and low-nicotine cigarettes is still 52 percent higher than for nonsmokers.[7] It has been estimated that an average of five and one-half minutes of life is lost for each cigarette smoked. This translates into an average reduction in life expectancy of five to eight years for cigarette smokers.[8] Dr. John Holbrook of the University of Utah Medical Center says, "When you light up, it's like exposing your whole body to a miniature chemical factory." The temperature within the glowing tip of a cigarette soars to 1800 degrees Fahrenheit, which produces an estimated four thousand chemical reactions between the paper and tobacco.[9]

---

[3]Jonathan E. Fielding, "Smoking: Health Effects and Control," *New England Journal of Medicine* 313, no. 8 (August 1985), 491.

[4]American Cancer Society, *Dangers of Smoking, Benefits of Quitting and Relative Risks of Reduced Exposure,* rev. ed. (New York: American Cancer Society, 1980), p. 5.

[5]Irvin Molotsky, "Congress Votes Stiffer Warnings of Tobacco Risk," *New York Times,* September 27, 1984, p. A1. Copyright © 1984 by The New York Times Company. Reprinted by permission.

[6]*Controlling the Smoking Epidemic,* Report of the WHO Expert Committee on Smoking Control, Technical Report Series 636 (World Health Organization: Geneva, 1979), p. 9.

[7]American Cancer Society, *Dangers of Smoking,* p. 11.

[8]Field, "Smoking," p. 491.

[9]David Holzman, "Where the Smoke Goes," *Washington Post,* March 20, 1985, p. 10.

I think historians will marvel at the fact that in the last few decades we have been panicking over the alleged health effects of things like DDT, aldrin, dieldrin, ethylene dibromide, nitrite in cured meat, saccharin, cyclamates, the asbestos in hair dryers, the chemicals in hair dyes. Yet we seem to tolerate a product which kills hundreds of thousands of us every year. No, we just don't tolerate it, we subsidize it and we advertise it and we promote it.

Source: Remarks by Dr. Elizabeth M. Whelan, A Symposium: Doctors and Smoking, "The Cigarette Century," *New York Times,* April 20, 1986, p. E8. Copyright © 1986 by the New York Times Company. Reprinted by permission.

Cigarette smoking has also been called the greatest threat to the health of American women. Smoking has been changing, it is claimed, from a man's to a woman's preserve, as it is estimated that more women than men will be smokers in about five years if present trends continue. In 1985 the American Cancer Society estimated that lung cancer killed more women than breast cancer, marking the first wave in what was called a rising tide of formerly "male" diseases among female smokers. The impact of this trend could be so severe, some demographers predict, that the edge in lifespan that women have had, which has been about eight years in their favor, will disappear because of women's smoking patterns.[10]

The response of the tobacco industry to these claims of increased mortality rates and incidence of disease is perhaps best represented by Walker Merryman, vice-president of the Tobacco Institute, who claims that the health studies relative to smoking aren't conclusive. The institute questions the statistical correlation between cigarettes and diseases and claims that nobody has clearly shown a cause-and-effect relationship between smoking and lung cancer. If smoking causes cancer, why do nonsmokers get it? he asks, and furthermore why don't all smokers get it if there is a clear cause-and-effect relationship? Merryman claims that studies done by the institute show that 90 percent of the heaviest smokers don't get lung cancer.[11]

Ann Bowder, assistant to the president of the Tobacco Institute, reports that the industry has provided $120 million in grants over the years for research through its Council on Tobacco Research. She also questions whether statistical studies show a causal relationship. She calls such studies "helpful, useful, and necessary" but adds that these studies show a correlation between smoking and disease but do not establish a causal connection. "If there were information beyond a shadow of doubt that the industry would have no doubts about—if they were able to induce lung cancer in an animal through the inhalation of tobacco smoke—that would put us out of business overnight."[12]

[10]"Smoking Called Biggest Health Threat to Women," *Dallas Times Herald,* November 11, 1985, p. A1.

[11]Bella Stumbo, "Where There's Smoke: On the Front Line with the Tobacco Lobby," *Los Angeles Times Magazine,* August 24, 1986, p. 14.

[12]"Mass Tort Litigation Predicted: Legal Attack on Tobacco Flares," *American Medical News,* September 20, 1985, p. 30.

Robert Stapf, the institute's leading media spokesperson, calls the antismoking crusaders a bunch of hypocrites who talk out of both sides of their mouths. They say that they want only to educate people about the risks of smoking, yet they refuse to look at the evidence objectively. Stapf claims that the antismoking advocates are out to scare people and make smoking so socially unacceptable that informed adults won't have a right to make their own choice because of laws and policies that restrict or ban smoking outright. People's right to a choice ought to be respected, whether they are nonsmokers or smokers.[13]

PASSIVE SMOKING

Much of the public's attention in recent years has been focused on the effects of passive smoking on human beings. Involuntary or passive smoking can be defined as the exposure of nonsmokers to tobacco-combustion products in the indoor environment. James L. Repace, a physicist at the Environmental Protection Agency, and Alfred A. Lowrey, a chemist at the Naval Research Laboratory in Washington, D.C., reviewed fourteen epidemiologic studies and reported that all but one study showed evidence of an elevated risk of lung cancer among nonsmokers exposed to cigarette smoke. Repace estimated that depending on the level of smoke one is exposed to, "there may be between five hundred and five thousand deaths each year from this disease [lung cancer] among nonsmokers thirty-five or more years of age, simply because they were exposed to side stream tobacco smoke."[14]

A University of Massachusetts researcher, Dr. S. Katherine Hammond, reported that "a filter cigarette will deliver less nicotine to the smoker but not to those present. Filter cigarettes dilute the smoke inhaled by the smoker, but emit the same ash and particles of a traditional cigarette into the surrounding air."[15] Repace concludes that current efforts to eliminate smoking in public places is justified owing to the estimated magnitude of the risk from passive smoke. The main targets for antismoking laws are schools, hospitals, theaters, convention halls, and public places where people have to stand and wait.

Joseph Califano, former secretary of the Health and Human Services Department, stated that studies show that five thousand Americans die each year because of second-hand smoke. A Japanese report concluded that nonsmoking wives of heavy smokers had an 80 percent higher risk of lung cancer than women married to nonsmokers. Other studies have associated involuntary smoking with pneumonia, asthma, bronchitis, and heart disease.[16] In 1986 a special committee of the National Research Council of the National Academy of Sciences reviewed the available scientific studies and concluded that nonsmokers incur considerable health risks

[13]Stumbo, "Where There's Smoke," pp. 12–13.

[14]"Effects of 'Passive Smoking' Lead Nonsmokers to Step Up Campaign," *Journal of the American Medical Association* 253, no. 20 (May 1985), 2937.

[15]Gayle Young, "Nicotine a Problem in Passive Smoking," *United Press International,* April 14, 1986.

[16]"Restrict Smoking in Public Places?" *U.S. News and World Report,* July 21, 1986, p. 65.

from passive smoking. The committee did not make any recommendations on whether smoking should be limited in public places or workplaces, stating that its charge was only to evaluate the scientific data available on passive smoking.[17]

Because of the concern with passive smoking, forty states have passed laws restricting smoking in public places. Thirty-three prohibit smoking in trains, buses, streetcars, or subways, and seventeen forbid it in offices and other workplaces. There are also about eight hundred local ordinances against the use of tobacco. These vary widely across the country. For example, in Cambridge, Massachusetts, smoking has been banned in just about all public buildings.[18] In Austin, Texas, every company is required to have a written policy on smoking, and if there is a dispute, the rights of the nonsmoker prevail. Every week seems to bring new rules and regulations.

SMOKING IN THE WORKPLACE

Smoking in the workplace is also an issue of recent concern because of the passive smoking issue. Proponents of a smoke-free workplace argue that restrictions on smoking will save lives and money by reducing absenteeism, health insurance costs, property maintenance, and legal liability. The problem for employers is one of balancing the rights of smokers and nonsmokers and the responsibility of the employer to provide a healthy work environment. This is not an easy problem to solve, as many employers are discovering, but more and more companies are dealing with it in some fashion. A poll taken by the Administrative Management Society in 1986 found that 42 percent of the firms surveyed had some kind of smoking policy, up from only 16 percent at the beginning of the decade.[19]

Many companies have designated smoking areas for their employees, which would seem on the surface to be a reasonable solution to the problem. But some companies have found the cost of doing this was too expensive, and so they have banned smoking entirely. For example, in 1985 Pacific Northwest Bell, which employs about fifteen thousand people some 25 percent of whom are smokers, became one of the largest public employers to ban smoking in any of its facilities. A spokesperson for the company said that employees "have to go outside if they want to smoke," a prospect that was admitted to be unpleasant because it rains so often in that part of the country.[20] Robert E. Mercer, chairman of Goodyear Tire and Rubber Company, has predicted that "we'll get to the point where nonsmoking is a condition of employment."[21]

Indeed, USG Acoustical Products Company did just that, by announcing that employees working in its plants must give up their smoking, even at home, or lose

[17]Alan L. Otten, "Passive Smoking Heightens Health Risks for Nonsmokers, a Federal Study Says," *Wall Street Journal,* November 17, 1986, p. 68.

[18]"Where There's Smoke," *Time,* February 23, 1987, p. 22.

[19]Ibid., p. 23.

[20]Jube Shiver, Jr., "Smoking: A Burning Work Issue," *Los Angeles Times,* November 21, 1985, p. 1.

[21]"A Burning Issue on the Job and Off," *Newsweek,* January 13, 1986, p. 9.

their employment. Mineral fibers used in the production of acoustical tiles were believed to be especially hazardous to smokers. The company planned to conduct lung tests to make sure workers were complying with the ban, and those who didn't quit smoking would be fired. This policy affected about two thousand workers in eight states, and it was the first time a company attempted to regulate smoking off the job. Employees were given the opportunity to enroll in a company-sponsored program to help them quit smoking or could elect to enroll in a program of their own choosing at company expense.[22] Later, under pressure from various groups concerned about this invasion of privacy and lack of respect for worker's rights, the company backed off and announced that the employees who didn't quit smoking would not necessarily be fired but that each situation of this sort would be reviewed on a case-by-case basis.[23]

Smoking is also becoming more hazardous to careers in business. Instead of being a socially acceptable practice, smoking is increasingly seen as a character defect indicating weakness and lack of self-discipline. Thus, in some companies smoking is becoming an impediment to the climb up the corporate ladder.[24] In other cases, job seekers are finding that smoking can prevent them from getting work. Classified newspaper advertisements sometimes specify that employers are looking for nonsmokers only, while in other situations, one of the first questions asked of job applicants is whether they smoke.[25]

Employers justify these actions because they believe tobacco users take too many sick days and raise insurance premiums. Employees who smoke cost too much in health-care benefits, lost productivity, and office maintenance. Companies are revising their definition of work performed to include not only how well individuals perform their jobs but whether they are good corporate citizens. The opponents of this practice believe that it results in discrimination against smokers and will, no doubt, lead to lawsuits. Thus far, however, employers have had wide latitude to regulate company policy with regard to smoking. The federal courts have focused their efforts on employment discrimination based on race and sex and have not had occasion to establish a firm legal framework with regard to the smoking issue.[26]

ADVERTISING

The Federal Trade Commission estimated that spending for cigarette advertising in 1980 reached $1.24 billion, making cigarettes one of the most heavily advertised and promoted products in the world.[27] People who are against smoking argue that

[22]Mark Weaver and Nora Zamichow, "Company Tells Smokers: Quit or Be Fired," *Dallas Times Herald,* January 21, 1987, p. A1.

[23]"Company to Relax Plan That Would Ban Smokers," *Dallas Times Herald,* January 28, 1987, p. A3.

[24]Alix M. Freedman, "Harmful Habit: Cigarette Smoking Is Growing Hazardous to Careers in Business," *Wall Street Journal,* April 23, 1987, p. 1.

[25]"Thou Shalt Not Smoke," *Time,* May 18, 1987, p. 59.

[26]Shiver, "Burning Work Issue," p. 1.

[27]"Skimming Cream from the Crop," *Advertising Age,* January 31, 1983, p. M11.

for over sixty years cigarette firms have used unfounded health claims to encourage people to smoke regardless of the risk or harm involved. Misleading ads were placed as far back as 1929 in some of the leading publications. One Luckies ad, for example, showed a fist labeled "American intelligence: breaking the chain of ignorance" and promised "No throat irritation—no cough" to smokers of Lucky Strike cigarettes. In later years smokers were urged to protect the delicate tissues in their throat by using Luckies. Then, as evidence began to mount linking smoking with disease, cigarette makers used medical themes to promote smoking. American brands claimed that 20,679 physicians said Luckies were less irritating to the throat. R. J. Reynolds responded by claiming that "More doctors smoke Camels than any other cigarette!"[28]

One of the most deceptive cigarette advertising campaigns occurred with the introduction of Kent cigarettes in 1952. It was claimed that these cigarettes had less tar and nicotine than most competing brands and provided "the greatest health protection in cigarette history." The levels of tar and nicotine were so low that addicted smokers complained that smoking Kents was like "smoking through a mattress." By 1955, however, Kent cigarettes had quadrupled in nicotine content and increased sixfold in tar delivery. The public was not informed about this change and was deceived into believing they were using a "safe" cigarette.[29]

Some believe that the advertising of cigarettes today remains deceptive but in a more subtle manner. Advertising still is believed to communicate the message to the public that it is reasonably safe to smoke. The industry has conducted major publicity campaigns to create doubt in the public mind about the relationship between smoking and disease. One report accused the industry of adopting a strategy of quoting scientists out of context and selectively citing evidence to make it appear that there was a controversy within the scientific community over the effects of smoking, where none really existed.[30]

Because ads may be having a diminishing effect on men, they have been increasingly targeted at young women, projecting smoking as liberating and glamorous. Nonsmokers argue that every freedom, including freedom of speech, entails some responsibility to warn people about the possible dangers of using their product. The industry cannot think just about itself but also needs to consider the health risks and possible deaths associated with smoking.[31]

Since 1971 there has been a ban on the advertising of cigarettes on radio and television. Antismoking groups want a ban on all forms of cigarette and tobacco advertising. In 1986 a bill was introduced into Congress that would have banned all advertising and promotion of tobacco products, including newspaper and magazine ads, athletic sponsorships, billboards, posters, and matchbook covers. The measure would have covered cigarettes, cigars, pipe tobacco, snuff and chewing tobacco.

[28]Joe B. Tye, "Cigarette Ads Reveal a History of Deceit," *Wall Street Journal,* August 5, 1986, p. 26.

[29]Ibid.

[30]Joe B. Tye, "Cigarette Marketing: Ethical Conservatism or Corporate Violence?" *New York State Journal of Medicine,* July 1985, p. 324.

[31]Tye, "Cigarette Ads," p. 26.

Promotional activities would have been prohibited, from the manufacturer down to the retailer.[32] This bill did not pass. Previously, the American Medical Association had called for a ban on the advertising and promotion of cigarettes and smokeless tobacco. Its 371-member policy-making body had voted almost unanimously to back such a sweeping prohibition of cigarette advertising because the health risks were believed to be so great.[33] The AMA also asked for increased educational efforts to attain the goal of a "smoke-free society by the year 2000" and for enlarging that goal to aim for a completely tobacco-free society.[34]

The industry believes that there is no real evidence to support the claim that advertising of tobacco products leads to further consumption. They claim that advertising is not used to entice nonsmokers into smoking but is used to promote brand loyalty within the existing market and to get people to switch brands, not to start smoking.[35] Cigarette makers like to argue that the advertising issue is one of free speech. Any attempt to restrict their efforts to promote smoking is portrayed as a violation of their First Amendment rights. The tobacco industry believes that it has the right, like any other manufacturer, to advertise its product.[36]

The American Newspaper Publisher's Association and the Magazine Publishers Association have supported this position with the following statement: "Products that can be legally sold in our society are entitled to be advertised; if it is legal to sell a product, it should be legal to advertise it. This 'commercial speech' is constitutionally protected."[37] The American Advertising Federation has also opposed the suggested ban on all cigarette advertising, stating that "the Federation traditionally has been opposed to all attempts to restrict the freedom to advertise legal products. The AMA resolution is misguided and ill-advised in terms of public policy."[38] Barry W. Lynn, Legislative Council for the American Civil Liberties Union, commented on the AMA resolution as follows:

> The American Civil Liberties Union believes that the First Amendment does not permit a prohibition on truthful advertising of products which may lawfully be distributed and sold. Thus, we will oppose new efforts to expand the prohibitions on tobacco advertising to billboards or to newspapers and magazines, while supporting

---

[32]"Law Introduced to Forbid Ads for Tobacco Products," *Dallas Times Herald,* June 10, 1986, p. A4.

[33]"Setting Off the Smoke Alarm," *Time,* December 23, 1985, p. 56.

[34]"AMA Calls for Ban on Tobacco Products Ads," *Dallas Times Herald,* December 11, 1985, p. A1.

[35]"Setting Off the Smoke Alarm," p. 56.

[36]The Supreme Court issued a ruling in 1986 that seems to support the AMA position that a ban on cigarette advertising is constitutional. In a 5–4 ruling, the court upheld a Puerto Rico ban on gambling advertisements stating that such a ban does not violate the First Amendment protections for commercial speech. The majority opinion stated that states may ban advertising of products and services that are legal to sell, so long as the legislature also has the power to ban their sale outright. See *"Supreme Court: Ad ban does not violate First Amendment speech protections,"* *American Medical News,* July 18, 1986, pp. 2,34.

[37]"AMA Calls for a Ban," p. A1.

[38]"AAF President Opposes AMA Call for Cigarette Ad Ban," American Advertising Federation Press Release, December 10, 1985.

requirements for including warnings about the dangers of smoking. There is not sufficient proof of the claims that eliminating advertising will significantly decrease smoking to meet the standard set by the Supreme Court for limiting commercial speech. Eliminating much of the speech of the tobacco industry from the public arena is no way to have a fair, robust debate on smoking in our society.[39]

The industry also opposes using the words *addictive* and *death* in warning labels on cigarette packages, claiming that evidence is lacking to support the inclusion of those terms. Cigarette makers have fought against the use of the word *addictive* in particular because of its legal implications. By arguing that smoking is not addictive and that smokers have a free choice to quit at any time, the tobacco industry has managed to win every lawsuit brought against it thus far. They have successfully argued that people smoke voluntarily and are thus responsible for any injury to their health that may result.[40]

In December of 1985 a jury ruled in favor of R. J. Reynolds Company in a $1 million product-liability suit. The suit was brought by the family of John Galbraith, who had died in 1982 from heart and lung ailments after smoking for fifty years. The jury was not convinced that Galbraith had been addicted to cigarettes or that he had died of tobacco-caused disease.[41] In April of 1986 the U.S. Court of Appeals for the Third Circuit in Philadelphia said that the federally mandated health warning printed on cigarette packages protects the industry from claims that it failed to warn smokers adequately that cigarettes are dangerous. The court also denied the claim that advertising had the effect of negating this warning. This decision overturned a lower court ruling in a case filed by the estate of Rose Cipollone, who died at the age of fifty-eight from lung cancer allegedly caused by smoking.[42] The Supreme Court allowed this ruling to stand without comment.[43]

These victories were important for the tobacco industry, but the industry will have to defend itself in dozens of similar cases. Even a single verdict against one of the tobacco companies could trigger thousands of other lawsuits seeking compensation for smoking-related deaths or diseases. Because of this threat tobacco companies have been strengthening their defenses, hiring the best law firms in the country to represent them and retaining psychologists, economists, physicians, and medical researchers to testify at trials. The cost of all this effort is unknown, but lawyers fees for only one trial were $3 million.[44]

[39]"ACLU Opposes Tobacco Advertising Ban," American Civil Liberties Union Press Release, December 10, 1985.

[40]M. F. Goldsmith, "Tobacco-Addiction Death Link Shown but Labels Don't Tell It," *Journal of the American Medical Association,* February 1986, pp. 997–98.

[41]"A Jury Takes Tobacco Companies off the Hook—for Now," *Business Week,* January 13, 1986, p. 36.

[42]Ed Bean, "Cigarette-Pack Warnings Protect Firms in Liability Suits, Appeals Court Rules," *Wall Street Journal,* April 10, 1986, p. 2.

[43]"High Court: Warning Labels Cut Tobacco Firms' Liability," *Dallas Times Herald,* January 13, 1987, p. A1.

[44]Patricia Bellew Gray, "Legal Warfare: Tobacco Firms Defend Smoker Liability Suits with Heavy Artillery," *Wall Street Journal,* April 29, 1987, p. 1.

Plaintiffs involved in lawsuits against the tobacco companies have claimed that the warning labels did not adequately inform them concerning the dangers or risks of contracting particular diseases by smoking. They also claim that industry advertisements directly challenge or criticize health warnings, encouraging smokers to disregard any warnings of health risks. These arguments are central to the product-liability cases still pending.

A three-judge panel of the U.S. Third Circuit Court of Appeals determined that tobacco companies are not obliged to issue health warnings that go beyond those required by the U.S. Cigarette Labeling and Advertising Act. The 1966 federal cigarette-labeling law preempts any state law tort claims that "challenge either the adequacy of the warning or the propriety of a party's actions with respect to the advertising and promotion of cigarettes."[45] In October of 1985, a new law went into effect requiring four rotating health warnings. Representative Albert Gore, Jr., (D. Tenn) called this legislation a true compromise between "keeping the essential elements of a comprehensive smoking education program while recognizing the legitimate concerns of the tobacco industry."[46] The new warnings specifically express a relationship between cigarette smoking and lung cancer, heart disease and emphysema and warn pregnant women that smoking might result in fetal injury and premature birth.[47]

FIGURE 1   Four Rotating Health Warnings

SURGEON GENERAL'S WARNING: Smoking Causes Lung Cancer, Heart Disease, Emphysema, And May Complicate Pregnancy.	SURGEON GENERAL'S WARNING: Cigarette Smoke Contains Carbon Monoxide.
SURGEON GENERAL'S WARNING: Quitting Smoking Now Greatly Reduces Serious Risks to Your Health.	SURGEON GENERAL'S WARNING: Smoking By Pregnant Women May Result in Fetal Injury, Premature Birth, And Low Birth Weight.

Legislative proposals have also attacked the current tax provisions that allow for deductibility for advertising and promotion of tobacco products. In 1986 such legislation was introduced in Congress by Senator Bill Bradley (D.-N.J.) and Representative Pete Stark (D.-Calif.). Senator Bradley contended that the tobacco industry spent about $2 billion annually on advertising and that the proposed law would add approximately $2.3 billion over the next three years to federal revenues.

[45]John Riley, "Smoking Suits Dealt a Setback," *National Law Journal,* April 21, 1986, p. 45. See also Kathleen Clute, "Cigarette Health Warnings Protect Tobacco Companies," United Press International, April 11, 1986.

[46]"4 Cig Warnings Backed," *New York Times,* May 18, 1984, p. A10.

[47]Molotsky, "Congress Votes Stiffer Warnings," p. A1.

Bradley said, "This is not a freedom of speech question. Tobacco companies can advertise all they want. They just aren't going to get my subsidy."[48]

ECONOMIC IMPACTS

The core sectors in the tobacco industry employed more than 414,000 persons during 1983 and paid total compensation of $6.72 billion to these employees. Supplier industries employed about 296,000 workers and paid out almost $7 4 billion in compensation. Combined, these industries employed 710,000 workers and accounted for $31.5 billion of gross national product. Another 1.59 million were employed to produce goods and services in all business sectors to meet the consumption demands of workers and their families who received income from the tobacco industry. This employment accounted for another $50.6 billion of gross national product.[49]

In 1979 alone Americans spent $21.3 billion for tobacco products, which generated a contribution of $57.6 billion to the gross national product. Directly and indirectly, tobacco accounts for 2.5 percent of all employment in the private sector. Tobacco also generates $22 billion in taxes for state and federal governments.[50] Any major decline in the tobacco industry would obviously affect the financial fortunes of a great number of people. Many of the people now employed in this industry might be left without a job, and thus the unemployment rate in the country as a whole would increase. Workers would have to be retrained as it is doubtful if many of the skills necessary to produce tobacco products would be readily transferable to other industries. The entire economy would suffer with the decrease in the gross national product that would result from a decline in the industry.

Advertising expenditures are already being affected. With sales slipping, cigarette companies are abandoning national magazine advertising and replacing it with discount coupons, sponsorship of sports events, point-of-sale displays, and more sharply focused promotional devices. It was estimated that at the end of 1986 $50 million in advertising revenue, or 12 percent of 1985's $434 million advertising budget, had been drained from the country's major magazines. This drop was on top of a 12 percent decline in spending in 1985.[51] Cigarette advertising on billboards also fell 7 percent in 1986 to $349.4 million, and even bigger cutbacks were made for 1987.[52]

---

[48]Robert Doherty, "Attack on Tax Deduction for Tobacco Advertising," United Press International, February 20, 1986.

[49]"The Economic Impact of the Tobacco Industry in the United States Economy in 1983," in *Chase Econometrics Letter: Business Trends Forecaster,* vol. 1 (Philadelphia: Chase Econometrics, 1983), p. 179.

[50]"Skimming Cream from the Crop," *Advertising Age,* January 31, 1983, p. M-11.

[51]"Good-bye to the Marlboro Man," *Forbes,* June 2, 1986, pp. 207–8.

[52]Ronald Alsop, "Billboard Firms Lure New Ads as Tobacco, Liquor Sales Slide," *Wall Street Journal,* May 7, 1987, p. 29.

On the other hand, nonsmokers are questioning the economic burden they are being forced to bear to provide medical care for smoking-induced illnesses. Legal restrictions on smoking are following these changes in attitude. Indirect losses from reduced productivity, earnings lost from excess morbidity, and disability and premature deaths are estimated to cost the country $37 billion annually.[53] The U.S. Public Health Service has concluded that within a single year cigarette smoking has caused in excess of 81 million person days lost from work and 145 million person days spent ill in bed. Twenty-five percent of the disability days for men between the ages of forty-five and sixty-four are associated with cigarette smoking. Women who smoke reportedly spend 17 percent more ill days in bed than women who have never smoked.[54]

> Smoking results in a considerably increased morbidity rate, with its consequent loss of working days, absenteeism and excessive demands on medical services, both for primary and for hospital care. The cost to the community of premature death, increased illness, and loss of productive capacity resulting from cigarette smoking is very high in countries where the habit has been common for a long time.[55]

In the United States the per capita cost for smoking-related disease is estimated at $454 annually. The total costs of smoking represent approximately 11 percent of the comparable aggregate costs of all illnesses in the United States. In 1976 total out-of-pocket health-care costs for smoking-related diseases was estimated at $8.2 billion or approximately 8 percent of all U.S. health-care costs.[56] In March 1987 the surgeon general of the U.S., C. Everett Koop, stated that smoking costs the nation $65 billion a year in health care and lost productivity.[57] In February of the same year the American Lung Association stated that smoking costs the nation $30.4 billion a year in lost work and productivity and another $23.3 billion a year in medical care.[58]

PUBLIC-POLICY ISSUES

There are several key value issues involved in this controversy. In a society that values freedom so highly, to what extent should steps be taken to prevent the spread of harmful substances throughout the community? To what extent should individuals be allowed to engage in dangerous self-destructive behavior that entails

[53]Fielding, "Smoking," p. 491.

[54]American Cancer Society, *Dangers of Smoking*, p. 14.

[55]*Controlling the Smoking Epidemic*, WHO, p. 10.

[56]American Cancer Society, *Dangers of Smoking*, p. 62.

[57]Sharon Eglebor, "Koop: Smoking Costs Too High," *Dallas Times Herald*, March 28, 1987, p. A1.

[58]"Cigarette Smoking Kills 350,000 in U.S. a Year, Report Says," *Dallas Times Herald*, February 21, 1987, p. A1.

personal, social, and economic consequences for other people. People's rights are affected by the steps that are taken to deal with this issue. Nonsmokers want a healthier environment free from cigarette smoke. They want specific areas designated for them, where smoking is prohibited. Smokers, on the other hand, resent having their freedom restricted in this manner and feel it is unfair and unjust to be allowed to smoke in only designated areas of public places. Smokers' preferences are being ignored, and smokers are now considered, in a manner of speaking, to be second-class citizens. Their rights are no longer considered so important.

Types of legislative efforts that have been suggested and, in some cases implemented, to control smoking include the following: (1) control of advertising and sales promotion of cigarettes and other tobacco products; (2) placing health warnings and tar and nicotine content labels on tobacco products; (3) restricting smoking in public places, including workplaces; and (4) initiating preventive action to discourage smoking by young people, for instance, making it mandatory that high schools educate students on smoking and its dangers. These efforts are aimed at (1) decreasing cigarette consumption; (2) providing a basis for effective educational campaigns on smoking and health, particularly among young people and high-risk groups such as pregnant women; (3) protecting the rights of nonsmokers by allowing them to breath clean air; and (4) establishing nonsmoking as the social norm. Proponents of these measures hope to bring about a healthier society.[59]

Another complaint brought by nonsmokers is that the tobacco industry, which markets one of the most dangerous products sold in the United States, is the only industry that has been sheltered from product liability. It has been suggested that the tobacco industry's failure to warn the public of the dangers that smoking entails is an "unparalleled display of corporate indifference" and exposes the tobacco industry to civil liability.[60] Because of this problem it has been suggested that the tobacco industry be made financially liable to nonsmokers who are injured or killed in cigarette-caused fires in hotels, hospitals, airplanes, and other public places. Health-insurance members also insist that smokers pay a fair share of extra tobacco-related health-care expenses and that smokers make up for the extra costs of Medicare, Medicaid, and veterans' benefits inflicted upon nonsmokers. These measures are expected to act as deterrents for those who are considering smoking, although their effect on teenagers is doubtful.[61]

The federal government began regulating smoking on airplanes in 1973, when the now defunct Civil Aeronautics Board required airlines to provide separate sections for nonsmokers. Ten years later, in 1983, all smoking was banned from small aircraft and cigar and pipe smoking was banned on large commercial flights.

[59]R. Roemer, "Combating the Smoking Epidemic: Why Legislation?" *Proceedings of the Fifth World Conference on Smoking and Health,* vol. 1., W. F. Forbes, R. C. Frecker, and D. Nostbakken, eds. (Winnipeg: Canadian Council on Smoking and Health, 1983), pp. 593–602.

[60]D. W. Garner, "The Legal Implications of Cigarette Smoking," *Proceedings of the Fifth World Conference on Smoking and Health,* vol. 1.

[61]J. F. Banzhaf, "The Socio-Economic Implications of Smoking and the Non-Smokers' Rights Movement," *Proceedings of the Fifth World Conference on Smoking and Health,* vol. 1.

Many are urging that all forms of smoking be banned on all domestic flights.[62] Smoking ordinances have also been established in many other public places, such as hospitals and restaurants, where smoking is allowed only in designated areas. Thirty-eight states now have ordinances against smoking on public transportation and in public places, including schools, hospitals, auditoriums, theaters, and government buildings. Five states and about a dozen cities or counties regulate smoking in the workplace, whether a public or private facility.[63] Smokers do not seem to have any kind of united front to retain these rights.

Philip Morris, the nation's largest cigarette manufacturer, has begun a counterattack against the nonsmokers and other opponents of smoking. It is trying to get those who are against tobacco usage to ease the pressure they are placing on smokers, who are being shunted away from more and more nonsmoking areas and accused of harming other people with their habit. The company argues that if smokers want to enjoy a cigarette, they should be able to do so in peace. It appears to some that the antismoking advocates are making smoking into more of a civil-rights issue than a health issue, and smokers believe the whole issue is getting blown out of proportion. In response, the company publishes a free quarterly magazine that it sends to smokers and has put inserts into cigarette packages urging smokers to rebel against tobacco taxes.[64]

CONCLUSION

The primary factor initiating this confrontation between smokers and nonsmokers was the medical discovery that smoking did indeed entail certain health risks. This information caused a division between those who smoked and those who wanted it eliminated for health reasons. Despite this issue, the tobacco industry continues to maintain a profitable business and to promote the use of cigarettes and other tobacco products, acting as if no serious problem existed. Meanwhile, the antismoking campaign persists and continues to cause problems for the tobacco industry.

The industry uses two main arguments in the fight against the antismoking campaign. The first argument is that everyone has had fair warning about the possible negative health effects of smoking, and the second is that the link to adverse health effects has not been scientifically established. John Strauch, an attorney for R. J. Reynolds, says: "We've got to draw the line somewhere on what we're going to require from people in the way of accountability for their own choices." The industry's first line of defense, he says, is this issue of personal

[62]Laurie McGinley, "Ban on Smoking Sought for Flights by Airlines in the U.S.," *Wall Street Journal,* August 13, 1986, p. 6. See also "AMA Will Urge Ban on Smoking in Planes, Fines for Violations," *Wall Street Journal,* June 26, 1987, p. 9.

[63]"Effects," *JAMA,* p. 2938.

[64]Trish Hall, "Smoking Guns: Philip Morris, Seeking to Turn Tide, Attacks Cigarettes' Opponents," *Wall Street Journal,* February 4, 1986, p. 1. See also "Breathing Fire at the Antismoking Campaign," *Business Week,* August 19, 1985, pp. 55–56; and Robert Bruce Slater, "One Magazine We Can Do Without," *Business and Society Review,* no. 60 (Winter 1987), pp. 45–47.

responsibility.[65] So the battle continues as legal and medical coalitions form to pool information, strategies, theories, and money. There are currently an estimated 125 cases pending against the tobacco industry. A single defeat could lead to an avalanche of costly lawsuits that could swamp the companies in litigation costs even if they won most of them.[66]

> The current round of litigation reflects the growing belief among plaintiffs' lawyers that the time is now right. They cite sweeping changes in product-liability law, important new medical evidence, and, perhaps most significantly, a changing social climate due in no small part to 20 years of denunciations of tobacco by the U.S. surgeon general.[67]

In anticipation of a decline in tobacco sales, major tobacco companies are diversifying. Phillip Morris, marketer of Marlboro, the country's biggest selling cigarette, acquired Miller Brewing Company in 1969. More recently, R. J. Reynolds acquired Nabisco, and Phillip Morris merged with General Foods. These mergers represent diversifications into product areas or lines that have a close fit with the strong consumer marketing required of cigarettes and utilize the same primary distribution channels. These responses by the tobacco industry, however, will not alleviate the pressures of the antismokers. They are more in the nature of defensive strategies designed to help the industry survive in case the tobacco market does collapse at some point.[68]

Advertising has been geared toward people who already smoke, to avoid the accusation of trying to convince nonsmokers, especially young smokers, to start smoking, but this effort will obviously not expand the market. At a time when current users are trying to quit or are finding their use of tobacco severely restricted, tobacco companies will have difficulty in keeping sales up if they are not trying to expand the market and find new uses for their product.

The future of the tobacco industry depends mainly on what the courts will decide in the many product-liability suits filed against major tobacco companies. Many analysts believe that no strong precedent has been set in the cases that have been decided thus far and believe that pending cases in Texas, New Jersey, and Boston will be the crucial tests. The industry's future also depends on how the general public will respond to new research findings of the hazards of smoking and, most important, the hazards of inhaling secondary smoke.

For the time being, however, the tobacco industry is still in good shape. While unit sales dropped about 7 percent from 1982 to 1985, after peaking in 1981, at least three of the nation's six cigarette manufacturers reported record profits in

---

[65]Ed Bean, "Tobacco Industry's Court Victories Fail to Slow Product-Liability Suits, *Wall Street Journal,* January 30, 1986, p. 29.

[66]William P. Barrett, "Smoldering Lawsuits: Smokers Want Tobacco Companies to Pay for Their Illnesses," *Dallas Times Herald,* September 8, 1985, p. A1. See also "Caveat Fumator," *Time,* September 7, 1987, p. 43.

[67]Ibid.

[68]Tobacco Takes a New Road," *Time,* November 18, 1985, pp. 70–71.

1986 because of price increases and cost-cutting measures. The companies have sought acquisitions to lessen their reliance on tobacco while implementing manufacturing efficiencies to boost margins in their core business. Twenty years ago, cigarette-rolling machines were capable of producing twelve hundred cigarettes per minute. Today's new machines have the capability to produce eight thousand cigarettes per minute. Thus, the short-term outlook for the cigarette industry is said to be pretty healthy.[69]

The companies are also benefiting from the increasing popularity of American brands in international markets, where unit volume has increased roughly 5 percent a year.[70] Potential smokers make up more than one-half the world's population. Governments in Third World countries will not be so quick to spend already scarce funds on antismoking campaigns, and they will be ever more reluctant to give up tax revenues from tobacco sales. Cigarette manufacturers are not required to provide warning labels on products exported from the U.S. unless they are going to a U.S. military base.[71]

Nonetheless, the surgeon general predicts that for all its enormous economic power, the cigarette industry will virtually disappear over the next twenty years. The tobacco industry is currently a formidable adversary and is the biggest obstacle to the antismoking campaign in this country. But as per capita cigarette consumption continues to decline, the surgeon general claims that the industry will become less and less formidable with every tomorrow.[72] Thus, the threat of a smoke free society is one that the industry cannot ignore because its very existence is at stake.

QUESTIONS

1. Can you distinguish between facts and values in this case? What are the facts of the situation regarding the health effects of cigarette smoking? How do you account for the differences between the antismoking movement and the tobacco industry regarding the facts about cigarette smoking? Are these differences simply differences in values rather than facts? Are changing values responsible for the plight of the industry?

2. How would you go about establishing the facts about cigarette smoking and its health effects? Is statistical evidence conclusive in showing the relationship between health problems and smoking? What kind of cause-and-effect relationship would be conclusive in proving the facts regarding smoking and health problems such as cancer or lung diseases? Would these facts be acceptable to the Tobacco Institute?

3. Are cigarettes an ethical product? If not, are the people who work in this industry unethical people? If cigarettes are an ethical product, how does

[69]"Tobacco Company Profits Just Won't Quit," *Business Week*, December 22, 1986, pp. 66–67.

[70]Ibid.

[71]American Cancer Society, *Dangers of Smoking*, p. 63.

[72]Eglebor, "Koop," p. A1.

smoking contribute to the welfare of people and promote human fulfillment? Why do people smoke? What does the promotion of smoking say about the values of the industry? What values do the antismoking advocates hold?

4. Would a benefit-cost analysis help in making decisions about the advertising of tobacco products and the banning of smoking in public places? Where would values enter into these calculations? Is benefit-cost analysis a useful decision-making tool in these complex situations? Why or why not?

5. What are the rights of smokers and nonsmokers with regard to the provision of nonsmoking areas or the outright banning of smoking in public places? Are companies that ban smoking in their facilities guilty of discrimination? Are they violating any laws with regard to the rights of smokers? What is the future likely to hold with respect to the question of the rights of smokers versus nonsmokers?

6. Do tobacco companies have the right to advertise their product? Was the banning of such ads from television an unethical action? Why or why not? Should advertising of tobacco products be banned entirely? Is this an issue of free speech, or is it one of responsibility? What ethical criteria should take precedence in this decision?

THE DALKON SHIELD: SELF-INTEREST

BEGINNINGS

On Christmas day in 1967 two longtime friends and their families gathered at the traditional holiday dinner. One of these friends was Dr. Hugh Davis, who was then an assistant professor of medicine at Johns Hopkins University in Baltimore and an expert on birth control. The other friend was a man named Irwin "Win" Lerner, who was an inventor with his own research facility, called Lerner Laboratories, located in Stamford, Connecticut. Lerner had an electrical engineering degree from Oklahoma A&M University.

Among the topics of conversation at the dinner was the research Davis was conducting into intrauterine devices (IUD). An IUD is inserted into a woman's uterus to prevent the development of a fertilized egg and thus the conception of children. IUDs are generally made of plastic and are less than an inch wide, so they can be inserted easily. Most IUDs have a tail several inches long that serves as a signal to an attending physician that the IUD is properly in place. The tail also aids in removal of the IUD from the uterus.

Many experts had hailed the IUD as the cure for the worldwide population explosion because they were relatively easy to use and seemingly very effective. They were unlike birth-control pills in that there was nothing to be taken every day and they did not have to be monitored very frequently. Since the IUD was largely a mechanical device, many people preferred its use to birth-control pills, which contained strong drugs and also became suspect of causing some serious side effects. However, the pregnancy rate—the percent of women using a birth-control method who did become pregnant during the year—was generally much lower for pills than for use of the IUD.

Thus, the IUDs on the market in 1967 were not satisfactory to all doctors. Besides being ineffective in some cases, the IUD ripped the walls of the uterus in some women, causing infection and serious bleeding at irregular intervals. There was also the possibility that the tail of the IUD could act much like a wick, drawing bacteria up from the unsterile vagina to the sterile uterus. This could cause extensive infection of the uterus and surrounding areas. It was believed that this wicking effect could be inhibited by the use of a very thin, single-strand tail, which would utilize the mucus normally present in the cervix to block any ascending bacteria.

Davis had been working at improving the performance of the IUD for several years. In fact, he had applied for a patent on an IUD called the Incon Ring only the year before. But since he was not a manufacturer, he had no way of translating this research into a marketable product. Thus, the relationship with Lerner was a perfect fit for both parties. While Lerner had never worked on devices for bodily insertion, he was an inventor who had the facilities to turn Davis's ideas into a marketplace reality.

By the time the Christmas dinner ended, the two friends had agreed to develop a better IUD for the market. At the end of the following summer, they had already developed a device they called the Dalkon Shield. This name for the device apparently reflected the last names of Davis, Lerner, and a lawyer of Lerner's by the name of Robert Cohn. The Dalkon Shield looked much like a crab with eight extended legs, making it radically different from other IUDs, which were longer and thinner by design. (See Figure 1.) The single-strand tail, which was standard on most IUDs, was replaced by a multifilament tail containing two hundred to four hundred strands surrounded by a nylon sheath that was open at the lower end.[1]

The device was tested on women who were patients at the family-planning clinic that Davis operated at Johns Hopkins Hospital. These tests began in September of 1968. While the tests were being conducted, Davis, Lerner, and Cohn were working out the financial arrangements connected with production and marketing of the device. They eventually formed the Dalkon Corporation in January of 1969, with the sole asset being the Dalkon Shield device. The stock of the new company was split between the three parties with Lerner getting 55 percent, Davis 35 percent, and Cohn 10 percent.[2]

The study Davis was conducting was completed by the summer of 1969, with about 640 women participating. According to Davis, the pregnancy rate for the Dalkon Shield was 1.1 percent, which was as low as or lower than the rate for birth-control pills. The results of this study were written up and submitted to the Ameri-

---

[1]William P. Barrett, "Testing of Dalkon Shield Questioned by Doctors," *Dallas Times Herald*, February 17, 1985, p. A22.

[2]Ibid.

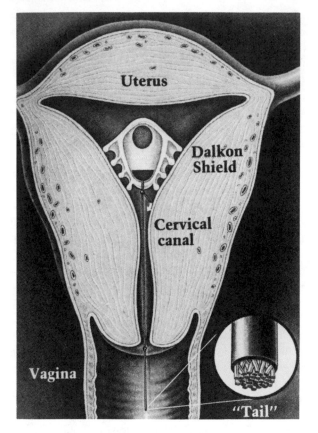

FIGURE 1   The Dalkon Shield   Source: Subrata N. Chakravarty, "Tunnel Vision," *Forbes,* May 21, 1984, p. 218. Reprinted by permission of *Forbes* magazine, May 21, 1984. Copyright © Forbes Inc., 1984.

can Journal of Obstetrics and Gynecology. The article was published in the February 1, 1970, issue under the title "The Shield Intrauterine Device: A Superior Modern Contraceptive." The article carried a great deal of prestige because of Davis's affiliation with Johns Hopkins, but nowhere did the article mention that Davis had a financial interest in the device he was evaluating. Thus, to the uninformed reader it appeared that Davis was conducting an objective study with no possible conflicts of interest that might impair that objectivity.

The timing of the article couldn't have been better as far as its impact was concerned. The nationwide scare about birth-control pills had about peaked with the committee hearing in the United States Senate about the side effects and safety of pills. Davis was called as the lead-off witness at these hearings and proceeded to blast birth-control pills as dangerous and present the IUD as the preferred method for controlling the birth of children. Davis was asked if he had a commercial interest in any IUD, and Davis replied that he did not. When asked about this several years later, Davis explained that he had answered the question negatively because he had not at the time of the hearing received his stock certificates in the Dalkon Corporation.[3]

The Dalkon Corporation formally started marketing the device in March of 1970, but sales were very disappointing. The Dalkon Corporation did not have an established sales organization, with salespeople scattered around the country and around the world, that could promote the device. It did not have the money to mount an extensive advertising campaign. Nor did it have access to medical offices all over the country. Without these ingredients, the Dalkon Shield was headed into oblivion.

ENTER A. H. ROBINS COMPANY

The New Jersey General Practitioner Association held its regular convention in the middle of May 1970 at Host Farms, Pennsylvania. At this convention the medical director of the Dalkon Corporation, who was promoting the Dalkon Shield, drew the attention of a salesman for the A. H. Robins Corporation by the name of John McClure. Robins was a small ($133 million sales) Richmond, Virginia, manufacturer of pharmaceuticals and other products, best known for Sergeant's Flea and Tick collars, Robitussin cough medicine, and Chap Stick lip balm. The salesman contacted his boss, a vice-president at Robins, three days later and forwarded information about the device, including the Davis article that reported the 1.1 percent pregnancy rate for the shield.

This information triggered a great deal of activity at Robins, including in-house meetings about the Dalkon Shield, consultation with outside experts, and a visit to Ohio to watch the insertion of the device. Apparently, the key visit came on June 8, 1970, when the medical director of Robins, Dr. Fred Clark, Jr., traveled to Baltimore to see Davis and review his files. Upon reviewing this information, Clark raised questions about the reported pregnancy rate, stating that data given him for the first fourteen months covered 832 insertions with twenty-six pregnancies, which produced a pregnancy rate of 3.1 percent or higher—three times that of birth-control pills, the IUD's chief competitor.[4]

Clark also noted that Davis and Lerner had made design changes in the Dalkon Shield that made it thinner and more flexible. Thus, the study performed by Davis that claimed a 1.1 percent pregnancy rate applied to a different model. Other questions were raised by Jack Freund, who was vice-president of the medical department. Freund apparently stated that the Davis study was "not long enough" and that he had been told by Lerner that the actual pregnancy rate with a follow-up period increased to 2.3 percent. While Freund lauded the Dalkon Shield for its other characteristics, he did refer to its possible higher pregnancy rate when compared with birth-control pills.[5]

[3]Ibid.
[4]Ibid.
[5]Ibid.

W. Roy Smith, the director of product planning for Robins, wrote on June 10 that he was concerned about marketing "a device not identical in composition to that on which the paper was based." Smith noted that copper had also been added to a later model to improve effectiveness by producing an added drug effect for the device. This statement was later disputed by the company, which argued that copper had been added only to help hold together the plastic material in the shield and not to increase the contraceptive effect. The difference was crucial as at that time the FDA required extensive premarket testing of drugs but not of devices. Thus, if the copper addition was considered to be a drug to promote contraception, it could be subjected to three years of testing before the device could be sold.[6]

Smith was also concerned about the lack of hard data concerning the Dalkon Shield. "We have relatively limited information on the Dalkon Shield in terms of length of usage, overall cases published, etc.," he wrote in a memo, referring to "this relatively limited total case history."[7] Thus, the people in Robins were aware that the Davis study was the only information they had about the effectiveness of the Dalkon Shield and that this study had problems that needed investigation. It was clear that there was some mystery regarding the way the study was completed.

Despite these concerns, the company went ahead and bought the rights to the Dalkon Shield from the Dalkon Corporation on June 12, 1970, barely three weeks from the time they had first heard about the device. Robins paid $750,000 for these rights and agreed to pay Davis, Lerner, and Cohn a total of 10 percent of future royalties. Davis was to be hired as a consultant to Robins at a salary of $20,000 per year. All profits made off the device after June 15 went to Robins. The company immediately drafted plans to begin marketing the device using its own sales force. Production costs were estimated at 36¢ for each device. The cost to doctors was set at $4.35 less discounts for bulk purchases.[8]

PROBLEMS BEGIN

Almost immediately after buying the rights, the company started hearing about problems with the device. The marketing department surveyed doctors who had been using the shield produced by the Dalkon Corporation and reported that some of these doctors were quite displeased. Reactions to the device were found to be varied and inconsistent. Two weeks after they purchased the rights, a company official noted that there might be a problem with the tail, which was reported to have a wicking tendency. Thus, the potential for wicking problems was apparently known by the company early in the summer.

Sometime toward the end of July 1970 the company agreed to make further changes in the product in response to Lerner's recommendations. The width of the device was reduced slightly, and the legs were fattened and rounded. These changes

[6]Ibid.
[7]Ibid.
[8]Ibid.

were not tested before they were marketed and mentioned in promotional material. Robins, which had never manufactured a birth-control device before and had no gynecologist on its staff, apparently concluded that it did not need to test these changes. Robins later claimed it had consulted with experts and talked with enough doctors to satisfy itself that the changes would not be adverse.[9]

So Robins geared up its nationwide sales network for the debut of the Dalkon Shield, even though several company officials expressed concern about the lack of thorough testing to support the effectiveness of the model that was about to be sold in the marketplace. The company engaged in an extensive advertising campaign. A patient brochure that was distributed starting on January 1, 1971, when the national marketing campaign began, stated, "You can relax and enjoy the luxury of a truly superior birth-control method." Thousands of reprints of the Davis study that found a 1.1 percent pregnancy rate were distributed. These reprints bore the all-important Johns Hopkins imprimatur.[10]

Other pregnancy-rate studies, all involving earlier models than the one being sold, were also publicized. One study by Dr. Thad J. Earl reported a startlingly low 0.5 percent rate, but Earl, like Davis, had an undisclosed financial interest in the Dalkon Shield. Another study that reported a 1.1 percent rate was conducted by Dr. Donald Ostergard, a Los Angeles-area physician. A third study was conducted by a Dr. Mary Gabrielson, who computed a 1.9 percent pregnancy rate, which she called comparable to the Davis study. As a result of follow-up studies, however, she revised the rate to 4.3 percent, a figure Robins did not report for several months.[11]

These marketing efforts paid off. The Dalkon Shield captured an impressive 60 percent of the American IUD market in less than a year. Figure 2 shows how sales of the device took off and stayed relatively high for three years despite mounting evidence that the device had serious problems. Because of the questions that were being raised about the safety of birth-control pills, the market was ripe for an alternative method of controlling pregnancies. However, a significant turn of events was about to take place.

Up to this point, concern had focused on the effectiveness of the Dalkon Shield and on whether the limited information that was available about pregnancy rates was accurate and thus could be believed. After the product was introduced, however, questions began to be raised about its safety as well. At least one competing salesman was telling customers that the tail of the Dalkon Shield was multilayered so that the inner core would act as a wick to induce infection into the uterus.

[9]Ibid. In relation to these changes the company made the following statement: "After Robins acquired the patent rights to the Dalkon Shield in June, 1970, the company, at Dr. Hugh Davis' suggestion, made three additional minor changes in the Shield: (1) the tie point for the tailstring at the base of the Shield was strengthened; (2) the standard size Shield was narrowed by two millimeters; and (3) the appendages were rounded or 'tear-dropped.' Each of these improvements was designed to increase tolerance and reduce expulsion. There is no evidence that these changes affected the safety of the Shield or pregnancy or medical removal rates associated with it." See A. H. Robins, "Summary History of the Development and Marketing of the Dalkon Shield," undated, footnote 2, p. 9.

[10]Barrett, "Testing of Dalkon Shield," p. A22.

[11]Ibid.

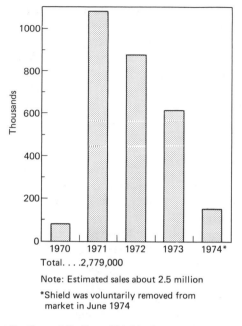

Total. . . .2,779,000

Note: Estimated sales about 2.5 million

*Shield was voluntarily removed from
market in June 1974

FIGURE 2   U.S. Distribution of Dalkon Shield   Source: Bill Barrett, "Testing of Dalkon
Shield Questioned by Doctors," *Dallas Times Herald,* February 17, 1985, p. A22.

Someone else, by the name of Wayne Crowder, was also coming to the same
conclusion. Crowder was a quality-control supervisor at the Chap Stick Company,
which was the wholly owned subsidiary manufacturing the shield.

Crowder conducted a simple experiment by hanging some shields in such a
way that their tails ended in a glass of water. The next day Crowder found that he
could milk water from the end of the tails. He subsequently informed his superior at
Chap Stick about the problem. Crowder suggested a way of sealing the ends in order
to avoid wicking, but this suggestion was rejected by the president of Chap Stick
because it would increase the cost of the product. Crowder was later fired—in
1977—but because of his efforts the tail received closer attention from company
officials. They began to view it as a serious problem and were motivated to actively
search for a tail replacement.[12]

It wasn't long after the Dalkon Shield was first marketed that medical complaints started to arrive at company headquarters. In February of 1971 it was
reported that two Dalkon Shield wearers had developed pelvic inflammatory disease. This infection can, however, be caused by many different things. In June of
that same year a physician's wife in Kentucky who was wearing the device developed pelvic inflammatory disease and required a hysterectomy. A Torrington, Connecticut, doctor reported two infections several months after insertion. A doctor in
Utah reported five pelvic infections by wearers of the Dalkon Shield, three of which

[12]Ibid., p. A23.

were severe enough to require hospitalization. And finally, according to a study conducted by the Maryland Health Department, one out of every fourteen Dalkon Shield patients became infected.[13]

In early 1972, it has been alleged, Robins became aware of another safety problem but did not inform the medical community. Some medical personnel in the company found that the nylon sheath could deteriorate over time from the effect of bodily fluids, and this deterioration made it easier for bacteria to ascend the filaments into the uterus. Robins officials were informed that three baboons had died in a recent animal study using the Dalkon Shield, an unacceptably high figure. Kenneth Moore, the project manager for the shield wrote in reference to this deterioration, "We have a problem. We are desperately searching for a suitable material to replace our currently used nylon string." On March 11, 1971, the Robins research committee recommended that "the string be removed or replaced."[14]

The problems continued. Five doctors who were treating cases of pelvic inflammatory disease suggested that the shield be withdrawn from the market. Meanwhile, more questions continued to be raised about its effectiveness. A doctor in Richmond said that 8.5 percent of his patients who used the shield became pregnant. An army doctor, Russell J. Thompsen, blasted the advertised pregnancy rate studies as "pathetically inadequate" because of the short time period involved. The real pregnancy rate, Thompsen suggested, was closer to 10 percent.[15]

The company responded to these allegations by modifying its advertising to say the pregnancy rate was "approximately" 2 percent but that "in a few isolated studies" higher rates had been reported. Robins also changed its labeling, adding infection to the list of possible side effects. In October 1971 Allen Polon, a project coordinator for Robins, wrote that an eight-page Robins ad, which included the 1.1 percent pregnancy rate found by Davis, was "outdated and . . . no longer valid." He asked that the company stop using the figure. However, the company continued to use the figure for more than a year after this question was raised.[16]

By the end of 1973 the company was aware of the deaths of six women associated with septic or infected abortions. In early 1974 Robins held a septic-abortion conference, consisting of experts in the field, to reach a decision about continued sale of the shield. The company did not share with these experts any of the information it had accumulated about tail wicking. Five of these doctors said use of the Dalkon Shield increased the risk of septic abortion, five said it did not, and two abstained. One of these doctors, Dr. Howard Tatum of the Population Council,

---

[13]Ibid. The company has continued to insist on the safety of the device by making strong statements about medical evidence and conclusions from this evidence. For example, in a report issued by the company, the following statements appear: "By 1970, the medical literature was *unanimous* in its conclusion that not only was there no association between IUD use and pelvic inflammatory disease, but that there was no difference between tailed and non-tailed devices in this regard. . . . Because of the *consensus* in the medical literature that there was no association between IUD use and pelvic inflammatory disease, the interviews concentrated more on other events associated with IUD use, including expulsions, medical removals, and pregnancies." (Italics mine.) See "Summary History," p. 10.

[14]Barrett, "Testing of Dalkon Shield," p. A23.

[15]Ibid.

[16]Ibid., p. A24.

further examined the tail of the shield and notified the FDA about the potential wicking problem.

Pressure against the shield was building. Robins sent a "Dear Doctor" letter on May 8, 1974, in which it publicly warned for the first time of a link between the Dalkon Shield and septic abortion. Robins officials considered taking the shield off the market that same month but were warned by their lead lawyer that such a move would be a "confession of liability" that would cause Robins to lose many of the lawsuits pending against the company at that time. Finally on June 26, 1974, the head of the FDA wrote Robins that "because of its questionable safety" the company should stop selling the device. Two days later, the company announced that it was "voluntarily" withdrawing the product from the market. The company did not, however, issue a formal recall of all shields then in use and stated in a press release that "performance has clearly been satisfactory."[17]

THE CONTINUING BATTLE

The failure to issue a recall would cost the company millions of dollars. Many of the women who later filed lawsuits against the company claimed an injury after 1974 when the company withdrew the product from the market. The announcement about the suspension of sales was not as widely publicized as a formal recall would have been, and as a result, hundreds of thousands of women continued wearing the Dalkon Shield apparently unaware that there was a medical problem. The first Dalkon Shield trial took place in Wichita with a settlement of $85,000 against the company. Several months after this trial the company announced that it would not remarket the product but continued to maintain that the shield was safe and effective when properly used.[18]

Lawsuits continued to be filed against the company. A Denver jury in 1979 awarded $6.8 million to the plaintiff, $6.2 million of it in punitive damages. A jury in Los Angeles in 1980 awarded $600,000 to the plaintiff. Three years later a jury in Miami awarded $2.75 million, subsequently reduced to $1.45 million, $500,000 of it in punitive damages. In 1983 a Minneapolis jury awarded $1.75 million in damages, of which all but $250,000 was punitive damages.[19]

The company was severely criticized for some of their trial tactics, particularly their habit of questioning plaintiffs about their sex lives. The company maintained that its actions were necessary to rule out other possible sources of infection. Roger Tuttle, the chief Dalkon Shield lawyer from 1971 to 1975, later expressed regrets for his role as architect of what he called the company's "hard-nosed, ask-them-lots-of-questions-about-their-sex-life strategy." Tuttle was demoted in 1975 after the company lost its first trial and eventually moved to Oral Roberts College in Tulsa, a Protestant fundamentalist school, where he is a law professor. He ex-

[17]Ibid.
[18]Ibid.
[19]Ibid.

plained that he had displayed a misplaced zeal for his former employer and now saw that a lawyer had a higher obligation to society.[20]

Tuttle also later revealed that in 1975 the company had destroyed documents culled from the files of top corporate officials in the spoiled-products incinerator that the company maintained in the basement of its Richmond headquarters. Tuttle maintained that the purpose of the destruction was to help the company deny that Robins's executives knew about the problems with the pregnancy rate or the tail wicking. Such documents obviously would have helped the plaintiffs in the cases filed against the company. The company later denied these allegations and claimed that the management never ordered or permitted the destruction of Dalkon Shield documents.[21]

In January 1985 Robins was also found guilty of perjury by a federal appeals court. The court ordered a new trial for a Florida woman who had lost a jury trial in Tampa because of the testimony of an expert witness for Robins, Dr. Louis Keith of Chicago. Dr. Keith testified that he had conducted wicking studies on the Dalkon Shield and that the tail did not wick as was believed. However, eight months later, he testified in a California case that he had never performed any such studies. Robins lawyers said the appeals court had misconstrued the testimonies, and they characterized the discrepancies as "minor inconsistencies."[22]

In September 1980 in another "Dear Doctor" letter, Robins advised all women to have their Dalkon Shields removed, citing a possibility of infection from an obscure bacterium. No mention was made of pelvic inflammatory disease. The company again declined to issue a recall of the device and refused several requests by wearers for payment of removal expenses.[23] Then the Center for Disease Control in Atlanta conducted a study that found that wearers of the Dalkon Shield had a five times greater chance of contracting pelvic inflammatory disease than nonwearers. This finding came from a large study of contraceptive methods used by women hospitalized with pelvic inflammatory disease.[24]

Despite the growing litigation and negative scientific studies, the controversy surrounding the Dalkon Shield dropped from the news for several years until a judge by the name of Miles Lord decided to speak his mind about the conduct of corporate executives. Lord had presided over a number of Dalkon Shield cases in his Minneapolis courtroom and was becoming exasperated with Robins executives. When asked to approve the settlement of seven Dalkon Shield cases for $4.6 million, Lord demanded that the three top Robins executives appear before him in his courtroom. When they did appear on February 29, 1984, Lord proceeded to denounce the firm's legal tactics and alleged that the interest earned by delaying the settlement of cases covered all the legal fees of the company.

[20]William P. Barrett, "I Hang My Head in Shame: Ex-Robins Lawyer Regrets Company's Hard-Nosed Trial Tactics," *Dallas Times Herald,* February 17, 1985, p. A23.

[21]Ibid.

[22]Francine Schwadel, "Witness for Robins Probed for Perjury on Dalkon Shield," *Wall Street Journal,* April 9, 1985, p. 19.

[23]Barrett "Testing of Dalkon Shield," p. A24.

[24]"Dalkon Shield Warning," *FDA Consumer,* July–August 1983, p. 2.

The judge's speech received nationwide publicity (see appendix 1), and even though a federal review court struck the speech from the record in response to a protest by the company, ruling that the judge had been out of line, the episode focused new attention on the A. H. Robins Company and was followed by new action.[25] In October 1984 the company agreed to pay the bills for women who had the shield removed and mounted a $4 million advertising campaign to spread the word across the nation. (See appendix 2.) Also in October, Robins asked the federal court in Richmond to restrict punitive-damage awards across the country. The company sought a single nationwide trial on punitive damages to be held in its hometown. And in November, Robins settled 198 cases in Minneapolis for a total of $38 million.[26]

At the beginning of 1985 Robins and its insurer had paid more than $300 million to settle the claims of about 7700 women. At that time the company still faced more than 3700 lawsuits and claims across the country. The nationwide total was growing by about 30 each week. Payment of these suits was done for business reasons, according to one of Robin's lawyers, and was not an admission of guilt. The company could not defend against 10,000 suits, it was maintained. Robins has still never formally recalled the device and has maintained its position that the Dalkon Shield was neither defective nor unreasonably dangerous.[27] Some of the specific allegations made by the plaintiffs and the company's responses include the following:

> Robins told doctors, regulators and patients that there were no problems with the Dalkon Shield even though its staff had identified the suspected defect and was frantically seeking to correct it. The company says a seemingly damning set of memos is being wrongly interpreted.

> Robins, which never before had manufactured birth-control devices and had no family planning experts on its staff, put the Dalkon Shield on the market with design changes that had not been tested. The company says it took all reasonable steps in light of the information then available, and that in any event, plaintiffs never claimed these changes caused any injury.

> Experts testifying on behalf of the women suing, contend that the wider tail with 200 to 400 strands, which was unusual among IUDs, facilitated wicking, particularly because the sheath could keep the bacteria-smothering mucus away from the strands. This is a contention Robins rejects.

> Copper was added to the Dalkon Shield to increase its contraceptive effect but, to avoid costly delays for government-mandated testing, Robins falsely told federal

---

[25]"A. H. Robins Hauls a Judge Into Court," *Business Week,* July 16, 1985, pp. 27–28. Robins executives filed a complaint with the U.S. Eighth Circuit Court of Appeals, arguing that the judge had "methodically destroyed their personal and professional reputations" and "grossly abused his office." They charged that Lord's diatribe was an example of judicial irresponsibility at its worst. The complainants asked that he be reprimanded. Five federal judges, including the chief judge of the eighth circuit heard the case, and three other federal judges gave statements in Lord's defense. "A Panel Tries to Judge a Judge," *Time,* July 23, 1984, p. 88.

[26]Barrett, "Testing of the Dalkon Shield, p. A24.

[27]Ibid., p. 22.

regulators the metal had been added only to increase its strength. The company says the copper had no contraceptive effect and that no deception was committed.

In promoting the Dalkon Shield, Robins published a favorable study conducted by a co-inventor of the product without revealing his financial interest in the device and while the company had its own doubts as to the validity of his data. Plaintiffs' lawyers contend that Davis falsified the data by selecting women only after they had had favorable experiences. In a statement under oath, Davis was unable to say who picked the women for the study, saying only that many people in his office were involved in the process. Plaintiffs also allege that Davis improved the results of the study by instructing new patients to use contraceptive foam, a substance which kills sperm, during the first few months of usage. Davis denied this but later conceded that the initial set of instructions published when the Dalkon Corporation first marketed the device recommended that wearers use foam. This recommendation was also made to Robins. The company maintains that Davis conducted an honest study and that such financial disclosures were not customary in those days, and that a Dalkon Shield critic who had invented a rival IUD did the same thing.

In promotional material, Robins cited studies that did not exist and made claims for which no research had been done. The company says any such errors were inadvertent. Robins is also alleged to have continued to publish studies showing low pregnancy rates after its officials knew the data were false, misleading or otherwise invalid. Plaintiffs' lawyers maintain that the pregnancy rate problems should have made Robins suspicious of the Dalkon Shield in general. The company denies this allegation, and argues that the pregnancy rate problems are irrelevant to the infection issue.

Robins officials ordered the destruction of incriminating company documents in an effort to reduce potential liability. The company says that its former lawyer who so testified, Roger Tuttle, was lying.[28]

Thus far, lawyers for the plaintiffs bringing suit against the company concede that they have uncovered no documents or testimony suggesting that top Robins executives knew their product would cause as much harm as it may have done. Moreover, Robins initially won twenty-four out of the fifty-two cases that have gone to trial, usually by showing that the plaintiff's injury in a particular case was not linked to the Dalkon Shield. And in only eight of these cases have juries awarded punitive damages.[29]

RECENT DEVELOPMENTS

The legacy of the Dalkon Shield has continued to haunt the company. On April 2, 1985, the company set aside $615 million to cover expected losses from the thousands of suits that were still pending and would be filed in the future against the company. Robins's chief financial officer called the sum ''a reasonable estimate of the minimum cost'' of legal fees and compensation in current and anticipated suits

[28]Ibid.
[29]Ibid.

filed in the United States. Legal experts stated that the fund was the largest ever established to handle medically related product-liability claims. The fund wiped out the company's net worth, creating a deficit of $128 million, which required the suspension of dividends until 1987 because of a Virginia law prohibiting dividend payments until the deficit is eliminated. Robins had paid a quarterly dividend of nineteen cents a share. The company earned $58 million in 1983 but was expected to post a $461.6 million loss for 1984.[30]

At the time the fund was established Robins had already paid $314 million to settle some 8300 suits, with about 3800 more still pending. Robins estimated that over the next seventeen years an additional 8300 cases could be brought against it in the U.S. courts alone. The average payment in each case through the end of 1984 was about $37,900. The company estimated an average of $53,200 for pending cases and $52,400 for future ones. New lawsuits were being filed at the rate of about seventy a week, the highest rate in the company's history. Company officials attributed this increase to an advertising campaign designed to encourage women still wearing the device to have it removed at the company's expense. Robins claimed that it had paid $1.08 million for 4437 removals.[31]

The fund was designed to pay compensation only to plaintiffs bringing suit in U.S. courts. The company did not assess how much might be required to cover liabilities to women who used the shield in foreign countries. Of the 4.6 million devices that Robins sold before the product was taken off the market, 1.7 were sold in overseas markets. The fund also did not cover punitive damages because of the difficulty of measuring potential exposure to this kind of award.[32] Punitive damages aren't covered by product-liability insurance, and by the end of 1984, Robins had only about $70 million left in compensatory-claim insurance.[33]

In addition to establishing the reserve fund, the company also announced that it had settled a stockholder suit that claimed that Robins and three of its officers had made misleading statements about the Dalkon Shield. The company agreed to pay a total of $6.9 million to shareholders who had bought the stock between March 8, 1971 and June 28, 1974, and who still held their shares at the end of that period.[34]

Five days after establishment of this fund the Agency for International Development (AID) released a report that established the agency as the world's largest

[30] "How Robins Will Go On Paying for the Dalkon Shield," *Business Week*, April 15, 1985, p. 50.

[31] William P. Barrett, "Dalkon Shield Maker Concedes Possible User Injuries," *Dallas Times Herald*, April 3, 1985, p. A8. In May 1985 a jury in Wichita, Kansas, awarded nearly $9 million to a Topeka woman who claimed the use of the Dalkon Shield had forced her to undergo a hysterectomy. The jury awarded $1.43 million in actual damages and $7.5 million in punitive damages. See "Woman Awarded $8.9 Million in Damages from Dalkon Maker," *Dallas Times Herald*, May 5, 1985, p. A11. In a suit filed in Austin, Texas, the plaintiff sought $2 million in damages for pain and suffering and $50 million in punitive damages. Robins asked the judge to rule against such a large punitive damage award. See William P. Barrett, "Dalkon Maker Issues Plea to Judge," *Dallas Times Herald*, May 10, 1985, p. A22.

[32] "How Robins Will Go On Paying," p. 50

[33] Francine Schwadel, "Robins Sets $615 Million Pool to Cover Dalkon Shield Claims, Halts Dividend," *Wall Street Journal*, April 3, 1985, p. 2.

[34] Ibid.

single buyer of the Dalkon Shield. The agency stated that its large purchases contributed to the product's "illusion of success." The agency had purchased 697,292 Dalkon Shields or 15.5 percent of the worldwide total of 4.5 million. The devices were distributed in about forty countries through AID itself, various family-planning agencies of foreign governments, and private institutions. Half of the stock that was purchased by AID remained in warehouses and never reached users. The agency claimed that it "moved aggressively" to retrieve unused intrauterine devices once Robins took the product off the U.S. market.[35]

This claim was disputed by Martina Langley, an Austin, Texas, lawyer who said she had once worked in a Central American medical clinic. The lawyer was convinced that in the three countries she knew best, El Salvador, Guatemala, and Nicaragua, most of the women who received a government-funded Dalkon Shield were still wearing them. She claimed that doctors in El Salvador were prescribing the shield as late as 1980, six years after Robins had discontinued sales in the United States and five years after AID said it had retrieved all unused shields. Langley was critical of the decision not to launch Third World publicity programs to have Dalkon Shields removed.[36] In response to this criticism, the agency ordered new studies to help determine whether many women in foreign countries are still using the device.[37]

The results of two new studies funded by the National Institutes of Health were released in April 1985 and provided additional ammunition to those who were suing the company. The studies were critical of the Dalkon Shield stating that the device posed a three-to-eleven-times greater risk of infertility than other devices. One of the studies found that 5 percent of the infertile women in the population studied had used the Dalkon Shield, while only 1.4 percent of the fertile women had used the device. The other found that Dalkon Shield users represented 14.5 percent of all cases of infertility, while they represented only 2.5 percent of fertile women.[38]

Despite these difficulties, company officials maintained that the company was financially sound. When asked at a news conference whether the firm would file for bankruptcy, a senior vice-president replied, "We are not in danger of that. We are operating today just as we did yesterday. It's business as usual." Some Wall Street analysts agreed. Barbara Ryan of the Bear, Stearns brokerage firm said, "This will cost Robins a lot of money, but the company's survival is not in question."[39]

In spite of these optimistic projections, however, the company did file for bankruptcy in August of 1985, citing the mounting cost of the 5100 claims that were

---

[35]William P. Barrett, "IUD Sales Success Boosted by Agency's Purchases," *Dallas Times Herald,* April 7, 1985, p. A9.

[36]William P. Barrett, "Foreigners Using Dalkon Shield, Lawyer Claims," *Dallas Times Herald,* April 21, 1985, p. A6.

[37]William P. Barrett, "U.S. Agency to Study Dalkon Shield Use in 4 Countries," *Dallas Times Herald,* April 25, 1985, p. A7.

[38]Michael Waldholz and Francine Schwadel, "IUDs, Especially Dalkon Shield, Pose Increased Risk of Infertility, Studies Say," *Wall Street Journal,* April 11, 1985, p. 38.

[39]"The Big Payout," *Time,* April 15, 1985, p. 86.

pending against Robins at the time. This action paralleled that of Manville Corporation, which had filed for protection under Chapter 11 in 1982 as a way of dealing with the mounting claims of workers who claimed they were injured as a result of exposure to asbestos. The bankruptcy filing brought a halt to further action regarding the claims already filed and prohibited the filing on any new claims anywhere except in federal bankruptcy court. The president and chief executive officer of Robins, E. Claiborne Robins, Jr., stated that "the continuing burden" of Dalkon Shield litigation forced the company to seek bankruptcy-law protection. The filing was made "to ensure that all persons to whom the company has an obligation are treated fairly, to preserve the assets of the company and to maintain its current operations."[40]

As of June 30, 1985, the company and its insurer had paid $378.3 million to dispose of 9320 cases involving the Dalkon Shield. Legal fees amounted to another $107.3 million. Since new cases were being filed at the rate of about 370 a month, the company expected thousands more to deal with in addition to the 5100 that were pending.[41] Since the company's request to consolidate thousands of claims for punitive damages into a single proceeding had been denied, the company would have continued to face separate awards for these damages that could have exhausted its finances. This filing was opposed by women's groups who filed suit asking the bankruptcy court to dismiss the company's request, claiming that by filing for bankruptcy, Robins was only trying to delay and diminish compensation to plaintiffs. They charged that injured women would receive less compensation under a Chapter 11 settlement than they would if each case went to trial separately.[42]

Subsequently, U.S. District Judge Robert Merhige of Richmond set a deadline of April 30, 1986, by which time women who used the Dalkon Shield must have filed damage claims or be barred from suing. A. H. Robins Company agreed to pay about $4 million to mount a three-week advertising campaign across the country to notify women of this deadline and an additional $1 million for publicity in more than ninety other countries. This effort included thirty-second announcements that would be shown 41 times on network television and 171 times on major cable superstations. Ads were also placed in 225 daily newspapers and eight national publications.[43]

Even in bankruptcy proceedings, however, Robins's troubles continued. When in bankruptcy, a company must obtain court approval before using any company assets to make payments to creditors or company officers for any debt incurred prior to the filing of the petition. Such a requirement is necessary to protect the interests of the remaining creditors, who must wait for court approval of a reorganization plan for paying off debts. Yet the company went ahead and made about $1.2 million of

---

[40]Francine Schwadel, "Robins Files for Protection of Chapter 11," *Wall Street Journal,* August 22, 1985, p. 3.

[41]William P. Barrett, "Dalkon Shield Maker Files for Bankruptcy," *Dallas Times Herald,* August 22, 1985, p. 1.

[42]"Dismissal of Robins's Chapter 11 Petition Sought by Plaintiffs," *Wall Street Journal,* August 26, 1985, p. 4.

[43]William P. Barrett, "Deadline Given for Claims from Dalkon Shield Users," *Dallas Times Herald,* January 5, 1986, p. A8.

deferred-compensation payments to executives, spent about $600,000 in other expenses, and paid $5 million to settle contract debts for computer services and royalties on drug patents and trademarks, all without court approval.[44]

The company claimed that it hadn't had adequate advice from its outside law firm, which it subsequently dismissed, and that the officers hadn't realized immediately that the payments were improper.[45] Judge Merhige ordered Robins to retrieve these payments and considered appointing a trustee to run the company.[46] Such an independent trustee can be appointed if the court finds evidence of "fraud, dishonesty, incompetency, or gross mismanagement" or if a court decides that such an appointment would be in the best interests of the creditors.[47] The amount involved was subsequently expanded to $22 million by federal investigators.[48] The judge stopped short of appointing a trustee, however, and instead ordered the appointment of an examiner with broad authority to monitor the activities of the company while it was in bankruptcy-law proceedings. The examiner would review Robins's financial data, investigate allegations of any misconduct by company officials, and report to the court on his findings. But management would retain control of the company's operations.[49] In September 1986 the examiner asked for and was granted an extension until February 5, 1987, for the company to submit a reorganization plan to the court.[50]

Before this date was reached, American Home Products Company offered to bail out A. H. Robins from bankruptcy proceedings by acquiring the company and assuming its liabilities for the Dalkon Shield product. American Home expected to pay at least $20 for each of Robins's 24,175,000 shares outstanding or a total of $484 million.[51] American Home would also have established a huge trust fund for settling the hundreds of thousands of pending claims related to the Dalkon Shield device. Just a few days later, however, American Home Products withdrew this bid, sending Robins's stock into a sharp decline. Initially, the company cited the lack of guarantees that it would be protected against future Dalkon Shield claims and the difficulty of combining the two companies, which would apparently take longer than American Home executives had thought.[52] Eventually, it was disclosed that

[44]Sonja Steptoe, "U.S. Requests That Robins Be Operated by Court Appointee; Spending Is Cited," *Wall Street Journal,* March 14, 1986, p. 4.

[45]Sonja Steptoe, "Robins Officials Dispute Firm on Payments," *Wall Street Journal,* June 6, 1986, p. 4.

[46]Sonja Steptoe, "Robins Is Ordered to Seek Retrieval of $6.8 Million," *Wall Street Journal,* March 31, 1986, p. 34.

[47]Sonja Steptoe, "U.S. Expands Payments Case against Robins," *Wall Street Journal,* June 5, 1986, p. 4.

[48]Ibid.

[49]Sonja Steptoe, "Judge Orders Appointment of Examiner to Monitor Activities of A. H. Robins Co.," *Wall Street Journal,* August 6, 1986, p. 4.

[50]Sonja Steptoe, "Robins Examiner Receives Extension in Chapter 11 Case," *Wall Street Journal,* September 30, 1986, p. 47.

[51]"American Home Products Is Proposing to Buy Robins in Chapter 11 Bailout," *Wall Street Journal,* February 5, 1987, p. 2.

[52]Michael Waldholz and Alix M. Freedman, "American Home Withdraws Robins Bid, Citing Risks Involved in Going Forward," *Wall Street Journal,* February 13, 1987, p. 2.

what may have really torpedoed the negotiations were the escalating financial requests by Robins. Apparently Robins wanted five-year employment contracts and severance payments for about fifty top executives and supplemental consulting contracts of about $100,000 a year each for its chairman, E. Claiborne Robins, Sr., and his son, E. Claiborne Robins, Jr., the company's president.[53]

As a result of this failure, the bankruptcy judge took steps to prevent Robins from sabotaging any future acquisition offers. He expanded the powers of the court-appointed examiner and ordered the company to cooperate in the event of another rescue offer. If Robins failed to comply, it could face the threat of a court-appointed trustee negotiating on its behalf.[54] In April 1987, just before Robins was to face two further motions in court that would threaten its ability to survive as an independent company, Robins submitted its own reorganization plan.[55] The plan would create a $1.75 billion trust fund for settling claims against the Dalkon Shield and about $100,000 million for paying other creditors. Initial funding for the trust would come from a $75 million cash payment from Robins and a five-year, $1.68 billion letter of credit from a group of banks.[56]

The latest development in this continuing saga was a $2.6 billion bid from Rorer Group Inc. to merge with Robins. Rorer indicated that it was proposing a true merger rather than a buyout and promised to leave Robins's Richmond operations substantially intact. Rorer offered to issue one share of new convertible preferred stock with a stated value of $30 for each share of Robins stock outstanding. If Rorer's common-stock price reached or exceeded $48 in the open market, Rorer would issue 0.625 common shares to Robins's holders. The combined company would have sales of about $1.6 billion and would rank sixth among U.S. non-prescription-drug makers. The board of Robins signed a letter of intent to accept this proposal, but the proposal also had to be accepted by all parties to the bankruptcy proceedings, a process that could take months to resolve.[57]

CONCLUSION

Why was Robins so reluctant to announce a recall as Procter & Gamble did with Rely tampons when there was an indication that the product might be linked to toxic shock syndrome, another disease caused by vaginal infection? Perhaps part of the answer lay in the fact that the Dalkon Shield was an extremely profitable product. The shield generated a profit margin of over 40 percent in the United States and over

---

[53]Sonja Steptoe, "Robins Demand Cited in Failed Takeover," *Wall Street Journal,* February 17, 1987, p. 6.

[54]Ibid.

[55]Sonja Steptoe, "Robins's Chapter 11 Plan Derailed Sale but May Delay Settling of IUD Claims," *Wall Street Journal,* April 20, 1987, p. 2.

[56]Sonja Steptoe, "Robins's Reorganization Plan Specifies Added Debt of $1.35 Billion, Asset Sales," *Wall Street Journal,* April 6, 1987, p. 6.

[57]Sonja Steptoe, "Robins Accepts Rorer's $2.6 Billion Bid; Dalkon Claimants' Lawyer Reacts Coolly," *Wall Street Journal,* July 6, 1987, p. 3.

70 percent overseas. And sales of the device were good, perhaps even outstanding. From January 1971 until sales were suspended in the United States at the request of the FDA in June of 1974 and overseas in April of 1975, Robins sold some 4.6 million shields worldwide, making the Dalkon Shield the largest selling IUD in the world.[58]

Perhaps the words of Roger Tuttle, the company's former laywer who managed the defense of the shield, put the problem into perspective. In an article that appeared in the *Oklahoma Bar Journal,* Tuttle wrote: "Robins entered a therapeutic area with no prior experience, no trained personnel, and reliance on statistics from an admittedly biased source. Although the device was based on sound scientific principles, Robins over-promoted it without doing sufficient clinical testing in an effort to ride the crest of a marketing wave for financial gain."[59] Morton Mintz in his book *At Any Cost* states: "The Dalkon Shield created a disaster of global proportions because a few men with little on their minds but megabucks made decisions, in the interest of profit, that exposed millions of women to serious infection, sterility, and even death."[60]

QUESTIONS

1. Where did the A. H. Robins Company go wrong? Why did they not concern themselves more with thoroughly testing the Dalkon Shield before it was marketed, particularly by an unbiased researcher who did not have a financial interest in the product? Were they motivated solely by profit, or were there other factors involved?

2. Why wasn't the product recalled after evidence began to mount about its adverse health effects? What makes this case different from the Rely Tampon situation where the product was withdrawn by Procter & Gamble after a suggested link with toxic shock syndrome? Was Robins right to defend the product and never admit there might be a problem?

3. What role did the regulatory agencies play in this situation? Should they have taken a more active role early in the controversy? What can government do to protect the public from unsafe products? Is the role government agencies can play in this respect limited? If so, in what ways?

4. Did the judiciary play a key role in this case? What decisions do the courts have to make in product-liability cases? Did Judge Lord overstep his authority as district court judge when he lectured Robins executives? Do you applaud or condemn this action? Why? Are judges accountable for their actions?

5. What is the difference between compensatory and punitive damages? Should punitive damages be assigned in this situation? Why? What purpose do they serve? Do you support Robins's contention that all punitive

[58]Subrata N. Chakravarty, "Tunnel Vision," *Forbes,* May 21, 1984, p. 218.

[59]Ibid.

[60]Morton Mintz, *At Any Cost: Corporate Greed, Women, and the Dalkon Shield* (New York: Pantheon Books, 1985), p. xiii.

damages ought to be consolidated in one case? Why do you think they made this suggestion?

6. What role can consumers play in being diligent about the purchase and use of products? Are consumers at the mercy of producers in the modern complex and sophisticated marketplace? How can consumers protect themselves from misleading or outright false advertising and unsafe products?

APPENDIX 1   *A Plea for Corporate Conscience*

From a speech delivered by Federal District Court Judge Miles W. Lord in his Minneapolis courtroom on February 29. Lord made his remarks in approving a $4.6 million product-liability suit against the A. H. Robins Company, manufacturer of the Dalkon Shield intrauterine contraceptive device, which has been found to cause serious, and sometimes fatal, pelvic infections in many of its users. This settlement satisfied 7 of the 9000 claims that have been brought against Robins. Lord's remarks were addressed to E. Claiborne Robins, Jr., the firm's president; Carl D. Lunsford, senior vice-president for research and development; and William A. Forrest, Jr., vice-president and general counsel.

Mr. Robins, Mr. Forrest, and Dr. Lunsford: After months of reflection, study, and cogitation—and no small amount of prayer—I have concluded that it is perfectly appropriate to make this statement, which will constitute my plea to you to seek new horizons in corporate consciousness and a new sense of personal responsibility for the activities of those who work under you in the name of the A. H. Robins Company.

It is not enough to say, "I did not know," "It was not me," "Look elsewhere." Time and again, each of you has used this kind of argument in refusing to acknowledge your responsibility and in pretending to the world that the chief officers and directors of your gigantic multinational corporation have no responsibility for its acts and omissions.

Today as you sit here attempting once more to extricate yourselves from the legal consequences of your acts, none of you has faced up to the fact that more than 9000 women claim they gave up part of their womanhood so that your company might prosper. It has been alleged that others gave their lives so you might prosper. And there stand behind them legions more who have been injured but who have not sought relief in the courts of this land.

I dread to think what would have been the consequences if your victims had been men rather than women—women, who seem, through some quirk of our society's mores, to be expected to suffer pain, shame, and humiliation.

If one poor young man were, without authority or consent, to inflict such damage upon one woman, he would be jailed for a good portion of the rest of his life. Yet your company, without warning to women, invaded their bodies by the millions and caused them injuries by the thousands. And when the time came for these women to make their claims against your company, you attacked their characters. You inquired into their sexual practices and into the identity of their sex partners. You ruined families and reputations and careers in order to intimidate those who would raise their voices against you. You introduced issues that had no relationship to the fact that you had planted in the bodies of these women instruments of death, of mutilation, of disease.

Gentlemen, you state that your company has suffered enough, that the infliction of further punishment in the form of punitive damages would cause harm to your business, would punish innocent shareholders, and could conceivably depress your profits to the point where you could not survive as a competitor in this industry. When the poor and downtrodden commit crimes, they too plead that these are crimes of survival and that they should be excused for illegal acts that helped them escape desperate economic straits. On a few occasions when these excuses are made and remorseful defendants promise to mend their ways, courts will give heed to such pleas. But no court will head the plea when the individual denies the wrongful nature of his deeds and gives no indication that he will mend his ways. Your company, in the face of overwhelming evidence, denies its guilt and continues its monstrous mischief.

Mr. Forrest, you have told me that you are working with members of the Congress of the United States to find a way of forgiving you from punitive damages that might otherwise be imposed. Yet the profits of your company continue to mount. Your last financial report boasts of new records for sales and earnings, with a profit of more than $58 million in 1983. And, insofar as this court has been able to determine, you three men and your company are still engaged in a course of wrongdoing. Until your company indicates that it is willing to cease and desist this deception and to seek out and advise the victims, your remonstrances to Congress and to the courts are indeed hollow and cynical. The company has not suffered, nor have you men personally. You are collectively being enriched by millions of dollars each year. There is no evidence that your company has suffered any penalty from these litigations. In fact, the evidence is to the contrary.

The case law suggests that the purpose of punitive damages is to make an award that will punish a defendant for his wrongdoing. Punishment has traditionally involved the principles of revenge, rehabilitation, and deterrence. There is no evidence I have been able to find in my review of these cases to indicate that any of these objectives has been accomplished.

Mr. Robins, Mr. Forrest, Dr. Lunsford: You have not been rehabilitated. Under your direction, your company has continued to allow women, tens of thousands of them, to wear this device—a deadly depth charge in their wombs, ready to explode at any time. Your attorney denies that tens of thousands of these devices are still in women's bodies. But I submit to you that he has no more basis for denying the accusation than the plaintiffs have for stating it as truth. We simply do not know how many women are still wearing these devices because your company is not willing to find out. The only conceivable reasons that you have not recalled this product are that it would hurt your balance sheet and alert women who have already been harmed that you be liable for their injuries. You have taken the bottom line as your guiding beacon and the low road as your route. That is corporate irresponsibility at its meanest. Rehabilitation involves an admission of guilt, a certain contrition, an acknowledgment of wrongdoing, and a resolution to take a new course toward a better life. I find none of this in you or your corporation. Confession is good for the soul, gentlemen. Face up to your misdeeds. Acknowledge the personal responsibility you have for the activities of those who work under you. Rectify this evil situation. Warn the potential victims and recompense those who have already been harmed.

Mr. Robins, Mr. Forrest, Dr. Lunsford: I see little in the history of this case that would deter others. The policy of delay and obfuscation practiced by your lawyers in courts throughout this country has made it possible for you and your insurance company to put off the payment of these claims for such a long period that the interest you earned in the interim covers the cost of these cases. You, in essence, pay nothing out of your own pockets to settle these cases. What corporate officials could learn a lesson from this? The only lesson they might learn is that it pays to delay compensating victims and to intimidate, harass, and shame the injured parties.

Your company seeks to segment and fragment the litigation of these cases nationwide. The courts of this country are burdened with more than 3000 Dalkon Shield cases. The sheer number of claims and the dilatory tactics used by your company's attorneys clog court calendars and consume vast amounts of judicial and jury time. Your company settles those cases out of court in which it finds itself in an uncomfortable position, a handy device for avoiding any proceeding that would give continuity or cohesiveness to this nationwide problem. The decision as to which cases are brought to trial rests almost solely at the whim and discretion of the A. H. Robins Company. In order to guarantee that no plaintiff or group of plaintiffs mounts a sustained assault upon your system of evasion and avoidance, you have time after time demanded that, as the price of settling a case, able lawyers agree not to bring a Dalkon Shield case again and not to help less experienced lawyers with cases against your company.

Another of your callous legal tactics is to force women of little means to withstand the onslaughts of your well-financed attorneys. You target your worst tactics at the meek and the poor.

If this court had the authority, I would order your company to make an effort to locate each and every woman who still wears this device and recall your product. But this court does not. I must therefore resort to moral persuasion and a personal appeal to each of you. Mr. Robins, Mr. Forrest, and Dr. Lunsford: You are the people with the power to recall. You are the corporate conscience.

Please, in the name of humanity, lift your eyes above the bottom line. You, the men in charge, must surely have hearts and souls and consciences.

Please, gentlemen, give consideration to tracing down the victims and sparing them the agony that will surely be theirs.

APPENDIX 2   *Public Notice*

An Important Health Warning To Women Using An IUD

The Dalkon Shield

I f you are still using an intra-uterine birth control device (IUD) inserted in the early to mid 1970s, this message is for you. Many women had an IUD called the Dalkon Shield inserted during that time. It is important that each Dalkon Shield be removed, since there is substantial medical opinion that its continued use may pose a serious personal health hazard. If you are still using a Dalkon Shield, A. H. Robins Company will pay your doctor or clinic to remove it.

A. H. Robins ceased distribution of the Dalkon Shield in 1974. Many claims have been made that the device causes health problems, including pelvic infections, that may result in serious injury or death. In 1980, A. H. Robins advised doctors to remove the Dalkon Shield from any woman still using it. In 1983, the U.S. Food and Drug Administration and other government agencies issued the same advice based on their concern about pelvic infections among Dalkon Shield users.

A. H. Robins will pay your doctor or clinic for any examination needed to find out if you are using the Dalkon Shield. If you are, A. H. Robins will pay the cost of having it removed.

WHAT TO DO

If you know you are using a Dalkon Shield IUD, or if you are using an IUD inserted in the early to mid 1970s and are unsure of the kind, call your doctor or health clinic for an appointment. Your call will be in confidence, and there will be no cost to you.

If you have further questions, please call A. H. Robins Company toll free. The number is **1-800-247-7220.** (In Virginia call collect **804-257-2015.**)

A·H·ROBINS

1407 Cummings Drive, Richmond, Virginia 23220

Reprinted by permission of A. H. Robins Company.

APPENDIX 3   *Calendar of Events*

August 1968: Irwin Lerner and Hugh Davis agree to invent Dalkon Shield.

Feb. 1, 1970: Davis publishes article reporting 1.1 pregnancy rate with Dalkon Shield.

SOURCE: "Chronicle of the Dalkon Shield," *Dallas Times Herald,* February 17, 1985, p. A23.

June 9–10, 1970: Two Robins officials consider purchasing Dalkon Shield and question pregnancy rate.

June 12, 1970: Robins buys Dalkon Shield from company owned by Lerner and Davis.

June 29, 1970: Robins officials warned about possibility of wicking in shield tail string.

Jan. 1, 1971: Robins begins national marketing of Dalkon Shield.

Feb. 15, 1972: Robins hears warning that Dalkon Shield may deteriorate in the body.

June 23, 1973: Robins consultant reports five cases of septic abortions, which are infected miscarriages.

June 26, 1974: Food and Drug Administration asks Robins to remove shield from the market.

June 28, 1974: Robins "voluntarily" withdraws Dalkon Shield from market.

Aug. 8, 1975: Robins announces it won't remarket Dalkon Shield.

July 30, 1979: Denver jury returns $6.2 million verdict against Robins.

Sept. 25, 1980: Robins recommends for the first time that women wearing Dalkon Shields should have them removed. However, Robins will not pay any of the costs.

Feb. 29, 1984: U.S. District Judge Miles Lord denounces Robins officials in Minneapolis court.

July 30, 1984: Roger Tuttle, attorney for Robins, testifies that he helped burn incriminating company documents about the Dalkon Shield nine years earlier.

Oct. 21, 1984: Robins asks federal judge in Richmond, Va., to consolidate all punitive claims into one trial.

Oct. 29, 1984: Robins says it will pay for removal of Dalkon Shield and begins $3.8 million advertising campaign.

Nov. 14, 1984: Robins pays $38 million to settle 198 cases in Minneapolis.

THE TYLENOL CRISIS: SELF-REGULATION

Trust forms the basis of successful marketplace transactions. Employees trust that they will be paid for services rendered. Creditors trust that they will be paid principal and interest for money loaned. Managers trust that employees will put in an honest day's work for wages and salaries received. And consumers trust that the products they buy are safe to use as directed. The trust that consumers place in the products they buy on the marketplace is perhaps the most essential trust for a free-enterprise system to function and for companies to earn a profit on the goods and services they produce.

The federal government has long been concerned about various aspects of the products consumers buy, and consumer protection has deep roots in this country. Since 1906 with the passage of the Pure Food and Drug Act, Congress has seen fit to pass consumer-protection legislation and establish regulatory agencies and procedures to deal with product-related problems. During the 1960s and 1970s, however, Congress passed more consumer-protection legislation than at any other time in its history. This legislation led to the creation of new regulatory agencies and the addition of new responsibilities to existing agencies.

For example, the Consumer Product Safety Commission was created to deal with the safety of products not previously regulated. The National Highway Traffic Safety Administration was established to deal with automobile safety and set mileage standards. The Food and Drug Administration was given additional responsibilities to regulate medical devices in addition to its traditional responsibilities for drug safety and efficacy and food safety. The Federal Trade Commission established new regulations pertaining to advertising so that consumers could have more faith in the claims being made by advertisers.

Against this background of consumer protection, it would seem that the consumer is fairly safe when he or she goes to the marketplace to purchase products. Indeed, the average consumer demonstrates an almost blind trust in the products that are offered on the market. It is this blind trust that claimed the lives of seven Chicago-area residents who ingested Extra-Strength Tylenol laced with cyanide, a poison so deadly that it kills within minutes.[1] It is also this blind trust that was shaken for several frightening months throughout the country and made consumers wary of the products they were buying.

BACKGROUND

Johnson & Johnson with its subsidiaries is one of the world's largest and most diversified manufacturers and distributors of health-care products, including surgical dressings, prescription (tranquilizers, anti-inflammatory agents, sedatives) and nonprescription drugs, oxygen and blood-pressure monitoring systems, lotions and related items for babies, anesthetics, and specialty surgical products for hospitals. Products for international markets are modified as required to reflect local requirements and needs. They are made by subsidiaries in about forty-six foreign countries and sold in most countries of the world. In 1982 consumer products provided 43.0 percent of sales, professional products 33.5 percent, pharmaceutical products 19.4 percent, and industrial products 4.1 percent of sales.

---

[1]Cyanide is the name given to metal salts containing a carbon atom linked to a nitrogen atom. It is so toxic that fifty milligrams—a fraction of a teaspoon—can kill in as little time as fifteen minutes. Lethal doses kill by disrupting the blood's ability to carry oxygen through the body, affecting the heart, lungs, and brain. It is not sold over the counter, but experts say there is little to stop any knowledgeable person from getting cyanide, even in rather large quantities. "The Tylenol Scare," *Newsweek*, October 11, 1982, p. 36.

Johnson & Johnson was incorporated in the state of New Jersey on November 10, 1887. On January 2, 1982, the company had 79,000 employees. The company operates 200 plants including 94 in the United States, 33 in Canada and Latin America, and 29 in Africa, Asia, and the Pacific. The company also has numerous offices and warehouses worldwide.

THE PRODUCT

Tylenol is a product of McNeil Consumer Products Company, which has been owned since 1959 by Johnson & Johnson. During the 1960s Tylenol, an acetaminophen-based analgesic, was introduced in the market as an over-the-counter product. It was considered a good substitute for aspirin since it does not irritate the stomach. Tylenol, therefore, was heavily promoted to doctors and pharmacists as an alternative pain reliever for individuals who suffer upset stomach or other side effects from aspirin. About the same time McNeil also began to advertise Tylenol to the public.

Tylenol was the best-selling product in the company and in all forms and strengths accounted for a 35 percent share of the over-the-counter analgesic market. The Tylenol line represented 8 percent of Johnson & Johnson's total revenue and 17 percent of corporate income. In only nine years, Tylenol captured 35 percent of the $1.3 billion analgesic market. Among its much-longer-established competitors, Anacin was second with 13 percent of the market, followed closely by Bayer with 11 percent, Excedrin with 10.1 percent, and Bufferin with 9 percent of the market. Figure 1 shows Tylenol's rapid growth in sales.

Of the total Tylenol sales, $125 million was sales of Extra-Strength capsules, which was the fastest growing segment in the Tylenol line. The capsules were a new phenomenon in over-the-counter drug products. According to marketing experts, consumers often consider such medicinelike drugs more effective than tablets, although the active ingredients may be identical.[2]

THE PROBLEM

"A nightmare, an absolute nightmare," said James E. Burke, the chief executive officer (CEO) of Johnson & Johnson, as he and other company officials watched an exceptional reputation in the industry vanish almost overnight.[3] Within a three-day period during the fall of 1982 seven people were found dead in the Chicago area. The apparent cause of death was eventually linked to cyanide in Extra-Strength Tylenol capsules, which were manufactured by McNeil Consumer Products Com-

---

[2]"Tylenol Containing Strychnine Is Found in California as Consumer Fear Mounts," *Wall Street Journal,* October 6, 1982, p. 2.

[3]Michael Waldholz, "Johnson & Johnson Officials Take Steps to End More Killings Linked to Tylenol," *Wall Street Journal,* October 4, 1982, p. 16.

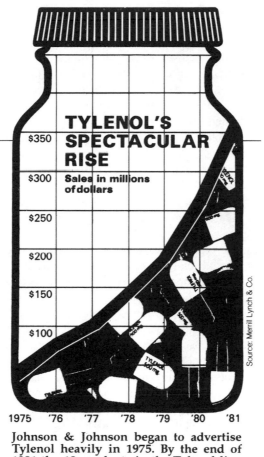

TYLENOL'S
SPECTACULAR
RISE

$350
$300 Sales in millions of dollars
$250
$200
$150
$100

1975 '76 '77 '78 '79 '80 '81

Source: Merrill Lynch & Co.

Johnson & Johnson began to advertise Tylenol heavily in 1975. By the end of 1981 the 12 products in the Tylenol line had taken an overwhelming 35% share of the total analgesic market, more than Bayer, Bufferin, and Anacin combined. After September 30 sales plunged 80%.

FIGURE 1   Source: Thomas Moore, "The Fight To Save Tylenol," *Fortune,* Nov. 29, 1982, p. 49. Copyright © 1982 Time Inc. All rights reserved.

pany, a subsidiary of Johnson & Johnson. Before the deaths, few people had been aware of the connection between Tylenol and Johnson & Johnson.

Over the past decade, razor blades buried in apples, cookies laced with LSD, and straight pins embedded in candy bars have been frequent Halloween "tricks" that caused nationwide concern. But product tampering reached a new high—or low—with the Tylenol incident. Although Tylenol was not initially suspected, the link between the deaths was made after two firefighters in different districts of Chicago compared information about the deaths and noticed that each victim had taken Extra-Strength capsules shortly before they died. Tests by the Cook County

Medical Examiner's Office found as much as sixty-five milligrams of cyanide in some capsules. Fifty milligrams is considered lethal.

At first, the possibility of a disgruntled employee tampering with the product during the manufacturing process was considered, but local authorities quickly discounted that assumption when it was determined that the bottles, which bore different lot numbers, were not from the same plant.[4] One bottle of capsules was manufactured in McNeil's Fort Washington, Pennsylvania, plant while the other bottle was from their Round Rock, Texas, plant. Subsequently, the Food and Drug Administration (FDA) publicly exonerated McNeil Consumer Products Company. In a letter to the company, the FDA said that contamination had not occurred at a McNeil plant. Investigators theorized that the capsules had been tampered with at distribution points, most likely after they reached retail shelves.[5]

Although the story of each of the seven victims was different, the end results were the same. Each died from taking Extra-Strength Tylenol capsules laced with cyanide. Mary Kellerman of Elk Grove Village, Illinois, was one of the first victims. This twelve-year-old girl awakened at dawn on Wednesday, October 6, 1982, with a sore throat and runny nose. Her parents gave her an Extra-Strength Tylenol capsule, and at 7 A.M. they found her dying on the bathroom floor. Doctors initially believed that she had died of a stroke.

Adam Janus, twenty-seven, was found by paramedics, collapsed in his home with his pupils fixed and dilated. Despite emergency-room efforts to keep him alive, he died, appearing to have suffered a massive heart attack. Later that day grieving relatives took Tylenol capsules found in a bottle in his home. Adam's twenty-five-year-old brother Stanley died that night. Stanley's wife of three months, Theresa, lived two more days until doctors abandoned efforts to save her life. Doctors grew suspicious when Janus's brother and sister-in-law were brought to the hospital with dilated pupils and very low blood pressure, which did not respond to treatment. After taking blood samples, it was discovered that there were tremendously high levels of cyanide in both victims.

Almost simultaneously, two off-duty firefighters linked Tylenol to the deaths. Jenna Kellerman, confused over her daughter's death, heard about the puzzling Janus deaths and called Arlington Heights firefighter Phillip Cappitelli, who was the relative of a friend, to see if he knew of any details. Cappitelli called his friend Richard Keyworth, a firefighter in Elk Grove Village. Keyworth remembered hearing from paramedics that Mary Kellerman had taken an Extra-Strength Tylenol capsule before she died. "This is a wild stab—maybe it's the Tylenol," Keyworth told Cappitelli. Cappitelli then learned from paramedics in Arlington Heights that the Janus family had also taken Extra-Strength Tylenol. Soon thereafter, police retrieved two bottles from the Kellerman and Janus homes, both bearing manufacturer's lot number MC 2880.

Officials at McNeil and Johnson & Johnson, who were alerted by Chicago authorities early Thursday morning, September 30, announced an immediate recall of all 93,400 bottles of Tylenol bearing the lot number MC 2880. This batch had

---

[4]"The Tylenol Scare," *Newsweek*, October 11, 1982, pp. 32–36.
[5]Ibid.

been produced in McNeil's Ft. Washington plant and shipped to thirty-one eastern and midwestern states in August. The company also sent nearly half a million Mailgrams to physicians, hospitals, and wholesalers informing them of the danger. But that afternoon another fatality was linked to Tylenol when investigators found five contaminated capsules in the home of thirty-one-year-old Mary McFarland of Elmhurst, Illinois. The bottle of cyanide-laced capsules bore the lot number 1910 MD, and another empty bottle marked lot number MC 2738 was found in her trash.

The case of the sixth victim was more perplexing. Mary Reiner, a twenty-seven-year-old of suburban Winfield, also died Thursday. Four contaminated capsules were found in her home, but Reiner, who had just delivered her third child, had mixed the Extra-Strength capsules with a bottle of Regular-Strength Tylenol, and the lot number was untraceable. By Friday McNeil's recall was expanded to include bottles of the 1910 MD lot, which had been produced at the Round Rock plant and shipped to Chicago and the western part of the United States. Since cyanide-laced capsules had been found in lots produced at both plants and contaminated capsules had turned up only near Chicago, investigators concluded that the tamperings took place after the shipments reached Illinois.

Chicago health and law-enforcement officials tried to warn area residents against taking Extra-Strength capsules. Volunteers also aided in this effort. Late Friday, thirty-five-year-old flight attendant Paula Prince was found by police, lying in her Near North Side apartment, only a few feet away from a bottle of Extra-Strength Tylenol capsules. Prince, who was the first victim found in Chicago and not its suburbs, had a bottle from lot number 1801 MD.

Two more bottles containing cyanide-laced capsules were discovered in Chicago. One was among those returned to the company by stores on the Near North Side, the neighborhood in which the last victim resided. The other bottle was turned in to Chicago police by Linda Morgan, who said she had bought the Tylenol on September 29, the day before the first deaths were reported. She attended a family gathering that day, and when she decided to take a pain reliever, her sister offered her Bufferin. She decided to take the Bufferin instead, and says she escaped death by "blind luck."

The victims could have been anyone. Death was random, as the poisoner had no way of knowing who his victims might be. Six of the bottles containing poisoned capsules were found in five drugstores and another in a grocery store. One of the stores was located in North Chicago, and the others were located in communities in the western suburbs, scattered roughly along a north-south line near Illinois state route 53. Investigators theorized that the killer had driven along route 53, turning off at randomly selected points, to place a poisoned bottle of capsules in each store.

PUBLIC REACTION

Within hours after the first three deaths, retailers in the Chicago area began to remove Tylenol Extra-Strength capsules from their shelves. Later, Mayor Jane Byrne ordered all Tylenol products removed from the city's retail shelves. By the end of the second day, the Tylenol-related poisonings in the Chicago area had attracted national media attention. A nationwide "panic" had begun, a serious loss was predicted for Johnson & Johnson by financial analysts, and marketing experts were sounding the death knell for Tylenol.[6]

Some experts feared that the episode might set off even more of a widespread panic among consumers, and in the wake of the Chicago deaths, there were signs they could be right. Poison-control centers as far away as San Francisco and New Orleans were flooded with calls from frightened citizens. Some consumers marched into local stores with boxes of Tylenol, demanding their money back or asking for other pain killers to replace Tylenol. In cities across the country, consumers threw away all the Tylenol on hand and many discarded other drugs as well. Health officials patiently explained to worried callers that if they were able to manage the telephone call, they probably did not have cyanide poisoning.

A wave of copycat crimes was creating further problems for law-enforcement officials around the country. Following the Chicago deaths, the Food and Drug Administration (FDA) received more than 270 reports from citizens suspecting product tampering in everything from food and drinks to medication. The FDA confirmed only thirty-six of the incidents to be "hard-core, true tamperings." Brands of hot dogs, caramel apples, and brownies were pulled off store shelves as a result of the reports. More than forty communities banned Halloween trick-or-treating, and many more issued warnings to parents to check all treats carefully. Police cruisers rolled through Chicago streets blaring warnings about the Tylenol incidents over loud speakers. Stories about the contaminated drug appeared on all three national television networks.

Only days after the first deaths occurred, the FDA became involved, advising consumers to avoid in prudence all bottles of the capsules.[7] Chicago's Mayor Jane Byrne took to television to urge her constituents not to take Tylenol. Residents in Chicago were asked to bring in suspect bottles for testing. Schools, churches, and even Boy Scout troops took it upon themselves to reach shut-ins and elderly people who might not have heard radio or TV warnings.

Soon after the Tylenol poisonings occurred, the Food and Drug Administration met to draft federal requirements for tamper-resistant packaging. Federal action was necessary to avoid a jumble of conflicting regulations among different states and municipalities, which could adversely affect and limit the distribution of over-the-counter products. The regulations that were eventually established require a statement on the label of over-the-counter drugs to make consumers aware of the specific tamper-resistant features of the package. These requirements went into effect on February 7, 1983. Legislation was also introduced on the Senate floor that would provide federal penalties for anyone who adulterates or tampers with an over-the-counter product.[8]

---

[6]Michael Waldholz and Dennis Kneade, "Tylenol's Maker Tries to Repair Good Image in Wake of Tragedy," *Wall Street Journal,* October 8, 1982, p. 1.

[7]"Poison Madness in the Midwest," *Time,* October 11, 1982, p. 18.

[8]Lawrence G. Foster, "The Johnson & Johnson Credo and the Tylenol Crisis," *New Jersey Bell Journal* 6, no. 1 (Spring 1983), p. 2.

MEDIA REACTION

The Tylenol tragedy quickly captured the nation's attention. Queries to Johnson & Johnson from the press exceeded 2500. Two news-clipping services generated in excess of 125,000 clippings. One of them said the Tylenol story had resulted in the widest domestic coverage of any story since the assassination of President John F. Kennedy. Associated Press and United Press International gave it second place as the impact story of 1982, second only to coverage of the nation's economy.[9]

The television and radio coverage was staggering. The story became something of a communications media monster, as 80,000 separate news stories in U.S. newspapers, hundreds of hours of national and local television and radio coverage, and more than 2000 phone calls to Johnson & Johnson from media representatives were made seeking information related to the Tylenol crisis. According to a study conducted by the company, more than 90 percent of the American public knew about the Chicago deaths from cyanide-laced Tylenol within the first week of the crisis, an unusually large percentage for any news story. It was, in the words of a newspaper columnist, one of the most heavily covered news events since Vietnam.[10]

Paralleling this massive outpouring of print, radio, and TV coverage, were the company's own programs to reach out and inform its various publics, including the media, on matters related to the Tylenol crisis. Johnson & Johnson had to use a variety of communication methods to get its message out on the evolving Tylenol story.

COMPETITOR'S REACTIONS

Competitors who had previously been left dormant by the runaway success of Tylenol seized the opportunity to improve sales. Datril ads were back on the air, telling consumers, "Look for extra-strength Datril in its tamper-proof packaging." Analgesic products such as Excedrin P.M., Pamprin, and Arthritis Pain Formula, which had never previously emphasized their ingredients, heavily stressed that they were "100 percent aspirin-free." The campaign was aimed at Tylenol users who had been advised by physicians to switch to acetaminophen from aspirin, which can cause an upset stomach.

Anacin-3 also gained from Tylenol's misfortune. The manufacturers issued a press release on the "unprecedented demand" for increased production of Anacin-3 following the poisonings. They also aired previously prepared television ads saying, "Like Tylenol, Anacin-3 is aspirin-free." According to one Tylenol competitor, "They went right for the jugular."[11]

[9]Ibid., p. 3.

[10]*The Tylenol Comeback*, a special report from the editors of *Worldwide*, a publication of Johnson & Johnson Corporate Public Relations, undated, p. 5. Reprinted from *Johnson & Johnson Worldwide* 17, no. 5, (December 1982.)

[11]Dennis Kneals, "Rivals Go after Tylenol's Market, But Gains May Be Only Temporary," *Wall Street Journal*, December 2, 1982, p. 31.

The Tylenol incident also prompted several companies to speed up introduction of new products. In January St. Joseph's Aspirin-Free tablets for adults were advertised on television. Sterling Drug, Inc., the makers of Bayer Aspirin, considered introducing Panadol, which was its top-selling nonaspirin pain reliever in the United Kingdom. Adria Laboratories introduced a new product called Effercin, with television ads promoting "fast relief . . . contains no aspirin or acetaminophen." The ads also pointed out that Effercin came in "three-way tamper-resistant packaging."[12]

COMPANY IMPACT

The damage sustained by Johnson & Johnson because of the Tylenol tragedy was substantial. Before the crisis, Tylenol accounted for about 8 percent of Johnson & Johnson's corporate revenue and 17 percent of corporate net income in 1981, which totaled $468 million. Of this amount, 40 percent was contributed by the sale of capsules. The parent company's stock had risen in the last two years from the low 20s to 46⅛ the night before the poisonings. McNeil executives were confident that Tylenol would take over 50 percent of the market by 1986. In short, Tylenol was big and getting bigger.[13]

Of course, this growth came to a screeching halt in the wake of the poisonings. The cost to McNeil to "right the wrong" was substantial. One immediate cost was the distribution of Mailgrams (500,000) to doctors, hospitals, and distributors. McNeil also incurred costs in voluntarily withdrawing all thirty-one million bottles of Tylenol capsules on the market, with a retail value of over $100 million. Further, McNeil paid for shipment of the "tainted" capsules to a disposal site where they were destroyed. Legal costs also plagued McNeil, with four class-action suits filed against Tylenol the week following the deaths. Requested damages by surviving family members at the time totaled $35 million. One of the suits, brought by Marie Kusner of Highland Park, Illinois, demanded refunds for everyone who had bought Tylenol products in the entire country for the year 1982, which her lawyer estimated at $600 million. Though this suit was not expected to be won by the plaintiff, Johnson & Johnson had to incur substantial costs just to defend itself.[14]

The costs did not stop here. As expected, Johnson & Johnson's stock dropped in price from 46⅛ on September 29 to 42⅝, a paper loss of $657 million.[15] In addition, extra staff was needed to handle the crisis, increasing McNeil's costs even further. Advertising was halted and rewritten to meet new needs. But the most devastating blow received by Tylenol was its loss of a foothold in the analgesic market and, of course, the trust of the consumer in the product. Tylenol, which had

[12]Ibid.

[13]Thomas Moore, "The Fight to Save Tylenol," *Fortune,* November 29, 1982, p. 45.

[14]"Murder by Remote Control," *Time,* October 18, 1982, p. 19.

[15]"Lessons Emerge from Tylenol Disaster," *US News & World Report,* October 18, 1982, p. 67.

dominated the analgesic market with a 35 percent market share, dropped to a 7 percent market share.

Polling of consumer attitudes by Young and Rubicam, Johnson & Johnson's oldest advertising agency, revealed that 94 percent of the consumers surveyed were aware that Tylenol had been involved in the poisonings. The public was also learning that Tylenol was a Johnson & Johnson product. According to the survey, less than 1 percent of consumers said they knew that Johnson & Johnson was the parent company behind Tylenol prior to the poisonings. Now more than 45 percent were aware of that fact. The problem for the company was how to protect its name and not incite whoever poisoned the capsules to attack other products of the company. Other results of the survey showed that 87 percent of those surveyed acknowledged that the maker of Tylenol was not responsible for the deaths; however, 61 percent said they were not likely to buy Extra-Strength Tylenol capsules in the future, and 50 percent felt the same way about the tablets.[16]

Thus, while public opinion was not negative toward Johnson & Johnson, once it was established that the product tampering was done in the store and not in the plant, consumer confidence was severely shaken. The loss of consumer confidence affected not only Tylenol products but all drug products that could be easily tampered with on store shelves. Because of the Tylenol tamperings many consumers across the country became extremely suspicious of all over-the-counter products. Consumers began checking packages and questioning even the most minor defect.

COMPANY RESPONSE

The chairman of Johnson & Johnson decided to spend whatever millions it would cost to voluntarily withdraw thirty-one million bottles of Tylenol capsules from store shelves across the nation. This action was taken against the advice of government agents. Food and Drug Administration officials feared that the recall would increase the panic touched off by the deaths of the Chicago-area residents. The FBI argued that such an expensive action would demonstrate to potential terrorists that they could bring a $5.9 billion corporation to its knees. The recall cost $50 million after taxes.[17] Besides the recall, the company also took the following actions.

> Instead of being defensive about the deaths, the company was open with the public. A team to aid in the prompt release of accurate information was set up at its McNeil Consumer Products subsidiary including McNeil chairman, David E. Collins, a legal expert, a public relations specialist, and a security expert. Chairman Burke of Johnson & Johnson appeared on "Donahue" and "60 Minutes" to answer questions about the crisis. Other executives were interviewed for articles in *Fortune* and the *Wall Street Journal*.
>
> The company fully dedicated itself to the investigation. The company sent security people and several scientific employees to set up a lab to assist local authorities in analyzing Extra-Strength Tylenol capsules.

[16]Moore, "The Fight to Save Tylenol," p. 48.

[17]"Tylenol's Miracle Comeback," *Time*, October 17, 1983, p. 67.

The company established a toll-free consumer hot line in the first week of the crisis to respond to inquiries related to the safety of Tylenol. During the first eleven days after the line had been established, over 136,000 calls were made to the company. The number of calls proved to be many more than McNeil management had anticipated. An appeal was made to McNeil employees to pitch in and handle the phones on a volunteer basis during the weekends. Within an hour, enough people had volunteered to handle the entire weekend. Additional arrangements were made for the weekend by adding other consumer hot lines located at Johnson & Johnson facilities in New Jersey. A total of eighty-eight telephones were eventually utilized—thirty-three at McNeil and fifty-five at other locations.

Over 500,000 Mailgrams were sent notifying doctors and hospitals about the contaminated capsules. Also, about 15,000 retailers and distributors were notified.

In October, Johnson & Johnson communicated by letter on two separate occasions with its domestic employees and retirees, keeping them updated on important information and expressing thanks for continued support and assistance. In part, the communication urged employees and friends of the company to request that Tylenol tablets be returned to those local drug stores and retail outlets where they had been removed.

Consumers were offered the opportunity to replace Tylenol capsules with a free bottle of Tylenol tablets. Customers who had thrown away bottles of Extra-Strength capsules could obtain Tylenol tablets by calling a toll-free number set up for that purpose.

A $100,000 reward was offered by the company for information leading to the arrest and conviction of any person or persons who tampered with the capsules. Members of the corporate relations department of Johnson & Johnson also visited more than 160 Congressional offices in Washington to voice support for federal legislation making product tampering a felony and endorsing public service announcements by the FDA on tamper-resistant packaging.[18]

Despite the setbacks Tylenol experienced, the company never lost faith in the product and retained confidence in its ability to rebuild the business. The option of dropping Tylenol completely or marketing it under a new name was considered only briefly. Despite the long odds many outside marketing experts gave against a complete comeback, company executives said they never had any real questions about whether to bring back Tylenol. "It will take time, it will take money, and it will be very difficult; but we consider it a moral imperative, as well as good business, to restore Tylenol to its preeminent position," stated James E. Burke, chairman of Johnson & Johnson.[19]

That decision left many questions open about how to go about a comeback. It was obvious that changes of some sort were inevitable and even more obvious just how vulnerable the consumer really is to product tampering. The weakness of the product was the insecure packaging.

Early in the first stage of the crisis, Chairman Burke formed an emergency strategy group to meet twice a day to make decisions on rapidly developing events and to coordinate companywide efforts. In addition to Burke, the emergency strategy group included David R. Clare, president; Wayne K. Nelson, company group

---

[18]*Tylenol Comeback,* pp. 5–6.
[19]Ibid., p. 1.

chairman; Arthur M. Quilty, executive committee member; George S. Frazza, general counsel; David E. Collins, chairman of the McNeil subsidiary; and Lawrence G. Foster, corporate vice-president of public relations.

A key decision emerging from this strategy group was to hold a teleconference on November 11, 1982, to announce the reintroduction of Tylenol capsules in tamper-resistant packaging. This teleconference, which was beamed to twenty-nine cities via satellite, received extensive coverage on television news shows throughout the country. In explaining the decision, McNeil president, Joe Chiesa, said, "The problem with consumer research is that it reflects attitudes and not behavior. The best way to know what consumers are going to do is put the product back on the shelves and let them vote with their hands."[20]

The announcement explained that the capsules would be reintroduced in new triple-sealed packages that would have glued box ends, a plastic band around the bottle cap, and an aluminum seal across the bottle opening. The box and the bottle carried the printed warning, "Do Not Use if Safety Seals Are Broken." Thus, the company was the first in the industry to respond to the national mandate for tamper-resistant packaging, preceding the new regulation from the FDA. Company officials would not comment on the costs of the new packaging, but experts said that adding tamper-resistant features to products would cost an average of only one to two cents for each retail package.[21]

In an effort to regain consumer confidence before Tylenol went back on the market, the company replaced its previous television commercials with one that featured McNeil's medical director describing the situation and asking the viewer to trust Tylenol. An estimated 85 percent of all TV households in the United States saw the commercial an average of 2.5 times during the first week of airing.[22]

Within ten weeks of the recall, the company began putting capsules back on the shelves in the new packages. The sales force was aided by sales personnel from Johnson & Johnson's other pharmaceutical subsidiaries, who helped supply facts to the trade. More than 2250 sales people from domestic affiliates in the professional category were asked to make presentations to physicians and others in the medical community in support of the Tylenol capsule reintroduction. An estimated one million presentations had been made by the end of the year. The importance of the professional market to the Tylenol recovery is underscored by the fact that more than 70 percent of all Tylenol users have at some time received a recommendation from their physicians to use Tylenol.[23]

In an effort to encourage the American consumer to become reaccustomed to using Tylenol, the company provided the opportunity of obtaining free $2.50 coupons good toward the purchase of any Tylenol product. Consumers simply phoned a

[20]"A Death Blow for Tylenol," *Business Week,* October 18, 1982, p. 151.

[21]"Johnson & Johnson's Re-Entry Plan for Tylenol," *Chemical Week,* November 17, 1982, p. 23.

[22]*Tylenol Comeback,* p. 6.

[23]Ibid., p. 2.

special toll-free number to be placed on the list of those receiving the coupons. According to the Johnson & Johnson annual report, as of the first week in December, 1982, the coupon offer generated 210,000 calls by American consumers.

These efforts paid off, and consumer confidence was reestablished. Tylenol eventually regained more than 95 percent of the marketplace share it held before the still-unsolved poisonings. The company was given a great deal of credit for doing the right things to enhance its public image in what could have been a disastrous situation.[24] The costs of this effort, however, were not insignificant. According to Johnson & Johnson's 1982 *Annual Report,* "Withdrawal costs including disposal, handling, couponing and other associated costs resulted in an extraordinary after-tax charge in 1982 of $50 million or $.27 per share."[25] (See table 1.) Despite these costs, the company managed to maintain consumer and investor confidence by adopting an open approach in dealing with the situation and a willingness to consider the long-term benefits of their actions rather than short-term expediency.

To a large extent, Tylenol's comeback resulted from an early management decision not to let the product die.[26] "We have absolute confidence in our ability to rebuild this business," declared James Burke when the company announced its plans to reintroduce the product. He added, "We must not allow our lives to be ruled by terrorism."[27] No one believed the road to winning back consumer confidence in Tylenol would be easy. However, in November of 1982, less than six weeks after the nation had first learned the horrifying news of the Chicago deaths, McNeil Consumer Products Company, at an emotion-charged sales conference in New Brunswick, New Jersey, unveiled its plan for recovery of the product. "The fact that you are meeting here today, with your comeback plans in place, tells me that you are already 90 percent of the way there," noted Mr. Burke at the meeting.[28]

The results of the Tylenol crisis and the extent to which the company succeeded in facing the crisis were summarized in the chairman's annual letter to shareholders. (See appendix 1.) No crisis-management plan would have been sufficient in the face of the Tylenol poisonings because not even the best of managers could have planned for a tragedy of that proportion. When faced with this greatest crisis in its history, Johnson & Johnson relied on its corporate business philosophy as expressed in its credo for guidance in making the right decisions. (See appendix 2.) This philosophy established the company's priorities and defined its responsibilities to its constituencies. Although such a philosophy is not unique to Johnson & Johnson, it served the company immeasurably in responding to and managing one of the greatest crises ever to confront a corporation. The credo, according to the vice-president for Public Relations for Johnson & Johnson, "served the company

---

[24]"Tylenol's Miracle Comeback," p. 67.

[25]Johnson & Johnson *Annual Report,* 1982, p. 37.

[26]Michael Waldholz, "Tylenol Regains Most of No. 1 Market Share Amazing Doomsayers," *Wall Street Journal,* December 24, 1982, p. 1.

[27]"Re-Entry Plan," p. 22.

[28]*Tylenol Comeback,* p. 1.

TABLE 1. Two Years in Brief

WORLDWIDE

(Dollars in Millions Except Per Share Figures)	1982	1981	Percent Increase (Decrease)
Sales to customers	$5,760.9	5,399.0	6.7%
Earnings before extraordinary charge	523.4	467.6	11.9
Extraordinary charge (net of taxes)	(50.0)	—	
Net earnings	473.4	467.6	
Cash dividends paid	$ 182.4	158.6	15.0%
Additions to property, plant and equipment	470.2	388.5	21.0
Cash and marketable securities	587.6	620.5	(5.3)
Stockholders' equity	2,799.5	2,527.9	10.7
Per share			
Earnings before extraordinary charge	$ 2.79	2.51	11.2%
Extraordinary charge (net of taxes)	(.27)	—	
Net earnings	2.52	2.51	
Cash dividends paid	.97	.85	14.1
Stockholders' equity	14.80	13.51	9.5
Average shares outstanding (millions)	188.0	186.4	.9%
Stockholders of record (thousands)	43.0	38.2	12.6
Number of employees (thousands)	79.7	77.1	3.4

Source: Johnson & Johnson 1982 *Annual Report.*

better than any crisis-management plan could have. . . . It was the credo that prompted the decisions that enabled us to make the right early decisions that eventually led to the comeback phase.''[29]

CONCLUSION

Generally speaking, most Johnson & Johnson executives believed that the Tylenol comeback would not have been possible had the company failed in its responsibility to act quickly in the public interest as the crisis was breaking. (See appendix 3.) Looking back on the events in October, we see that they believed a number of decisions were critical to maintaining public trust. These included such actions as the early withdrawal of Tylenol capsules in Chicago, setting up a toll-free phone system to handle thousands of consumer inquiries pouring in at the height of the crisis, and rapid and frequent communication with the health-care community. Moreover, they believed it was a responsive, open public relations policy, carried

[29]Foster, ''The Johnson & Johnson Credo,'' pp. 1–2.

out at all levels, that helped minimize the spread of rumor and misinformation and provided valuable guidance to the media and consumers.

There is little area for disagreement about the way Johnson & Johnson handled the situation. Even the national media gave the company high marks for their response to the crisis. (See appendix 4.) While it could be argued that Johnson & Johnson managed the situation well because they weren't at fault, it should be noted that during the first few days this fact was unknown to them. The reasons Johnson & Johnson was successful in maintaining a good corporate image were their open approach in dealing with the situation—making public safety their primary concern—and their willingness to consider the long term benefits of such actions rather than short-term expediency.

Unlike other areas of public-policy decision making, this situation saw quick resolution in terms of public-policy formulation. In less than six months, FDA regulations were implemented requiring tamper-resistant packaging. Legislation was introduced in Congress to make tampering with food, drugs, and cosmetics a federal offense. Thus, the problem was dealt with quickly and decisively by both the private and public sectors.

However, the problem for consumers remains. "Consumers really don't have a defense against such random attacks," says Susan Bond, supervisor for the food and drug division of California's Department of Health Services, who followed the case closely. FDA deputy commissioner, Mark Novitch, conceded that for all the FDA's tests and standards and requirements, "there is no system we can devise to guarantee that people are protected against a bizarre situation." Some experts, including Bond, have long argued that all over-the-counter medicines should be individually sealed at the factory to guard against undetected tampering.[30]

But if individual medications need protective seals, perhaps so do individual fruits, vegetables, and a wide range of other products. Even then, there would be no guarantee of safety, and a maniac determined to harm consumers would surely find some way to thwart the precautions. "The magnitude of the possibilities is what frightens me," said Illinois Department of Public Health toxicologist John J. Spikes. "We know what we are dealing with. We just don't know when and how."[31] And most disturbing of all, why, and whether similar horrors can be prevented in the future.

EPILOGUE

Four years after its first Tylenol scare, Johnson & Johnson's nightmare began all over again. On the afternoon of February 10, 1986, the company received word that a woman, Diane Elsroth, had died two days earlier in Yonkers, New York, after swallowing two Extra-Strength Tylenol capsules laced with potassium cyanide. The

[30]"The Tylenol Scare," p. 35.

[31]Ibid., p. 36. See also Trish Hall, "Food Packaging May Be Improved, But Tampering Can't Be Prevented," *Wall Street Journal*, July 16, 1986, p. 21; and Cynthia Crossen, "Tamperproof Packaging: Inventors Say It Can't Be Done—But They Keep Trying," *Wall Street Journal*, February 26, 1986, p. 29.

company did not wait to hear details. It immediately notified retailers in the area to remove all Tylenol capsules. Employees went from headquarters in New Brunswick, New Jersey, to assist the coroners and investigators. The press office fielded calls throughout the night. Operators answering a toll-free phone number handled thousands of questions from consumers. And Johnson & Johnson suspended all Tylenol commercials.[32]

Concern widened when five more cyanide-laced capsules were found in a Tylenol bottle taken from a Woolworth store just two blocks from the store where Elsroth may have purchased her capsules. This bottle was from a different lot than the first bottle and had been filled at a different company plant. After these discoveries, New York along with several other states, banned the sale of all Tylenol capsules. Fifteen other states urged their voluntary withdrawal from stores. Johnson & Johnson, along with the FDA, issued a national alert against using Tylenol capsules.[33]

On Monday, February 17, 1986, the company announced that it would no longer sell any of its over-the-counter drugs in capsule form. In addition to Tylenol, the company made and sold capsule forms of Sine-Aid, a remedy for sinus congestion, and Dimensyn, a medicine for the relief of menstrual pain. Said Chairman Burke at a press conference: "We take this action with great reluctance and a heavy heart. But since we can't control random tampering with capsules after they leave our plant, we feel we owe it to consumers to remove capsules from the market."[34]

The decision cost Johnson & Johnson nearly $150 million to recall its capsules and scrap their production. The capsule form of Tylenol accounted for about 6 percent of the company's 1985 earnings of $613.7 million, or $3.36 a share on revenues of $6.42 billion.[35] During 1985 the Tylenol brand held a 34 percent share of the $1.6 billion pain-reliever market. To make up for this loss the company intensified its promotion of Tylenol in the form of caplets, which are smooth and elongated and far more difficult to adulterate than capsules because they are solid, like tablets. These caplets were first produced in 1983 after the Chicago poisonings and made up about 15 percent of all Tylenol sales when the capsules were abandoned.[36]

QUESTIONS

1. In a complex society based on mass production and distribution, there is no way to guarantee absolute protection against a maniac who is bent on planting poison somewhere in the vast array of products sold in drugstores and supermarkets. Do consumers need still more government legislation and regulatory agencies to protect them against death and hazards in the marketplace?

[32]"Drugs—Not Yet Tamperproof," *U.S. News & World Report*, February 24, 1986, p. 49.

[33]"A Replay of the Tylenol Scare," *Time*, February 24, 1986, p. 22.

[34]"A Hard Decision to Swallow," *Time*, March 3, 1986, p. 59.

[35]Michael Waldholz and Hank Gilman, "Tylenol's Maker to Stop Selling Some Capsules," *Wall Street Journal*, February 18, 1986, p. 3.

[36]"Hard Decision," p. 59.

2. What role did the government play in this situation? Was the role of government an important one in reestablishing consumer confidence? Has confidence in the over-the-counter drug market been restored? What guarantee do consumers have that their lives are not and will not be threatened by similar actions in the future? What responsibilities does the government have, if any, toward the seven victims of the tragedy?

3. Did Johnson & Johnson act responsibly in the Tylenol situation? Did the company consider itself to be a moral agent in responding to the crisis? What other courses of action could the company have taken in handling the situation? What lessons are there to be learned by other companies in responding to similar situations where consumer confidence is shaken?

4. To what extent should the producer of a product be responsible for the actions of a maniac? What is the appropriate relationship between the producer and the distributors as far as liability is concerned? Since neither the producer nor the distributor was at fault, does it make sense to argue that a loss-sharing relationship exists between them on the basis that a profit-sharing relationship exists between them under normal circumstances?

5. To what extent and in what form did the Johnson & Johnson Credo help them to face this unusual and unpredictable crisis? Did the company Credo really save the product and indicate the best way to handle the crisis? Or was it the fact that the public knew that the company was not guilty after only a few days of the crisis? Or were there other factors responsible for the successful handling of the situation? Is the Credo a good example of self-regulation that works for both the company and society?

6. Keeping in mind that the Credo was developed about forty years ago, what conclusions might be drawn in terms of the changes in public perceptions and expectations of corporations and the role of business in society? Could it be argued that what the public expected from Johnson & Johnson has not changed and that the principles embodied in the Credo are as relevant today as they were forty years ago? Will the Credo also work in the future without any need to adjust it to changing public expectations?

APPENDIX 1   *Excerpts from Chairman's*
              and President's Annual Letter
              to Shareholders

(Dated March 17, 1983)

We feel the theme of this year's annual report, ''An Eventful Year,'' dramatizes the validity of the principles articulated in that statement.

SOURCE: Johnson & Johnson 1982 *Annual Report*, pp. 2–3. Reprinted with permission.

While the Tylenol tragedy interrupted the consistency of our earnings growth in 1982, it was an event without precedent both in its impact on your corporation and on the American public.

The financial effect of Tylenol was obvious from our reported results. The combination of the $100 million cost of the capsule withdrawal and the loss of profit on lost Tylenol sales caused us to report profits in 1982 of $2.52 per share, or essentially the same as the previous year.

While our earnings increase in 1982 would have been within historic patterns if it were not for the Tylenol incident, the most important effect of the Tylenol experience on all of us in Johnson & Johnson was not financial but the dramatic reaffirmation of the philosophies by which we manage our business.

It is clear now to all of us that our unique form of decentralization worked for us in three ways. First, our employees at McNeil Consumer Products Company performed under extraordinary stress with unquestioned brilliance. The decisions they made and the speed with which they expedited the reintroduction of Tylenol capsules were undoubtedly due to the kind of concentrated management attention that created the Tylenol success in the first place.

At the same time, 13 sister companies of McNeil were mobilized to join in the massive effort to keep our customers in the trade and everyone in the medical profession informed of the basic facts in the Tylenol situation as they unfolded.

And finally, all of our companies worldwide rallied to increase their dedication to their own businesses, as they quickly understood the need for extra effort when one member of the Family of Companies was threatened.

Because Johnson & Johnson historically has been managed for the long-term, it was easier for all of us to make the costly short-term decisions so necessary to the future of Tylenol and the long-term strength of the corporation.

While the Tylenol tragedy dramatized the validity of these management principles, this annual report serves to remind us that it was indeed, but one event in a year of significant accomplishment of building for the future.

. . . To summarize, 1982 was indeed an eventful year. Despite the enormity of the Tylenol tragedy, we are impressed that our value system at Johnson & Johnson survived the challenge placed against it and served society well.

The public was served well because of the extraordinary cooperation that occurred among all the responsible elements of society. The regulatory agencies; the wholesale and retail parts of the distribution system; the various medical professions; the local, state, and federal law enforcement agencies . . . all worked together with the media to alert the public to the danger and to protect them in the process. It is well to remember that two unused bottles of poisoned Tylenol were recovered as a result of the withdrawal, so lives may have been saved.

We also would like to thank you, our stockholders. Your faith and confidence in us was remarkable, as evidenced by the value of our shares and the numerous letters of support for our Tylenol activities without a single letter of criticism.

And finally we would like to thank our employees—past and present. Their cooperation and unwavering support provided strength for all of us throughout the ordeal. We all learned during this experience that the reputation of Johnson &

Johnson, which had been built carefully for over ninety years, provided a reservoir of goodwill among the public, the trade, the medical professions, the law enforcement and regulatory agencies, and the media, which was of incalculable value in helping to restore the brand.

This reputation was built by our employees. It is because of their continued dedication that we are so confident about the future.

APPENDIX 2   *Johnson & Johnson Credo*

We believe our first responsibility is to the doctors, nurses and patients, to mothers and all others who use our products and services. In meeting their needs everything we do must be of high quality. We must constantly strive to reduce our costs in order to maintain reasonable prices. Customer orders must be serviced promptly and accurately. Our suppliers and distributors must have an opportunity to make a fair profit.

We are responsible to our employees, the men and women who work with us throughout the world. Everyone must be considered as an individual. We must respect their dignity and recognize their merit. They must have a sense of security in their jobs. Compensation must be fair and adequate, and working conditions clean, orderly and safe. Employees must feel free to make suggestions and complaints. There must be equal opportunity for employment, development and advancement for those qualified. We must provide competent management, and their actions must be just and ethical.

We are responsible to the communities in which we live and work and to the world community as well. We must be good citizens—support good works and charities and bear our fair share of taxes. We must encourage civic improvements and better health and education. We must maintain in good order the property we are privileged to use, protecting the environment and natural resources.

Our final responsibility is to our stockholders. Business must make a sound profit. We must experiment with new ideas. Research must be carried on, innovative programs developed and mistakes paid for. New equipment must be purchased, new facilities provided and new products launched. Reserves must be created to provide for adverse times. When we operate according to these principles, the stockholders should realize a fair return.

SOURCE: Lawrence G. Foster, "The Johnson & Johnson Credo and the Tylenol Crisis," *New Jersey Bell Journal* 6, no. 1 (Spring 1983), p. 7. Reprinted with permission.

"**W**e believe the consistency of our overall performance as a corporation is due to our unique form of decentralized management, our adherence to the ethical principles embodied in our credo, and our emphasis on managing the business for the long term.

This decision, like those we made with TYLENOL, stems from our management philosophy. They are difficult and costly, but we haven't the slightest doubt that they are in the best long-term interests of our stockholders."

— *James E. Burke, Chairman; Chief Executive Officer*

"**W**e have informed all our senior managers that they should continue to maintain long-term orientation in their decision-making ... We have been forced to reevaluate priorities and work within new circumstances, but we are keeping our traditional orientation."

— *David R. Clare, President and Chairman of the Executive Committee, Johnson & Johnson*

"**T**he American consumers have told us they believe in TYLENOL ... they've said bring it back in a tamper-resistant container and we'll buy it because it's a good product."

—*David E. Collins, Executive Committee member*

"**W**hat (McNeil) employees have demonstrated above all is the courage, skill and devotion that helped build this company — qualities that will now rebuild this company, to make us stronger than ever."

—*Joseph R. Chiesa, president of McNeil Consumer Products Company*

APPENDIX 4   *Media Reaction*

Editorials and columns in hundreds of newspapers commented favorably on the company's performance. Some said a new level of corporate responsibility had been achieved, while others suggested that a gap had been bridged between the news media and public relations in business. Some typical comments follow.

The Wall Street Journal: Johnson & Johnson, the parent company that makes Tylenol, set the pattern of industry response. Without being asked, it quickly withdrew Extra-Strength Tylenol from the market at a very considerable expense. . . . the company chose to take a large loss rather than expose anyone to further risk. . . . The anti-corporation movement may have trouble squaring that with the devil theories it purveys.

Washington Post: Though the hysteria and frustration generated by random murder have often obscured the company's actions, Johnson & Johnson has effectively demonstrated how a major business ought to handle a disaster. From the day the deaths were linked to the poisoned Tylenol . . . Johnson & Johnson has succeeded in portraying itself to the public as a company willing to do what's right regardless of cost.

San Antonio Express and News: In spite of the $100 million loss it was facing, the company never put its interests ahead of solving the murders and protecting the public. Such corporate responsibility deserves support.

St. Petersburg Evening Independent: The company has been straight-forward and honest since the first news of the possible Tylenol link in the Chicago-area deaths. Some firms would have tried to cover up, lie, or say ''no comment.'' Johnson & Johnson knows better that its first concern was to safeguard the public from further contamination, and the best way to do that was to let people know what had occurred by speaking frankly with the news media.

Savannah Morning News: Tylenol's makers deserve applause for their valiant attempt to recover from the terrible blow they have suffered.

SOURCE: *The Tylenol Comeback,* a special report from the editors of *Worldwide,* a publication of Johnson & Johnson corporate public relations, undated, p. 8. Reprinted with permission.

Index

A

A.H. Robins Company, 193–94, 201–6
Action agenda, 148
Adjudication procedures, 122
Adler, Mortimer J., 83–86
Agency for International Development,
    202–3
Altruism, 49
American Assembly of Collegiate
    Schools of Business, 33
American Cancer Society, 176
American Civil Liberties Union, 181–82
American Dental Society, 174
American Home Products Company, 205
American Medical Association, 181
Analytical ethics, 3
Animal testing, 91
Aristotle, 62
Asbestos, 153–54
    government usage, 157–58
    and insurance, 161–62
    victims, 156–57
Authority, 73–74
Ayer, A. J., 85

B

Benefit-cost analysis, 167
Bentham, Jeremy, 51
Bentley College, 131, 133
Berle, Adolf A., 149
Borel v. Fiberboard, 159–60
Burke, James E., 222
Business:
    as an ethical system, 27, 147
    performance, 17, 28

C

Califano, Joseph, 177
Caltex Petroleum Company, 170
Capitalism, 32
Cardinal virtues, 61
Carr, Albert Z., 95–96
Categorical imperative, 53, 85
Center for Business Ethics, 14
Cigarette smoking:
    advertising, 179–84, 188
    and airplanes, 186–87